Hal Myers became a cadet journalist immediately after leaving school at sixteen in 1940. His career, interrupted by three years' army service during World War II, soon took him to the London office of the *Sydney Morning Herald*, which later appointed him head of its Canberra bureau. He was also Australian correspondent of *The Economist*. Eventually resigning because of a dispute with his newspaper, he became a pioneer in public relations in Australia and helped build two of the country's most successful consulting firms.

Among various extracurricular activities, he was one of the founders of the Australian Document Exchange, a director of Film Australia and a member of the committee of the Sydney International Piano Competition. His main interests have been in the arts, travel and small-boat sailing. He and his wife have been married since 1950. They have a son and a daughter.

THE WHISPERING GALLERY

Hal Myers

Kangaroo Press

THE WHISPERING GALLERY

First published in Australia in 1999 by Kangaroo Press
an imprint of Simon & Schuster (Australia) Pty Limited
20 Barcoo Street, East Roseville NSW 2069

A Viacom Company
Sydney   New York   London   Toronto   Tokyo   Singapore

National Library of Australia
Cataloguing-in-Publication data

Myers, Hal
Whispering Gallery

   Includes index.
   ISBN 0 86417 985 5.

   1. Australia. Parliament — Reporters and reporting —
   History. 2. Journalists — Australia — Biography. 3
   Government and the press — Australia — History. I. Title.

070.44932092

Typeset by Midland Typesetters
Set in centaur 11.6 on 13.3
Printed in Australia by Australian Print Group

10 9 8 7 6 5 4 3 2 1

Front cover: Debate in the House of Representatives. Dr Evatt, leader of the opposition, standing on the right, is speaking. Prime Minister Menzies, seated opposite at centre table, shuffles papers. The formidable Speaker of the House, Archie Cameron, is in the chair. The author's friend Frank Green, Clerk of the House, is seated between Cameron and Menzies. Richard Casey, Minister for External Affairs, later Lord Casey, has walked across to speak to the Clerk. (*Australian Archives [ACT] CRSA 1200 L1736*)

whispering-gallery a usu. circular
or elliptical gallery situated
under a dome, whose acoustic
properties are such that a whisper
may be heard round its entire
circumference.
—*The New Shorter Oxford English Dictionary*

Contents

Introduction

This is a story from my early years going back to 1924, when I was born, and ending in 1955, when I suddenly turned my back on a career in journalism in Australia and Europe. It was a life which had given me a close-up view of events which already—I regret to say—can be called history.

Telling now of my experiences as a journalist, from nervous cadet to foreign correspondent, from columnist to critic, my years as a political correspondent in Canberra emerge as the biggest single element in the story. I was there during the great contest between Menzies and Evatt, who so narrowly failed to supplant Menzies as Prime Minister of Australia. It was the time also of the Petrov spy affair and the Royal Commission on Espionage, and the split in the Australian Labor Party.

This book, though, is not written as history but is personal, sometimes very personal. It is about an Australian life and the people in it—friends, rivals and associates, and the woman I married. The history is there because we were in it.

As to the politics, I have not tried to rehash the well-known events but have turned to the more shadowy tale (to me, equally interesting) of its contemporary chroniclers, the press gallery. This is the story of how as journalists we related to the politicians and contested among ourselves to uncover what was going on. We lived and worked together and against each other in a web of suspicions, hostilities and tensions, but also of friendships. These are my subject matter.

I must clarify a few details of my approach. The references to money and measurements in this book are all in pre-metric terminology without conversion or even explanation. I believe that everyone still has a rough idea of what a mile is; and, as for money, inflation has changed its value so much that 1940s and '50s figures could be even more meaningless and deceptive if converted to dollars and cents than when simply left in pounds, shillings and pence. I have also preserved some archaisms such as Persia and Ceylon, as we called Iran and Sri Lanka. In such matters I did not want to lose the flavour of the time.

In my quest for accuracy in this story I have gone back both to the records and to some of the participants in the events. Among them Stewart Cockburn, Menzies' press secretary in the early '50s, was of great help in setting me straight on various matters and filling in some details of which I was unaware. My former colleague Rodger Rea corrected and added to some of the detail, as did Thea Reid, wife of another colleague in the gallery, the late Elgin Reid. David McNicoll kindly gave me some information when I needed it. My wife has read my words ad nauseam and made many perceptive comments. A friend and former colleague who was not involved in the events of this book has nevertheless given me some most valuable suggestions. I refer to the journalist and historian Gavin Souter. And I am grateful for the care and interest shown by a perceptive editor, Carl Harrison-Ford.

In my search for photographs of scenes and people I have received great help from the staffs of the pictorial section of the National Library, the National Archive and the National Capital Authority. They took an immediate interest in my project and went out of their way to help me find what I was looking for.

PART I

Before

CHAPTER I

Start on Monday

1924 to 1940

It was when I was half way through high school that I first got the idea of being a journalist. A family friend, Garnet Bonney, used to call to see us occasionally and had what seemed an enviable life. He had gone to Adelaide in the early '30s as editor-in-chief of the evening newspaper, *The News*, and the Sunday paper, *The Mail*. In 1937 or 1938 he made a three-months' trip to the United States, travelling by sea and bringing back a big American car—a Pontiac—and lots of anecdotes. I decided that I, too, wanted to be a journalist and world traveller. Nobody in my family did anything like that.

Though I grew up in, technically, a half-Jewish household, my dad had no interest in the Jewish community and little active interest, for that matter, even in his own family. I saw something of the Myers family during my childhood, but it was always Mum who organised the meetings, as I doubt whether Dad ever made an effort to see anyone. The Myerses were a very mercantile group, as the stories of my favourite uncle George Solomon demonstrated. George, married to Dad's sister Ruth, displayed an imaginative talent for commerce right from his early days running a drapery store in the country: when trade was slow he cut up rolls of fabric to sell the pieces as remnants at higher prices.

The main family enterprise was an import firm called Myers and Solomon, directly opposite Sydney Town Hall on a site later occupied by Bebarfalds, a large furniture store, and then by Woolworths. Judging from its prominent position and from the character of the Myers and Solomon families, it must once have been a substantial and successful firm.

Alf Myers, my dad, was another story altogether. When he married Mum he was a commercial traveller on the North Coast of New South Wales. Not long before I was born he came to Sydney to try to save the family firm, and that was how his troubles began. They were inevitable, since his father, Henry, had continued to run Myers and Solomon until he was ninety, and it had been going downhill for years.

Henry Myers, widower and father of eight, was conditioned to a patriarchal role. Each weekday in his last working years he would put on his frockcoat, grasp his top hat and cane, and ascend into the horse-drawn carriage which took him to town. The rest of the world had no idea that the business could no longer afford his mode of transport, and that other members of the family were paying for it out of their own pockets so that he could keep up his front. He died at ninety-three, when I was four. I remember visiting this grey-bearded old man; he lived near us, but further up the Bronte slopes, in a house more impressive than ours but less so than the places he had once lived in when he still had his large family around him. It was a dark house, appropriate to his age.

When Henry Myers stopped working, Dad was the only member of the Myers or Solomon families who could be persuaded to come in to the firm to try to save it. But as its potential rescuer he was the worst possible choice, and he made a bad choice taking the job. He found that no proper financial records had been kept in the business for years, and he lacked financial experience himself. He also lacked the essential qualities of leadership and initiative, and the firm was able to struggle on solely because of the import agencies it held. It became an inevitable victim of the Depression.

The Myers' sense of position, at least, survived. It was notably displayed by Dad's unmarried sister Minnie, a tiny figure who was a leading contestant for the title of chief snob of the family. She was determined that I should understand what a wonderful family it was. There were other Myerses but we were the Maldon Myers, not to be confused with rivals or imposters. Maldon was in England, where the best of everything came from.

Minnie's rival in snobbishness was Rica, another of Dad's sisters, who lived in a large house in Potts Point. When I stayed there for a weekend Rica spent most of the time correcting my pronunciation so that I might acquire an accent suitable to a Maldon Myers. Her husband, Cecil Moses, corrected my grammar, meaning well.

I didn't see much of Mum's family at this time. Most of them lived in the country and my early memories of them come from my annual trip to

Grafton with Mum, for the first five years of my life, to stay with my grandpa and nanna and chase Nanna's chooks.

Most of the time I was growing up we lived in a semi-detached cottage in Gardyne Street, Bronte. We had moved there from Minto Avenue, Haberfield, where I was born—literally, for I was delivered in the bedroom there. I guess we changed houses to save money, but for me it was the right move, and Bronte was the place to grow up. There was no beach in Haberfield, and I could hardly keep away from the beach and the sea.

You could see the sea from our first semi, but only from the front verandah. The other rooms looked out on a high paling fence just three feet from the side of the house, and a brick wall at the back. But after a while our landlord, Mr Frewin, moved out of the other semi and we moved in. He had built the houses himself, so his own side had superior touches such as polished jarrah floors and leadlight windows. It cost us an extra two shillings and sixpence a week, but we could now see Bronte beach from almost every room. With our money problems at this time, we were lucky to live here.

When the Depression forced the closure of Myers and Solomon, the asset Dad was able to save from it was the agency for Pain's fireworks. This was what enabled him to offer something more than his own services to a new employer, and Mick Simmons, a sports store near Central Railway, took up the offer. Dad turned fifty-four in 1930, and at that age he would have had to go on the dole but for the fireworks agency. Instead, it kept him in a job through the Depression and until he retired.

Pain's was an English company that had a virtual monopoly of the big fireworks business in Sydney. Dad had to keep an eye on arrangements for the main fireworks displays and used to get free tickets to some events, taking me with him. For a couple of weeks before big fireworks nights he was so busy that Mick Simmons gave him a full-time assistant, so whenever he had to state his occupation after that he was able to say: 'Departmental Manager'. Minnie and Rica would have been relieved.

As the Depression deepened it affected us more. The days when Dad had a car were long gone, but we did have the telephone in Gardyne Street; now we had it cut off. Not that I minded the loss—the telephone seemed pointless to me. I couldn't understand why Mum sat for hours murmuring 'mmm … mmm … mmm … ' into it. Our rent was reduced but Dad's salary was reduced too, and though we never knew poverty we certainly knew the next thing to it. Unknown to Dad, Mum even pawned her engagement ring. She was terrified until she could put aside enough money to get it back.

Mum was the eldest child of Alex and Mary Walker. Alex's father George Walker migrated from Scotland and spent thirty years as a ship's captain in the Newcastle area of New South Wales. Mary's father Hugh Sweeny, an Irishman from County Cork, started his life in Australia building cottages for miners in the bush at Minmi, in the Hunter region of New South Wales, where a small mining village was beginning to spring up. What a pioneering story it must have been! Hugh's wife Agnes died after Mary was born, and Hugh must have been in Minmi alone with the infant Mary and her two sisters, only slightly older. But he must have escaped from this lonely bush workplace and gone to Newcastle in the early 1870s, for my grandmother grew up and was married there. When my mother, Beryl Walker, was two or three years old her parents moved to Grafton, and that was where she grew up.

Mum was the oldest of a family of eight, but soon after I began visiting Grafton only her youngest sister, Rea, was still at home. When I was ready to start school Rea was ready for university, so Grandpa and Nanna came to Sydney and rented a house near the Bronte shops. Looking back on their moves after that, the consistent element was that they kept getting closer to the Catholic church. After Grandpa died Nanna moved next door to it.

The Church of Mary Immaculate in Victoria Street, Waverley, was an austere building run by Franciscan priests. The Franciscans were the ones who didn't have any money. I was convinced that they were too poor even to buy proper clothes, and that this was why they went everywhere in brown dressing-gowns and sandals. The Irish influence must have been very comforting for Nanna; her favourite priest, old Father Griffin, had a rich Irish accent and Irish charm by the truckload. Nanna was so devoted to God and the church that Mum felt obliged to start sending me to mass. Father Griffin instructed me in the catechism when eventually I was to be confirmed, and told me that only people who believed in God went to heaven. 'What about people like the Aboriginals, or savages in other countries who have never even heard of God?' I asked. 'No, unfortunately those poor devils cannot go to heaven,' he replied authoritatively.

They were literal thinkers, these Irish Catholics. One of Alex Walker's brothers, like Alex himself, must have married one of them. He died before his wife, and when she too was on her deathbed the priest came to comfort her and administer the last rite. Her son spoke to Mum of her final hours, and with tears in his eyes told of the priest's last words. 'You are going to a better place, Mrs Walker,' said the priest. 'And when you get to heaven, please remember me to Mr Walker.'

Although I went through a short period of religious fervour as a child I could never attain such faith. As soon as I reached adolescence I became a sceptic.

When I was nine I had a test at school which was different from anything we had done before. It was, I was told later, an intelligence test, and on the result of it I was the only pupil from Clovelly public school invited to start the next year in an opportunity class in Woollahra. This was a significant shift in my prospects for a career. Woollahra school introduced me to a more competitive world, though I wasn't fully conscious of the change.

As far as I am aware there were only two opportunity classes for boys in Sydney at that time, and this was only the second year they had operated. The Education Department didn't really know what to do with us, but just by learning in a select group I was thrust into a more challenging arena, and responded to it. I did better than most of the class at Woollahra, and my results at the end of primary school were certainly better than they would have been if I had stayed at Clovelly.

At the end of 1935 I was ready to start high school, and my ambition was to get a selective place at Sydney High. But I wasn't confident, and it was at this time that we saw a paragraph in the *Sydney Morning Herald* about scholarships to Sydney Grammar school, so I applied. In the Primary Final examinations I got the marks I needed for Sydney High but won a scholarship to Sydney Grammar, too. Not knowing what to do, I consulted two rather distant cousins on the Myers side who had just finished at Grammar. They represented the school so well that I took up the scholarship.

Six in my year were scholarship winners. A scholarship was something to be proud of but I was sensitive about it, too. For all I knew, parents of the other scholarship boys might have been able to afford to send their sons to Grammar anyway, but mine certainly couldn't. Thus I imagined that my scholarship put me in the category of a charity case. I was embarrassed about Dad, and not only for this reason. I imagined that he wasn't only the poorest father at Grammar but also the oldest. Rising sixty now, he applied some super-glue every morning to fix a few strands of silver hair across his bald top. Around the house he shuffled and dragged his feet. In winter he wore thick, long-sleeved, long-legged woollen underwear, but even this wasn't enough. He tied a flannel belly-band around his waist to protect his kidneys.

Dad didn't read books and wasn't much help in my studies. Neither of my parents could, or tried to, guide me in my work. There was a good side to this: I was never pushed or criticised, just sustained in the warmth of parental approval. But I regret the lack of a good mentor, for I chose some of my school subjects badly and wasted a good deal of time.

This was the stage when the example of our friend Garnet Bonney began to turn my mind towards journalism. We saw him when he was setting out on his big trip to the United States and when he came back, fascinated by the American fantasy, by the drive, the achievement, the invention and the sheer eccentricity of it all. He sent us copies of articles he wrote for *The News* ... stories of the new phenomenon of hitch hiking, the emergence of the gigantic sculpted heads of presidents from the cliff-faces of Mount Rushmore, the restaurant owner who advertised: 'If your wife can't cook, keep her as a pet and eat here', and the Chicago man who told him reassuringly: 'I've lived in this town for twenty years and I ain't seen a guy bumped off yet'. Most Australians knew only Hollywood's America in the mid-'30s. I was greatly impressed by the richly entertaining opportunities that journalism had given Mr Bonney to see what seemed like the real America.

In my third year at high school our form master and English teacher, Toby Lumsdaine, invited a classmate and me to dinner in his bachelor establishment. Lumsdaine was a cultured extrovert who was as much at home teaching *The Merchant of Venice* as training the school cadets. Until then, in my experience, social contact between masters and boys did not exist. So this was a flattering invitation. My classmate and I, on best behaviour, were well fed and entertained. Then Mr Lumsdaine asked: 'Well, what do you plan to do when you leave school?' Even a few months earlier I would have hummed and hahed, but now I had an answer. 'I want to be a journalist,' I told him. 'Good!' he said. 'Now let me see ... if you're going to be a journalist you'll have to do English Honours next year.'

I've forgotten what other advice Toby Lumsdaine gave that night, but these were the most significant words of guidance I ever received at school. And for the next year I neglected almost everything else to try to read myself through the high points of literature for my English Honours course. Despite the exclusive Britishness of the literary diet that was served up to us, my reading that year was a wonderful start in the adult world of books. Then, of course, I wanted to write them myself, and was glad that I had chosen journalism as a career. I'd started with a childish attraction to it because of its imagined glamour, but now I was attracted to it because I thought it had something to do with literature.

The end of school was eventful. I won the English, Latin, French and

German prizes and some other awards. Prize-winners could chose their own books with the funds allocated to them, and the afternoon newspaper the *Sun* published a picture of me juggling with a pile of nineteen weighty books on Sydney Grammar's prize day. My results in the Leaving Certificate were good enough to win me one of 200 public exhibitions given yearly to Sydney University. For most students these were the only way of getting free university education in New South Wales at that time. Not that I could take full advantage of it. I couldn't ask my parents to go on supporting me for another three years or more, so I would soon have to get a job.

I had just turned sixteen, too young for the cadetship I hoped for on the *Sydney Morning Herald*. But George Solomon persuaded me to apply for one immediately, just to get my name before them. George, who was a well-known businessman in Sydney by then, gave me a reference. Our friend Garnet Bonney wrote a letter to the news editor, Angus McLachlan—who had served as a cadet under him on the Melbourne *Herald*—and commended me as the sort of lad he would employ. McLachlan interviewed me and wrote an encouraging response to Mr Bonney. Then I was called in again to meet the general manager, Rupert Henderson. I was so unworldly that I hadn't even rehearsed an answer to the most elementary question which he fired at me: 'Why do you want to be a journalist?' My unconfident reply was that I just wanted to, and had felt that way for a long time, and thought it was the right career for me. 'We want you to start on Monday,' he said.

There had never been a sixteen-year-old cadet before, but World War II was in its second year and the *Herald's* young journalists were beginning to join the forces. I realised afterwards that the management must have decided to hire younger cadets to get more use out of them before they, too, were lost to the services. But I felt like a prodigy at the time. Or at least until the next year, when the *Herald* gave a cadetship to a fifteen-year-old girl named Anne James.

Part II

Australia and Europe

CHAPTER 2

Critical Injuries

1941 to 1946

I was waiting one morning in January 1941 in the sub-editors' room at the *Sydney Morning Herald* for Mr Pile, the day sub-editor. The room was a scene of unexplained inactivity. Could this really be a newspaper office? I went to the far door to investigate the only sound I heard, and saw a machine typing noisily to itself. Long rolls of paper spilled out behind it on to the floor. As I peered into it I found that this equipment had been working all night, typing up its own account of what was happening throughout the world. To a real journalist the teleprinter was as mysterious as a nail or a doorknob, but to the newest cadet it was science fiction.

Mr Pile, however, didn't turn out to be in any way fantastic. I still don't know what he did as day sub-editor, coming into the deserted office in the mornings; he had the air of a family retainer kept on to shuffle documents in recognition of past services. But as the day progressed, people arrived who seemed more purposeful, and the newspaper office took on a more predictable appearance. I spent the next days wondering how I could become part of it, and by the end of the week I had the answer. My introduction to journalism would be in the sporting room.

The sporting editor, Jock Schofield, had a staff of three general hands whose incessant fights he treated with absolute indifference. Other part-time employees turned up irregularly. One was Mick Hayes, an ex-jockey who checked the track trials at Randwick racecourse at dawn and brought in lists of trial times, laboriously inscribed in huge handwriting on small sheets of copy paper. Alcohol had ended little Mick's riding career, and Jock Schofield had warned him: 'If ever I find you touching another drop, you're sacked.' But then Jock would have turned away to conceal a twisted smile.

The permanent staff were Harry Shearing, George Park and Charlie McQuillan. You could easily have found Jock and the three of them in a scene of London low-life as depicted in the Victorian novels I had read at school. Time had given character to Jock Schofield's face and redesigned his features. He had a rather large jaw and a face which receded at the mouth as if he had lost his teeth, but they had merely been worn down by his pipe, which was a fixture there. These lower features worked in with his eyes, usually to signify amusement, challenge or disbelief.

George Park was a small, spare man with the sharp features of a pickpocket or a music-hall comic. He had a storytelling routine drawn from his experiences in France during World War I, such as what a French prostitute said to him when he admitted at a too advanced stage that he didn't have any money. Harry Shearing, tall and overweight, with one stiff leg, disappeared early each afternoon for essential socialising in the sporting world. Charlie McQuillan was the least noticeable of this group, with no apparent peculiarities except for the mismatch between his dark hair and ginger moustache, which gave rise to pointless speculation in my mind as to the colour scheme in his pubic region.

The sporting room wasn't used to having a cadet, and my arrival was a bonus for Harry and George, as there was now someone else to take their calls in their absence—or, as I found, in their presence. They kindly allowed me to take down lists of results phoned in by every suburban and country sporting club in New South Wales. But Jock Schofield gave me other jobs to ensure that I would learn something from my time with him. He hinted that there was more to learn about life, too. 'My God, I wish I was your age and knew what I know now,' he said, but I was so naive that I couldn't really follow what he meant.

After a few months in the sporting room I was transferred to recording the shipping notices, the mails and weather information and the daily fruit and vegetable prices. One of my jobs was to supply an abridged version of the weather forecast for the news summary on page one. When the forecast included seemingly pedantic detail like 'north-easterly to south-easterly winds' I used my initiative to save space—easterly winds, I decided, was a fair summary and quite enough information for anyone. The news editor, Angus McLachlan, was a sailor. He gradually became perplexed by the number of times the steady sailing conditions being forecast for Saturday afternoons never eventuated. After some months he discovered that the Weather Bureau was not to blame.

Soon afterwards I began the cadet's customary term in the financial room, copying out the stock exchange prices and editing minor company statements. I didn't write an original line but was sustained by what I saw of other journalists whose careers seemed full of significance. Harry Kippax and Ian Bevan were among the younger ones; and I worked briefly alongside Noel Hawken, who became a distinguished journalist in Melbourne, and Roderick Macdonald and Bill Munday, both of whom were killed later as war correspondents in Europe. Bill sent home some of the best despatches of the war. Other journalists whom I would come to know were already away in the services or reporting the war, some of them from the London office, our main centre for overseas news. But the journalists I encountered were the kind of people I wanted to know and work with.

A week after I joined the staff another new cadet, Ross Westcott, arrived. Ross and I started eating together at the hamburger shop across the road in Pitt Street or adjourning for chocolate malteds at the milk bar opposite Wynyard station in George Street. On paydays we went to Darrell Lea's chocolate shop near the milk bar and stocked up with rocky road. The award salary for a first-year cadet was £2 9s. a week, a great improvement on the sixpence a week pocket money that I'd been getting as a schoolboy the year before.

I tried to juggle my job with a full-time Arts course at Sydney University while developing a social life, studying the piano and learning shorthand. The first to go was shorthand. It was a must for journalists, but I convinced myself of its dangers. Newspapers often required immediate verbatim reports of court cases and inquiries in which their own interests were involved. Some of these cases went on for weeks and I pitied some reporters I observed, who were efficient enough to get such assignments in those days before the tape recorder. My university studies lasted longer. Working 2 p.m. to 11 p.m. on the *Herald* I was able to go to morning lectures with the full-time students, but extra time for study was hard to find. So I backed out of the examinations at the end of the year, intending to organise myself better and take another chance in a second round of exams, the 'posts', which used to be offered in the new year.

The events of 7 December 1941, when the Japanese bombed Pearl Harbor and the war came to the Pacific, soon changed my plans. Three days later a military call-up was announced, and early in 1942 some of my fellow students who had gone into camp with the University Regiment for the Christmas vacation found that they were not coming out. Later in the year I would reach the critical age of eighteen, so for the time I put university studies out of my mind.

Ross Westcott, a year or so older than me, was the first of my friends to be called up. My birthday was on 16 September and a call-up notice arrived before the end of the month. I did a few final days' work at the *Herald* and presented myself at the Sydney Showground for army duty. It was more than three years before I worked at the *Herald* again.

If this were a book about my military career it would almost end here. For the army sidetracked me after putting me through a remarkably misdirected aptitude test. On the basis of this test it selected me for training as a radar mechanic, an occupation for which I had no practical aptitude at all. And I spent the rest of the war near Perth and Fremantle except for a period of infantry training at Bathurst camp, and two radar schools at Ingleburn, near Sydney. My job was to service the control equipment for searchlight batteries in the Fremantle area and beyond, in preparation for air attacks which never came. I had an introduction to the writer, Gavin Casey, in Perth, and through him met some of the local intelligentsia and supporters of left-wing causes. For a time I became more radical than most of them. I returned to Sydney after the war declaring my love for a girl named Joy in Perth, but distractions closer at hand set us both off in other directions after a few months of intense correspondence.

My time in the army had done something for my maturity but were three years lost in journalism. I was determined to catch up. For I had one and only one clear plan for the future: I would spend two years back at the paper to equip myself to work anywhere as a journalist, then I would go overseas. That was where the opportunities waited. Unlike other romantic notions about the future, this one had stayed with me through the war and survived in the peace.

Back at the *Herald* office in Hunter Street, Paddy the lift driver, a genuine drunken Irishman with a peg-leg, transported you to the second floor where journalists spilled out into marble corridors that led to the editorial offices. The management offices were on the first floor, and Paddy dropped executives there and listened to their conversations, hence his remarkable knowledge of events and confidential management decisions. He wasn't allowed to drop journalists at the management floor. If we had any business there we had to walk down from the editorial floor by an impressive curved terrazzo staircase. In front of the stairwell on the editorial level was a heavy oval table of great size. The music critic Neville Cardus always sat on one end of it to check his concert reviews before handing them in. A *Herald* photographer was credited with having had sexual intercourse on it late one Saturday night.

Herald men who had been war correspondents were still away, writing history in the present tense from London, New York, Germany, Paris, Tokyo, Indo-China, Manila and Indonesia. Ian Bevan had reported the end of the war in Europe and was headed for Nuremburg to cover the war crimes trials of Nazi leaders. Ian was only a few years older than me, and showed what a few years might do if you had the talent and opportunity.

My first real job after the war was no starring role but was exactly what I needed. I began writing the summaries for page one—a brief version of the main news in the rest of the paper. The advantage of the job was that I sat opposite the chief sub-editor, Ken Hacket, and saw every news story after it had been edited—or, in newspaper terms, sub-edited. Reporters typed their stories double-spaced on small sheets of copy-paper, one paragraph to a sheet, usually one sentence to a paragraph. The sub-editors—subs—never threw copy away. They simply ran a line through anything they deleted, whether words, paragraphs, or series of paragraphs. If there was an argument later, someone could always refer back to the original copy. So I saw both the first and the final versions of every story, and could see how reporters' copy was cut and polished. This was invaluable experience, as the *Herald* had no formal training: self-improvement by observation and practice was the only way to learn. After a few days Ken Hacket began to throw me minor stories to edit, and I graduated to the position of a junior sub.

Living back in Sydney I found that wartime shortages and wartime attitudes had a tenacious survival. It was news in the *Herald* when a shipment of whisky arrived from Scotland and beer from South Australia. Another *Herald* story listed the official alternatives for ex-servicemen who couldn't find civilian suits, a subject of some personal interest to me. We were advised just to continue wearing our uniforms, or to cut the buttons off and use civilian buttons instead, or to buy sports suits (sports coat with the invariable grey slacks). Luckily the moths hadn't destroyed my old clothes from 1942, so I didn't need to get civilian buttons for my army uniform.

In the Sydney to which I had returned, strikes were the state of normality and almost anything could cause them. Men in one coalmine walked off because the pit ponies didn't have time for a proper meal before work. This was nearly up the standard of a famous strike, later, by some miners who complained that the pit ponies had bad breath. A coal strike hit Sydney's electricity supply just before my first post-war Christmas. Trams were to run at half speed at night to save power, and only one hot meal a day was to be allowed in homes or restaurants. After there was a slight improvement in the situation three days before Christmas, the heading on the *Herald*'s front page lead story reflected the whole scene. 'More Power Cuts Eased', it read: 'Breakfast May Be Cooked'.

There were some depressing ideas about, too. William McKell, the Labor Premier of New South Wales, proudly announced a plan to improve Sydney's finest thoroughfare, Macquarie Street, starting with the demolition of some of its most outstanding buildings—the early colonial Parliament House, the Mint building, the Hyde Park Barracks and Sydney Hospital. There was enough protest to scuttle this proposal but it was dignified and muted protest: no Sydneysiders marched or demonstrated. Yet there was still a delight for me in this place. Sydney was a small and simple town in 1945, low-slung, unspectacular, run-down in parts, but human in scale and character, and not without its flashes of elegance.

In the office I was suddenly pulled out of the subs' room to go to the 2GB newsroom. Here the *Herald* staffed a small news organisation on its editorial floor for Sydney's leading commercial radio station. The service was run by Selwyn Speight, known as Dan, a former war correspondent. Dan welcomed me unconventionally by saying that he had objected strongly to my appointment. 'I don't want you to take this personally,' he said, 'but you're taking over from a very experienced B Grade journalist, and I've complained because I feel they are not taking the needs of this newsroom seriously enough if they don't give me a replacement who is just as experienced.' I was delighted. I said I could understand his feeling entirely.

Dan was a large man with a soft nature, despite the vein of stubbornness he had revealed, and a fortitude which had been tested in his time as a war correspondent in China. The punctilious honesty which he displayed with me was fixed in his character. He was conscientious, too, and set about helping me. A few weeks later he felt the time had come to revise his first judgment. 'Since I told you how I felt when you came here, I want to tell you now that you are doing just as good a job as X,' he said, mentioning the name of my older and more experienced predecessor. He reported this finding to Angus McLachlan.

The early morning news session from the Macquarie newsroom was essentially a rewrite of the news from the *Sydney Morning Herald*, and preparing it was an exercise in working quickly. When I was doing the early shift for the morning news I did much of the bulletin myself, having a good part of the breakfast-time news ready for handing over to a 2GB announcer by the time our later starters arrived. Afterwards, for the lunchtime and evening programs, we had to get around among the reporting staff and borrow their copy as they produced it. If events of special interest were happening we went out if possible to do our own reporting. Then we were not dependent on a *Herald* reporter's return to the office with his copy, the timing of which was unpredictable. The only certainty was that if an assignment ended late in the afternoon the reporter wouldn't appear with his story until well after the bars closed. Six o'clock closing ensured that the morning newspapers were published, but wasn't early enough for the Macquarie evening news.

Despite this peculiarity of newspaper offices I was impressed by the improbable process which converted the events of each day into a newspaper by the early hours of the next morning. When I heard people complain about the unreliability of the press I wondered how they themselves would perform in the conditions under which newspapers were produced. Yet I must confess that it was the engagingly inefficient side of the process that gave it its charm for journalists and its character for readers. Our office was more like a club than a production unit, and some of the *Herald*'s most interesting journalists had established a daily coffee ceremony. Soon I began to join Lindsey Browne, the critic, and Lou Kepert, a sub, in Frank's coffee lounge nearby in Pitt Street every afternoon. Lindsey was reviewing almost everything—plays, films and music. A share of some of the *Herald*'s complimentary tickets to concerts was a benefit for me from these meetings, but the best reward was in the conversation. Lou Kepert's interests were essentially in books and ideas, but he was also a talented practical newspaperman, attentive to his craft. I got to know him well after he followed Dan Speight into the Macquarie newsroom. The visit to Frank's coffee lounge caused a suspension of work for half an hour in mid-afternoon, after which there was another working session followed by the adjournment to the pub.

The pub ritual brought most of the 'literary' staff together—reporters, sub-editors, leader writers, feature writers, specialists. Most of them at that time went to the Grand Hotel in Hunter Street, just by the *Herald* building. Loyalty to a pub was essential, as good relations with a barmaid were the only guarantee that you could get your final round of drinks served as the crowd struggled to the bar just before six o'clock. Strange to say, the conversation in these uncivilised circumstances was civilised. Even the specialists among journalists tended to be people with broad interests and something worthwhile to say. Another attraction was that most of our journalists treated each other with goodwill. They followed their own course and didn't seem to be much diverted by jealousy of colleagues. But it was fortunate that there were no management consultants at this time. They would have ended the daily visits to bars and coffee lounges, and would probably have destroyed much of the informal contact that gave flavour to the organisation and the newspaper.

If the *Herald* staff was something of a club, the younger members formed an active branch of it and spent much of their free time together. Personal rivalries seemed to be excluded from this group, too. There seemed to be opportunity enough for all of us. The *Herald* had a policy of sending its bright young men to London or New York, and I simply hoped that my time would not be too long in coming—otherwise I would leave and get my experience of the world in some other way. I can speak only of 'bright young men' because few women journalists had the chance to work in anything but traditional women's news, and we didn't send anyone overseas for experience in that.

Soon after my return to Sydney I began to study the piano with Alexander Sverjensky, who taught many of the most successful students at the Sydney Conservatorium. I'd learned the piano as a kid, picked up a love of music later, and reached a fairly good standard on the piano for an amateur. Sverjensky tried to persuade me to leave the *Herald* and take up music professionally, as I could have taken advantage of a post-war study scheme for ex-service people. I was flattered but unconvinced. He wanted to turn out successful concert pianists and I didn't have the special kind of talent that concert pianism demanded. But with the advantage of my job on a newspaper I did aspire to become a music critic. Apart from being a war correspondent, and there was no war, I could think of little better in journalism at that stage than to have access to the pages of a major newspaper so as to become influential in the musical world. I set out to make this ambition known.

Neville Cardus, the *Herald*'s chief music critic, was a very distinguished one whom I had observed only from a distance. There was no apparent way to get to know him; he was seen only briefly in the office, after concerts when he called to drop in his reviews. Lin Browne was the second critic, but at times other writers had to stand in for one of them, and I hoped that I might be called on. Lin had started out as a cadet journalist as I had. He was rumoured while working in Canberra to have slept in the office for a year to save up to get married. When I first knew him he had also begun to produce crossword puzzles for the paper, and had used them to propose to his girlfriend. He devised two puzzles in such a way that the initial letters of all the ACROSS words spelt out I LOVE NANCY MOORE and WILL SHE MARRY ME. A few weeks later he used the final letters of the ACROSS words in another puzzle to complete the sequence. These spelt out simply: THE ANSWER IS YES. Some readers spotted the hidden messages, the story goes, and rang the *Herald* to show how smart they were. And by the time I came to know Lin, he and Nancy were married with two children.

When the *Herald* sent Lindsey to its New York office about the middle of 1946, presumably for his development as a critic, Angus McLachlan called me in to say that if I'd like to try my hand at music criticism they would give me the chance. Before I reviewed my first concert, however, Neville Cardus would like to talk to me. As far as I was concerned the great man could talk to me at any time. Cardus' stature was such that he was given a knighthood later, after he went back to his old post in England as music critic of the *Manchester Guardian*. Knighthoods have been conferred on some unworthy and even contemptible people, but to gain one from the power of one's pen, especially as a critic, is a testament to quality.

Cardus was a dark, slim man whom I assumed, quite wrongly, to lead an ascetic life, seeing him return alone to the *Herald* office after concerts, speak to no-one, then take off to his bachelor flat in Elizabeth Bay. He was on friendly terms with his wife, it was said, but they lived separately in Sydney. The truth, which I didn't suspect, was that Sydney women were paying him insistent attention, and he was in no danger of enforced celibacy.

For a music critic Cardus was surprisingly well known to the public, the reason being that he wrote with equal eloquence and authority on cricket. He had even been a professional cricketer, and I believe that his first writings for the *Sydney Morning Herald* were commentaries on a Test series in Australia shortly before World War II. On music he delivered judgment resoundingly. Cardus kept returning to the need for a worthy permanent conductor for the orchestra, but spared none of the possible candidates. 'The official conductor last night was E. J. Roberts, who, it is creditably reported, is a very good conductor in Perth ... ' was his lethal comment on one of them. Cardus was friendly with, but not sparing of, my teacher Alex Sverjensky. 'Last night in an almost crowded Conservatorium Mr Sverjensky began his recital diffidently, following the National Anthem with the Busoni arrangement of the Bach chorale, "I call on Thee, Lord", played so formally that I almost remained standing,' he wrote. 'Next he gave us a performance of Beethoven's Opus 57, shorn of grandeur and tumult, and at times inarticulate with wrong notes.' The rest of the review was more merciful towards the doyen of piano teaching.

I visited Cardus in his flat in Greenknowe Avenue, Elizabeth Bay. He was most agreeable, and gave me some words of advice which I have entirely forgotten. He apparently concluded that I was safe to experiment with. So in July 1946 I went to the Sydney Town Hall to review a concert by the Sydney Symphony Orchestra with three young soloists, winners of overseas scholarships given by the Australian Broadcasting Commission. I strove to conceal my self-importance, which was, naturally, matched by self-doubt—not enough of it, I would say now.

I was in effect becoming the *Herald*'s second critic, filling in for Cardus, as there had been no other regular critic behind Lindsey Browne. Of course I had nothing resembling Cardus' felicity of style and none of the accumulated knowledge of works and performances that are the foundation of a critic's standards. Cardus' experience also overcame, for him, the obstacle that the *Herald* placed in the way of good criticism by publishing its reviews the morning after the concerts. There was no time for the critic to reflect or rewrite. It was straight back to the office after the concert, straight on to the typewriter and straight into the subs' basket to catch the late edition of the next day's paper.

My first review was, apparently, good enough to keep me employed as a critic, and I reviewed many concerts as extra assignments in my spare time over the next few weeks. I didn't make any reputations but possibly helped to unmake a couple. Of one soprano I wrote that a public performer needed a certain minimum of vocal charm which she barely reached. A musician I knew heard her reaction: 'Damn that Myers!' she cried.

I was sent one day to review a lunchtime concert by a pianist named Paul Schramm. Schramm had appeared in Sydney some months before and was working hard to establish a place for himself there. He was very uneven musically but at first his technique and experience made a big impression. Lindsay Browne had described his playing as the best heard in Sydney since Schnabel—high praise, for this was a comparison with one of the outstanding musicians of his generation. Later reviews of his performances by Cardus and Ken McKenzie (Seaforth McKenzie, the novelist) had been favourable, though less unreservedly so.

Some aspects of Schramm's playing were a shock to me, and when I came to write my piece I did so without much inhibition. I described him as a pianist who frittered away his talents, criticised his 'popular history of music' program for displaying mainly what he could not do, and said that his Beethoven playing was completely out of style. 'Among his "modern" group,' I concluded, 'was his own composition, "Pistons". This is purely intended to make one gape so that the chewing-gum drops out, while one murmers: "Can he play!"'

This review was published unedited, and Angus McLachlan complained afterwards that my final comment was not quite in good taste by *Herald* standards. But he admitted that Cardus thought it was a good review. Soon afterwards I reviewed another recital by Schramm in which, I said condescendingly, he had 'somewhat redeemed himself'. I thought with some shame afterwards about my treatment of Paul Schramm, concluding that I had been little better than an immature smart alec. The popular concert that I had sneered at wasn't intended for highbrows. Schramm was trying to build an audience of people who enjoyed his kind of music-making. It was a perfectly legitimate one.

Schramm disappeared from the Sydney scene and I heard nothing more of him for years. Much later I was telling this story to my friend Elgin Reid, a Brisbane journalist working in Canberra. 'Exactly the same thing happened to me,' said Elgin. 'Paul Schramm went to Queensland when he left Sydney, and when I was younger I did some music criticism for the *Courier-Mail*. I reviewed Paul Schramm and criticised him pretty harshly, too. Afterwards I was sorry.' Elgin told me what had happened to Paul Schramm. He was dead—had died in Brisbane. Almost in the gutter, said Elgin. Perhaps with our help, I thought.

As my first year back at the *Herald* progressed I saw a great deal of Ross Westcott and two of the young women journalists on the staff. One was Pat Pearse, whom we had both known for several years. The other was a girl named Beth, whose potential to affect my life I did not at first realise. Pat and Beth had bought a sailing dinghy together, and we sailed, swam, picnicked, lunched, dined, partied, visited each other's homes, exchanged books and went to films, plays and concerts together. But while I was coming to know Beth, Ross and Pat were embarking on an affair which was soon destined for only one conclusion—marriage. As they began to spend more time together, Beth and I paired off. It was when she came to mean more and more to me that my fantasies about Joy, my girlfriend in the west, were forgotten. For Joy, too, something new in Perth had clearly supplanted thoughts of me. The letters between Sydney and Perth had become more rare; now they ceased.

CHAPTER 3

The Roosevelt

1946 to 1948

An English journalist, Stan Monks, joined the *Herald* in 1946 and began to share my role as backstop to Cardus. He was a versatile and well-trained newspaperman from a major British provincial paper, and had done some music criticism for it. So our musical readers lost nothing when I was posted soon afterwards to Canberra.

There was a disadvantage involved in this move, as I would see much less of Beth. But I would be able to get to Sydney fairly often, and welcomed the experience in Canberra. Arrangements for my transfer were in the hands of Tony Innes, the assistant chief of staff. Tony, a man in his forties, was a figure from another age. He might have come out of an early colonial painting: with a change of clothes you might have taken him for a commissioner for weights and measures. He was a short man, bulging a little, unathletic, with fine, black hair, close-grained black stubble and a rather large but thin, inquisitive nose.

It took an original mind to organise my move to Canberra as he did. You could get there in an hour's flight in a DC3, and every other journalist who went there took such a flight or drove. But Tony booked me on an overnight train in a sleeper. There was something vice-regal about this journey. You caught the train at Central station after dinner, went to bed and tried to sleep for a few hours. But you were awakened near dawn by jolting and clanking, only to find that you still weren't in Canberra, as it was on a branch line. With more jolting and clanking your carriage was unhooked and connected to another locomotive which took you to the national capital. You got up, dressed, and disembarked there at what was no more than a small country railway station.

The accommodation which Tony had booked for me was an upstairs bedroom in an unsophisticated suburban household in Manuka, where I felt like a man exiled to a far province. After a couple of weeks I organised a move to the Hotel Canberra, where politicians stayed. After this I must say that I became fond of Tony Innes when I came to know him better.

The head of the *Herald*'s Canberra office was Ray Maley. Ray was a big, loquacious man whom nobody can ever have disliked. If the world of politics is a jungle (a handy metaphor for the political columnist) Ray could only be described as one of the large herbivores, imposing enough to be left alone by the carnivores, easily domesticated, but certainly not a beast of burden. He had a sound mind for politics but liked to take things easy to a degree that amazed me. Once, he had to go to Sydney for some event but didn't reappear in Canberra for several days afterwards, leaving the inexperienced junior—me—alone in the office, as his assistant was on holidays. When Ray eventually returned one afternoon he sat on a desk and explained: 'I just thought I might as well stay up in Sydney to see the Test'—Australia was playing cricket against England at the time. Reassuring himself that everything was okay in the office (what else would I say?) he stood up again, patted his stomach and announced: 'I think I'll go and take the kids down to the pool for a swim.' I didn't mind. If I was there for experience, Ray Maley's way guaranteed that I would get it.

Maley lived with his wife Betty and two young sons in a house beyond the dreams of most journalists: a two-storey building at the end of Mugga Way, the street of ambassadors, high commissioners and only the most senior political correspondents. It was built on two and a half acres, and according to Ray had the largest garden in Canberra. Certainly it was Canberra's finest, having been designed with great imagination by its original owner. It was said that the *Herald* had bought the house for the convenience of the Fairfaxes during a period when they and the management were much involved with Canberra. Since then 29 Mugga Way had become the residence of the political correspondent. I dined there with the Maleys soon after arriving and commented on the size and style of the place. 'One day,' observed Ray encouragingly, 'this could be yours.' It could, I supposed. And when you moved into that house you had arrived.

I was also invited to the Bonneys' home. Garnet Bonney had been stationed in Canberra since 1940, when he was appointed Chief Publicity Censor, responsible for wartime security censorship of the Australian press and radio. Later in the war he became Director General of Information. The Bonneys lived in a rented government house, much less imposing than the *Herald*'s.

A government department, the Department of the Interior, not only governed Canberra but had built and rented out most of the houses in the city. These were clustered according to size and value, and allocated to public servants according to salary. If you were a public servant in a government house and your next-door neighbour was a public servant you knew that he was roughly on your own level. A public servant couldn't aspire to a government house above his station except through promotion. Garnet Bonney as a government employee lived among his like, in this caste system.

The interior of his house was unostentatious for a senior public servant and former editor of a major newspaper. The furnishing was unimpressive, although there were a few good paintings. I discovered later that betting on horses had kept Mr Bonney short of cash. But he liked art, and had bought the paintings at good prices during the Depression. His wife Minnie was anything but what I expected, an unintellectual type with a strident voice and no inhibitions about giving her opinions. But she was cheerful and kindly, and supplied a homely atmosphere in Canberra.

I also found companionship in the press gallery, but at times, mainly weekends, Canberra could be intensely lonely. The Hotel Canberra emptied. I was the only journalist staying there. The dining room was almost deserted, the waiters surly. For a change on Sundays I went to the only restaurant in the national capital, the Blue Moon Cafe at Civic Centre, reached after a long wait for one of the rare Canberra buses. But during the week, working at night in the press gallery, I had no cause to feel alone and displaced.

I saw Beth in Sydney as much as I could. We began to visit estate agents. We would get married in Sydney, we thought, and go overseas later—not too much later. Meantime there was movement at the *Herald* which seemed to reinforce my prospects of being posted to London or New York. Ian Bevan was back in Sydney after a spectacular run of assignments, shuttling backwards and forwards from the London office to Germany, Switzerland, France, Palestine, Greece—wherever there was an upheaval to report on. Harry Kippax succeeded him in London and was writing on theatre, music, books and international affairs. Would I follow Harry in London? And if I did, when? Overseas postings seemed to last for three years. I didn't intend to wait that much longer.

While I was in Sydney for Christmas I had a call from Dave Bailey, the acting news editor. 'We're bringing you back from Canberra for a very interesting assignment,' he told me. 'The *Herald* is going to start a column on page one, and the man we've brought in to write it is Syd Deamer. He asked for a bright young journalist to work with him to get the column started. Syd is a fine writer and a brilliant journalist. You'll learn a lot working with him, and I'm sure you'll enjoy it.' He walked me along the corridor and introduced me to Syd.

I knew something about Syd Deamer, who had been writing feature articles for the *Telegraph*—distinguished and perceptive profiles of interesting people, even Warwick Fairfax. The fact that Fairfax had agreed to be interviewed for an opposition newspaper was proof of the respect Deamer commanded; I don't believe that Warwick had another newspaper interview in his life. Probably his experience then was a major reason for the choice of Deamer to write this tradition-breaking feature, in which Warwick took a close interest. Introducing a front-page column to the *Herald* (which had published for well over a hundred years before recently putting news on the front page) was like the Catholics abandoning the Latin Mass. It was decided that the column would be called Column 8 and published under the signature 'Granny', as the *Herald* itself—Sydney's oldest newspaper—was known. Warwick Fairfax even drafted a first paragraph for the first column. 'Note for juniors:' it read 'I know very well how to suck eggs and a few other things.' The unfortunate wording ensured that his contribution was never published.

The juniors for whom Warwick's contribution was intended were the Sydney *Daily Telegraph* and its columnist David McNicoll. McNicoll was a clever newspaperman and, unusual for a real journalist, the man-about-town type, as his column showed. It was a smooth production from a man who seemed at home in the kind of Sydney society which held no interest for Syd Deamer. Syd was sociable but not social, choosing his companions for their personal, intellectual and conversational qualities. McNicoll displayed a sharp sense of news and reader interest, but Deamer would write a different kind of column, touching usually on more homely concerns.

An Englishman who had served in the Australian army in Gallipoli and France during World War I, Syd settled in Australia after the war. He had been editor of the Melbourne *Herald*, the Sydney *Daily Telegraph* and the *ABC Weekly*. After he left the *Weekly* he went back to the *Telegraph* under its new editor, Brian Penton, an uncomfortable reversal of their old roles. He was relieved to be offered a spot on the front page of the *Herald*.

Syd was full of quirks, ideas and judgments, and poured them all into Column 8. It first appeared without warning or explanation one Monday morning in January 1947, with a drawing of a sharp-nosed old lady in a bonnet at the top, and the signature, Granny, in shaky script at the bottom. Syd had worked hard to get together some material for the first few issues, but once the first column was published stories and suggestions came in from readers by mail and phone, and from journalists on the staff. Ideas that appealed to

him were followed up and worked over with the care that he would have given
to a major piece of writing. His Column 8 pars had clarity, elegance and
humour. Some arose from the everyday concerns of readers, like the strikes
and shortages of the time ('The leader-writers are having an easy time just
now. They merely have to cross out the word gas and put in milk; then cross
out the word milk and put in meat,' et cetera). And the little improbabilities.
The woman in furs who kept her taxi waiting while she collected her pension
cheque. The man who rode his white pony into a Canberra club to show it
off. 'Result—member suspended, pony out for life.' And there were some
sophisticated oddities, like this from an early column:

> Formation of the Foreign Press Association, reported in to-day's news,
> wasn't easy.
>
> The meeting was held at the home of Felix Naggar, French press
> representative.
>
> At one difficult stage the American representative said: 'We appear to
> have reached an impasse.'
>
> 'Impass, impasse!' said Mrs Naggar, echoing the American's pronun-
> ciation, 'What's that mean, impasse?'
>
> 'Cul de sac, my dear,' explained Mr Naggar, 'but only a Frenchman
> would think of saying dead-end.'
>
> And, wishing to ring Mr Naggar, I found that only the phone-book
> would think of calling him Nagger!

I didn't know at first about Syd's drinking. It was under control in the
early days of Column 8 but he soon slipped back, probably surprising only
me. I was working daytime hours and usually left the office before Syd
finished his column, so with evenings free I welcomed an opportunity of
doing some more music criticism. The first time I was given a concert to
review I also had my first experience of Syd's wayward behaviour. Music
criticism was something that I did in my own time, so I'd had no reason
to mention this evening assignment to him when he went out mid-afternoon
saying he would soon be back. But six o'clock, six-thirty, seven o'clock and
seven-thirty came, and Syd did not. I finally rushed up to the Conservatorium
at the last minute, leaving a note explaining my predicament. Syd presumably
returned, for Column 8 appeared the next morning, but when he arrived in
the office that day he attacked me for falling down on my responsibilities.
Column 8 was my job, he said, and I had no right to walk out on it like
that. I told him that he'd put me in an impossible position.

We soon sorted out our quarrel—in fact I believe that Syd's respect for me dated from our argument—but I was still, apparently, not measuring up to his professional standards. He rewrote some of my contributions and threw the rest away until I wrote one item which he accepted without amendment. It was this:

> The Friday Club of Progressive Women, a charitable organisation, met yesterday, Thursday, which was certainly progressive.
>
> It will always meet on Thursdays in future because it can't get a meeting room on Fridays.
>
> But members refused to change the name to the Thursday Club. Even progressive women are conservative about things like that.

We were sitting with a companion upstairs in the lounge of a hotel around the corner from the *Daily Telegraph* office. Syd had been a regular there for years. It was long after six o'clock closing time, the bars were darkened and empty, and we had gone upstairs through a side door. We were seated at a table when the licensee came up with three plates and put some crumbs on them. He spoke in a voice audible only to Syd, who translated afterwards. 'He wants us to look as if we've been eating,' Syd told us. 'Some of the Licensing Squad were here last night playing poker, and lost. He's expecting a raid tonight.'

The conversation suddenly swung away from illicit drinking. 'Yesterday this young man wrote a paragraph that I couldn't have improved on,' Syd suddenly declared. 'You have shown that you can write a piece for this column exactly as it should be,' he said, turning to me. 'I was proud of you.' My friendship with Syd Deamer had begun. Not because of the praise but because we were now colleagues. It may seem strange that he should make an issue of fifty words written on a matter of no consequence. But not everyone can tell a story with point in a few words. Syd took the art of this small literary form seriously.

Working with Syd was an introduction to a new nightlife of Sydney. He often joined the other *Herald* journalists at the pub, enjoying the conversation and getting ideas for his column. But I also experienced, with him, new bars, new people, new restaurants. I have no idea what his wife knew about the life he led but she certainly knew that you could never tell when Syd might go missing or for how long.

Eventually he came into the office one Monday morning, went out again before lunch and didn't return for a week. I kept the column going. Angus McLachlan always saw it before it went to press each night, so I took each day's collection to him for approval, saying nothing about Syd's absence and behaving as if he had just slipped out and I were merely the messenger. It would have been obvious that Syd was missing and why, but McLachlan said nothing to embarrass me. The following Monday morning Syd turned up without a word about the lost week.

I had used up most of his over-matter—copy previously set in type but not yet published—and filled up the rest of the week's columns with my own contributions. Syd immediately settled down to work on the next day's column and rebuild his stock of over-matter, doubtless for similar emergencies in future. But his unpredictability may have been one reason why he, unlike McNicoll in the *Telegraph*, hadn't been given a personal by-line on his column. The *Herald* may well have wondered if he would last. If he hadn't survived, the quality of Granny's column would have suffered, but there would have been no embarrassing disappearance of the *Herald*'s new front-page columnist. The name Granny could cover a multitude of alcoholic writers.

The first thing that Syd impressed on me as an inexperienced young journalist was the importance of pride in one's calling. You have to mix with people at all levels, he said, and you must never think of yourself as inferior to any of them, whatever their position; the role of journalists is just as important as that of the people they write about. But Syd expected a journalist to earn respect and not to assume it.

He also sought to pass on his love and care for the English language, and recommended many books. One was *Stephen Hero*, an early book by James Joyce that nobody knows. *Portrait of the Artist as a Young Man* is the one everyone does know, said Syd, but if you want to read the English language at its finest you must read *Stephen Hero*—'magnificent words from the pen of a boy of nineteen'. Magnificent. It was a word often on his lips.

I worked with Syd for three months until Column 8 was established, and stood in for him after that, not losing touch. 'When I leave Column 8, wherever you are and whatever you are doing, you will be the one they will call on to write it, because no-one else will be able to do it as well,' he told me. Of course it never worked out that way.

I had time then to spend many nights out of the office with him because my affair with Beth had come to an unhappy end. Our break might not have occurred if I had been more mature and able to handle difficulties. I cannot say that I was responsible for what happened but I was the one who took the final step, and felt that I had committed an act of betrayal.

On the international scene there were disturbing developments. Communists had won elections in Rumania and Poland which had clearly been rigged.

One could ignore such claims as propaganda but there were too many of them from sources that couldn't easily be dismissed. Books being published as serials in the *Herald* also helped to change my image of the world. We had already serialised *Animal Farm*, George Orwell's new satire on communist society, and soon published *A Room on the Route* by Godfrey Blunden, an Australian journalist who had been a war correspondent in Moscow and was now working in the *Herald* office in New York. Blunden's novel, telling of a Russian's attempt to escape surveillance and terror in a lovers' hideaway on the street leading to the Kremlin (the 'room on the route') made a worldwide impression; it reinforced the post-war disillusionment with Russia and its repressions. It made an impression on me, too, the novel seeming even more persuasive than the news stories.

I had hovered on the edge of the radical world, going to functions organised by the Australia-Russia Friendship Society and the Australian Writers' Federation, all of whose members seemed to be communists. A young poet, Muir Holburn, introduced me to the Writers' Federation. There I found myself among zealots who seemed to have difficulty in distinguishing fact from fiction. I happened to know something about one of their favourite subjects, the capitalist press—which, whatever its imperfections, was not as they painted it. They complained to me about a *Herald* report on a meeting in which they had been involved. The *Herald* had published deliberate lies about it, they said. They assured me that it wasn't the reporter's fault—it was just that the editors had twisted these things after they had been written. But I knew about this story. I knew that it had been written by Jack Flower, a most competent and honest colleague, and I knew that his report hadn't been twisted by anybody. If there was any twisting being done, these people must have been doing it. Perhaps they were shocked at seeing some of their friends' extreme statements so publicly exposed.

In contrast to this left-wing activity, the forces of conservatism were strong in Sydney, 1947. A colleague on the *Herald*, Lawson Glassop, had just had his war novel, *We Were the Rats*, judged obscene in a case in which a police sergeant swore that he found the word 'bloody' objectionable. This remarkable declaration was taken seriously, the publisher was fined and Lawson was finished as a serious novelist.

The *Herald* commendably started an annual competition for Australian novels. When we serialised the first winner, Ruth Park's *The Harp in the South*, there was such public outrage at the simple realism of its story of life in the slums of Sydney that Warwick Fairfax was moved to publish a signed article, 'Why we Print the Story', in defence of honesty in literature. But I don't want to be hard on culture in Sydney after the war. At least the *Herald* ran its competitions and published the books.

Also in Sydney then: Eugene Goossens was appointed conductor of the Sydney Symphony Orchestra; I saw opera, Shakespeare and modern plays; and I went to an exhibition at the Macquarie Galleries of five guinea (£5 5s.) paintings by Russell Drysdale, Donald Friend, Roland Wakelin, Elaine Haxton, Grace Cossington Smith and others. Almost as amazing to me now as the five guineas was the fact that I didn't buy any. I hadn't grasped the thought of acquiring original new art even at that price.

I busied myself now with work, friends, concerts and books. I became briefly involved with an older woman, then panicked when she made it clear that she had in mind a much longer attachment. But there was a much more significant figure in the background with whom I had a friendly though outwardly cool relationship. She was a young pianist named Leone Stredwick whom I'd heard play, during the war, with the Sydney Symphony Orchestra in the finals of the Australia Broadcasting Commission's concerto and vocal competition. I met her after that because her family had once been friends of my mother's in Grafton. Leone (known as Billie by family and friends) had come to Sydney on a scholarship to study at the Sydney Conservatorium with Alexander Sverjensky. That was how I also came to meet Sverjensky and take piano lessons with him after the war.

When I first met Billie she was a delectable sixteen-year-old, but from the vantage point of my twenty years, which I had just attained, I regarded her as dangerously under age. Any attempt to establish more than a friendly acquaintance, I thought, would probably destroy the chance of anything else later—and this was a possibility that I took seriously. After the war I saw her from time to time and still found her as enticing as ever, but she seemed to have other boyfriends, and I also was otherwise occupied. She now had an apparently serious boyfriend, a young painter studying at the Julian Ashton school. I told myself that I wasn't jealous of him.

At the *Herald* I reviewed some concerts, wrote Column 8 when Syd wasn't there, did a few offbeat news stories ('By a Special Reporter'—no personal identification to give a *Herald* journalist unwanted ideas) and went back to the subs' room. Late that year I was sent back to Canberra while Ray Maley and his offsider Cam Halliday took their holidays. I seemed to be identified as a prospective Canberra specialist, and that suited me. As before, there were enough reporters of my age in the press gallery to provide me with company, though the *Sydney Morning Herald* was the only newspaper that accommodated a junior in the select environment of the Hotel Canberra. Others lived in strictly one-star accommodation in the old Hotel Kingston, Hotel Civic or Hotel Ainslie, and one's social round moved among these scattered buildings, reached by bicycle, by Canberra's infrequent buses or by long walks. None of us had a car.

I made one lasting friendship then, with Rodger Rea, a contemporary of mine who worked for the Sydney *Daily Telegraph*. Rodger had recently been dumped by a girlfriend. In his case it was sex, not love, that had been at stake but we shared feelings of deprivation and were close companions in self-pity. Rodger came from Sydney but was becoming addicted to Canberra and politics.

It was mainly in press gallery conversations that I continued my political education, as Canberra was winding down for the year and parliament soon rose for the end-of-year recess. But it was a significant time politically. Labor's Prime Minister Chifley had just taken the step which would hang fatally over the rest of his term. It was the announcement of his plan to nationalise the Australian banking system. This would do more than anything else to defeat him.

Meeting Chifley, going to his press conferences and watching him in parliament had been my nearest approach to an intimate contact with politics. He remains one of the most engaging men I have encountered. As a speech-maker in parliament the one-time engine driver was unimpressive. His voice was a monotone. Journalists called it gravelly, and I can think of no better word to capture its quality. But Chifley had humanity and honesty, and a well-organised intelligence, and could always hold his own in debate or discussion. He was a courteous man, and at press conferences treated me and any other young reporters exactly as he treated the most senior member of the gallery. I haven't found anyone who knew him who didn't like and admire him personally.

There were two more years to go before Menzies would come back into office on a surge of public reaction. When I was working in the press gallery in Canberra in 1946, 1947 and early 1948, Chifley was undiminished and I was won over. If standard Labor policies were good enough for Chifley they were good enough for me, and I came to see the communists more as the opponent than, as I'd once believed them, the ideal. Through some of the unions they seemed to be set on wrecking the Chifley Government.

I saw much more, later, of Menzies, and often wished that he had Chifley's direct way of getting things done. Menzies had all the understanding but was more cautious, more attracted to waiting. Ray Maley, however, knew his virtues and encouraged me to go into the House of Representatives to listen whenever Menzies was to speak. 'If you listen to Menzies you always learn something,' he said. Years later he became Menzies' press secretary.

I had some time off in Sydney for Christmas 1947 and was asked to make up a party at a Christmas Eve ball at the Roosevelt nightclub with Billie Stredwick and her sister Maxine, Max's boyfriend Bob Spooner and a few others. I wasn't sure how I came to be asked. The others would have known that Billie had had a row with her steady boyfriend, but I had no idea.

The mood of that evening was fatal to the screen of caution which had set our unspoken rules of behaviour. Those rules were for the sixteen-year-old whom I had met three years before. They had nothing to do with the young woman I was with now, and in the early hours of the morning they collapsed forever. Hours later we were standing on the tiny back verandah of the Stredwicks' flat in Manly. It looked out on what remained of the lights along Manly beach but it was anything but a romantic spot. Indeed, as I held her she was leaning back against a sack of potatoes stored on the balcony. I was undeterred. 'This is for life, you know,' I told her. She did not demur. Then we spent every possible moment in each other's company until I had to go back to Canberra just before the new year.

I have never doubted that my future with Billie Stredwick was decided soon after I first walked into the Stredwicks' flat in Manly when I was still in the army. It was a destiny that was nearly rewritten by events, but I soon knew that if the opportunity arose, and if she felt as I hoped, there could be only one outcome. Working out a future for the two of us now, though, was not easy. Billie was trying to get a scholarship to study at the Juilliard School in New York. I would have been prepared to go to New York, too, but Frank Walker, who was a few years older than me, had recently been sent to our office there—despite Paddy the lift driver's claim that I had been going to get the job. And if I took myself overseas I couldn't get to New York anyway: Australia's currency restrictions and America's immigration laws made that impossible. But in Britain an Australian had unrestricted entry and the same rights as any Britisher. Australians *were* Britishers in 1948.

Billie's plans were a natural extension of what she had already done. When she was fifteen Sverjensky, visiting Grafton for the Australian Music Examinations Board, had been horrified to discover what was happening to her—or, more accurately, what wasn't happening. He pleaded with the Stredwicks to let her study at the Conservatorium and offered to teach her without fee until she could get a scholarship. They accepted the upheaval involved, which was great, as her mother Vera was an invalid and Billie's father Roger had no practical way of transferring to Sydney for his company at that time, and no desire to do so. So Vera, Billie and Maxie went to live in Manly with Lettie, a maiden aunt, to look after them. When Billie graduated two years later with the prize for the most distinguished student there was nowhere further that she could go at the Con. By the beginning of 1948 Leone Stredwick was one of Australia's best-known young musicians. This was a reality that had set her on a path which would soon diverge from mine. For how long, who could know?

Returning from my Canberra assignment, I discussed my situation at the *Herald* with Ian Bevan. I knew him best of the batch of journalists slightly older than me. I'd thought that he had a future at the top in the Fairfax organisation, but he was self-reliant and independent, and not inclined to wait for their or anyone else's favours. Our talk put me in a similar mood, and the next morning I checked the shipping notices in the paper and booked a passage to London. Then I saw Angus McLachlan and asked for extended leave to work overseas. He claimed that he couldn't give it to me, but said there was a good chance that they would send me to London soon. I was next on the list. 'As a matter of fact we nearly sent you to New York the last time,' he told me. I marvelled at Paddy the lift driver's inside knowledge and worried about the dilemma with which McLachlan had presented me.

McLachlan had always been helpful, but I was suspicious of the *Herald*'s management collectively. I took the risk, though, and uneasily watched the ship on which I'd been booked sail down the harbour, bound for Southampton. A month later Tony Innes told me to make arrangements to leave for London. 'Mr Henderson says you're to be there as soon as possible,' he said. 'Book yourself on a Qantas flight as soon as you can and we'll get the ticket.' On 15 April 1948 I stepped aboard a new Qantas Constellation aircraft scheduled to make the London flight in a mere four days. I left in a state of confusion; only a week before, Vera Stredwick had lain dead in Manly Hospital.

Vera Giovanelli met Roger Stredwick during World War I when Stred was a recruiting sergeant in Grafton, invalided out of combat duties after his horrors at Gallipoli. He had left school and home in Melbourne at fourteen and worked on the docks. He was tall, fair, handsome, strong, eloquent, gregarious, neurotic and, from some stage in his life, an alcoholic. He settled in Sydney with Vera when they married after the war and got a job on

Smith's Weekly, a paper which specialised in exposure stories. He chased up crime in an opium den in Chinatown and for one story took a job as a warder in what used to be called a lunatic asylum. Vera played the violin in a cafe, the Black Cat. She was a truly gifted player who under other circumstances could have had an outstanding career.

After Max and Billie were born Stred got a job with Atlantic Union (later known as Esso), went to Grafton and took a house near the Giovanelli family home. There, three unmarried Giovanelli sisters still lived together in the timber house that their Italian grandfather Giuseppe had built. Vera was the youngest. Stred was an untamed character, travelling the North Coast for Atlantic Union, staying in pubs and getting on the booze. One of his best drinking mates was Father McEvoy at Maclean. Stred knew how to live on expenses—that was one reason he had always refused a city job in head offfice. He sent his pay cheques to Vera.

Vera was killing herself with the housewives' favourite drug, APC, when I knew her. APC powders—aspirin, phenacetin and caffeine—were the headache cures in everyone's medicine cupboard. Bex, 'the better APC', even gave its name to a review called *A Cup of Tea, a Bex and a Good Lie Down*. Bex powders came in little sheets of paper, folded over, with about a teaspoonful in each. But Vera had her APC made up in bulk by the chemist and kept a big jar beside her as she sat on the couch from which she seldom moved. She doled it out to herself by the heaped desertspoonful. Later, phenacetin was found to be so damaging that it was banned, and APCs were no more. And Vera died suddenly aged forty-eight of a stroke, having already had thyroid surgery and lost a kidney, and no doubt with many other symptoms.

Billie and I sat up very late with Stred when Vera died. He retold much of his life as we sat together for hours. Billie had never really known him, and Vera's death was the start of a new relationship between them.

It was altogether a time of changing relationships. Mine was about to change once more. I was naive enough to embark on my travels in the belief that they were only an interruption to the course of true love and that destiny would find a way for Billie and me to come back together, 'for life' as I'd put it in my Christmas declaration on the back verandah in Manly. The risks of my being in London while she was in Sydney or New York were enormous, but I ignored them.

CHAPTER 4

The Dollar Licence

1948

My one-way air ticket to London cost the *Herald* £300 in 1948. Many people lived on that much a year. There was no economy class; the plane was all first class and half empty. Handsome new Boeing Constellations had just come on to the route, cutting the flight time from nine days to four, with three nights on the ground. We were put up in imposing style along the way: at the old Raffles Hotel in Singapore, one of the emblems of all that seemed enduring in the colonial presence; at some completely new hotel in Karachi which may even have been opened for the first time to accommodate us; and at the Heliopolis Hotel in Cairo, a monumental building of wide, echoing corridors and huge bedrooms made (I thought) for oriental potentates.

It was impossible not to yield to some sense of self-importance in this atmosphere of languid imperial privilege—especially as my journey to London was of mysterious urgency and therefore importance, though the reason for urgency had not been revealed. When I arrived I learned the truth. 'We don't know about any hurry for you to get here,' said Ken Hacket, who met me at the London air terminal. 'We just knew they were sending you over.' Ken himself had arrived recently, posted to London for a year 'to study British newspaper methods'. This meant to cool down after being sacked as chief sub. He welcomed me, guided me to the Cumberland Hotel near Marble Arch and took off back to the office.

Taking the bus down to Fleet Street afterwards, I found that every street was already embedded in my imagination. In one short journey the city sprang from literature into life. I gawked in succession at the signs: Oxford

Street, Regent Street, Piccadilly Circus, Drury Lane, Trafalgar Square, The Strand and Fleet Street itself, above it the unmistakable dome of St Paul's Cathedral on the hill.

The *Sydney Morning Herald* was on the first floor of the Reuter Building, 85 Fleet Street, where the Sydney *Sun* and the Melbourne *Herald* also had their offices. The Australian news agency, AAP, was on the floor above. The *Herald*'s team was a distinguished one. Irvine Douglas, the London editor, was a former news editor of the paper who had also served in the London office during the war. He was a big, ponderous man with the air of a chieftain, benevolent towards most of those who came under his direction. He was to be helpful to me, and would give me any opportunities he could. There was Colin Bingham, later to become editor of the *Herald*, who was its most experienced foreign correspondent. Colin was a sober middle-aged man who specialised in heavyweight international assignments such as the founding of the United Nations, and meetings of heads of state. Angus McLachlan had commended him as a wise man whom I should seek out and learn from, but we never quite clicked with each other. I think that the new arrival was too brash for his taste, and a sense of some such reaction produced a mild resistance in me. Then there was Harry Kippax, four years older than me, a journalist of the highest quality.

Ken Hacket was in the London office under protest. Because of his seniority and the circumstances of his presence he didn't seem to have any specific duties there; he amused himself in miscellaneous ways in the office and amused the rest of us with his stories. Ken knew some funny, or typical, or remarkable, or scurrilous stories about everyone. He didn't write much, but when a subject appealed to him he would produce an article about it, always with felicity and always entertaining.

Another Australian journalist, Ian Fawcett, was on the staff under an arrangement with the Melbourne *Age* to have one of its young men in the *Herald*'s London office. He was a twenty-six-year-old who had served as a squadron leader in the RAF—flying with the Pathfinders, who went in first on bombing missions to find and mark the targets. I think *The Age* had stationed him in London in recognition of his war service. Ian looked the part of the dashing risk-taker, tall and firm-featured. But he had also, in my mind, the air of a young man who had done his dash: thin, pallid, with rings under his eyes and a spirit of detachment from what we were doing. After a year so he resigned from the office. He stayed on in London but lost touch with all of us. I have always imagined him—hoping I was wrong—as one of that sad band of young men who find a heroic role in war, to which the rest of life can be no more than a postscript.

The London office expanded and many other journalists came and went while I worked there, but as far as I can remember this was the entire journalistic staff when I arrived.

The Cumberland Hotel was a monument to British stuffiness in more senses than one—with its hot, airless corridors and its cold, impersonal waiters—and I hurried to get out of it. At Ackroyds' agency in Jermyn Street, off Piccadilly, I leafed through scores of cards listing bed-and-breakfast establishments and places with rooms to let. I rang some of them and made an appointment to inspect a room with breakfast, dinner by arrangement if required, at 37 Eton Avenue, Swiss Cottage. It was the most expensive of those I'd rung, more than I wanted to pay, but the only one where anyone answered the telephone. I decided to move there temporarily, if it was acceptable, until I found something cheaper.

When I rang the bell at 37 Eton Avenue and asked for the owner, Madame Mulot, an English contralto voice informed me with careful emphasis, as if I might not otherwise understand the language: 'I am Madame Mulot.' I soon established myself in her remarkable household, and any thought of moving to save money disappeared. Some mornings the Irish maid woke me with breakfast on a tray. On other days I had to wake with the alarm to start work in Fleet Street at about six o'clock. The early shift was my main job at first. Harry Kippax, Ian Fawcett and I shared it but Harry was an insomniac who overslept after lying awake till four in the morning. When he started sleeping through two alarm clocks Irvine Douglas decided that the early shift should be shared between Ian and me, so I missed more hot breakfasts in Eton Avenue.

The *Herald*'s London news service was produced by a process of organised plagiarism. There were eight London morning newspapers and the *Manchester Guardian* for the man on the early shift to read, and our news service was lifted from them. I went through each of them and checked the copies of the AAP news coverage which had gone overnight to most of the Australian newspapers. Our job was to give the *Sydney Morning Herald* something individual. This was easy when there were so many British newspaper versions of most of the day's stories to choose from. We avoided copying any one paper's story so that our larceny would not be too obvious. A paragraph from here, a paragraph from there, an apt phrase from somewhere else, some judicious changes of wording, and we had our exclusive news service. By the time most of the staff got to the office the man on the early shift had already allocated a list of stories to each of them, keeping the most interesting ones for himself—or that was how it worked when I did the job. We almost never quoted the British newspapers and never acknowledged them as the source of any of our news.

Apart from New York, London was the *Herald's* only overseas office, and the main one. British news had special importance for Australia then, and Australia looked towards Britain for interpretation as well as fact in international affairs. The London office also covered Western Europe, the Iron Curtain countries of Central and Eastern Europe, the Middle East, the whole of Africa and most of Asia, especially India and China, as we had no other source of news on these places.

Doreen Mulot, my London landlady, was a North Country Englishwoman who went to a finishing school in France, married a Frenchman and left him when he brought his thirteenth mistress home. She was about forty, divorced and childless. She was on the stout side as a consequence of her own French cuisine. She could have been French, too, by appearance, with her sharp nose, the curve of the mouth and the small pointed jaw. Her father, Johnny, who lived next door, had a gaunter version of this sharp-featured face—very un-Anglo-Saxon. Thirty-seven Eton Avenue, on the edge of Hampstead, was one in a street of mainly handsome three- and four-storied red-bricked Edwardian houses built for well-to-do families, with large rooms and windows, high ceilings, servants' quarters and basements. Now it was a street of rooms and apartments to let.

My first dinner at Doreen's introduced me to three other paying guests. One was Kay Leather, a discontented French mistress from St Alban's school for girls. There was Muriel Grindrod, the Italian expert at Chatham House, otherwise known as the Institute of International Affairs. Muriel had, one must admit, a face that would sink a thousand ships, one of the worst jumbles of prominent upper teeth I have come across, and (as I thought) a supremely affected English accent, but as soon as I saw beyond the face and the voice I liked her. Unlike Kay she was happy and not frustrated, having a boyfriend named Hugh Latimer who also worked at Chatham House. It was a middle-aged romance, and I think he was her first lover. Hugh visited her twice a week. When I became more at home in this house I often sat and talked and drank vermouth with Doreen in the kitchen, directly under Muriel's bedroom. I regret to say that we smirked at the moans of ecstasy that could sometimes be heard through the ceiling and the floorboards above. Apparently they were not inevitable, though, for 'sometimes we just lie there and don't do anything', Muriel told Doreen.

Doreen, after marriage to M. Mulot, regarded such behaviour as unnatural and beyond comprehension. Hugh sometimes came to dinner. He was a modest and agreeable man who didn't leave any strong impression, except on Muriel.

The third guest on my first night at Doreen's was Muriel's ageing father, who sat silently at the table, staring. Mr Grindrod had spent some years in Burma. At one point during dinner he spoke, ignoring the subject of conversation to say that Burmese was a tonic language, and giving an example of a Burmese word which had three different meanings according to its pitch. After that, silence again. Mr Grindrod also walked the house knocking on doors, any time from six in the morning till late at night. 'Can you tell me the way to Rochdale?' he asked. He went out in his pyjamas, dressing-gown and slippers and asked people in the streets. I believe he said only one other thing during the rest of his life. That was when he claimed that a maid had come into his room and made lascivious gestures. Poor Daddy Grindrod, at least he was lucky in some of his fantasies.

Beyond Doreen's regency dining table, within the fold of a large bay window that faced the high-walled garden, was a grand piano. Doreen had hired this for the missing boarder, who was away. It was typical of her to do so, and just as typical that she should serve French wine with our dinner at her expense, so that we probably drank whatever small profit she made out of the food.

The missing person was a Frenchman of thirty named Freddy Lassalle. Freddy, I soon found, was short, dark, powerfully built, part Jewish, part French, part Portuguese. He had a kind of information job for the French Embassy and used to give a talk to English audiences entitled 'The Strange Ways of the French'. It was actually a funny and well-observed commentary on the strange ways of the English, something in the manner of the Hungarian George Mikes ('Continental people have sex lives; the English have hot-water bottles'). Freddy was away giving his 'Strange Ways' talk in provincial centres. He had met Doreen because she had spent much of the war working as secretary to his best friend, Jean-Louis Brillac, who was de Gaulle's information chief when the general had his Free French headquarters in London after the fall of France in 1940 (and who, incidentally, became a minister in de Gaulle's post-war government). Freddy was penniless when Jean-Louis got him the job in London. He had spent the whole time from the fall of France to the end of the European war in German prison camps. Life for him in post-war France was hard, especially as he was helping his sister and her two sons. Her husband had been killed by the Germans.

With people like this staying there, Doreen's place was a bilingual household which greatly helped my French and greatly increased, for me, the subsequent pleasures of France. A close friend of mine from Sydney, Mike Hutcheson, also contributed to my education in London. He was working for a big magazine publisher and living at his parents' house in Amersham, in Buckinghamshire—my introduction to the countryside of England. Mike also took me immediately to an exhibition from the Courtauld art collection and a show of cleaned masterpieces at the National Gallery. The Courtauld paintings gave me the electric shock that comes from a first encounter with the impressionists when you think you know them from reproductions. Suddenly there is a new vision which is as fresh as if the paint had not had time to dry. And at the National Gallery the delicate subtleties, no less than the colour (trumpet blasts of colour, in the case of the El Grecos) that had emerged from under the sludge of yellowed varnish on the old paintings was to me almost unbelievable. My visits with Mike to these two exhibitions changed most of my feelings about art.

I still saw Billie's and my separation at this time as no more than an interruption. And in my first months in London I met no-one to challenge our relationship. In Sydney, Billie was broadcasting, playing at music clubs, preparing for another ABC concerto competition and waiting to compete for the ABC's annual overseas scholarship. For this she was one of three finalists selected. Frances Moran from Perth was the surprising winner but, unexpectedly, this was not the end of Billie's chances of studying in America. The Grafton Rotary Club decided to sponsor an overseas scholarship fund for young people from the Northern Rivers district of New South Wales, with Billie its first beneficiary.

The pub next to the Reuter building was a meeting place for Australian journalists. Any of our staff who were about at the end of the day would call there. We met the Sydney *Sun* and Melbourne *Herald* people, too, even the Melbourne *Herald*'s London editor, Trevor Smith, who disdained juniors and didn't speak to me. His behaviour made difficulties for colleagues who knew us both, as it required them to carry on two separate conversations simultaneously. The Melbourne *Herald* seemed to specialise in people like that: Harold Cox, head of their Canberra office, was the same. The only other journalist with whom I had friends in common, and who also refused to acknowledge my presence, was Guy Harriott of the *Sydney Morning Herald*, whom I used to encounter in the *Herald* pubs in Sydney. Guy put some of my amiable colleagues there through the same uncomfortable process of conducting two dissociated conversations. Trevor Smith was something of a special case, though. He must have been astonished (as I was) when we met at a dinner in London for Old Sydneians—old boys of Sydney Grammar School. He was quite friendly afterwards.

The Sydney *Daily Mirror*'s office was around the corner from Fleet Street but sometimes their people visited our pub. I got to know their London editor, Eric Baume, in this way; he came to meet Ken Hacket there. Eric was famous among newspapermen, an adventurer, an outsized personality; he spilled out millions of words in newspaper copy, novels and, later, talk, for he became one of the big performers in early commercial television in Australia. Eric had been in London for some years. The foreign affairs specialist in his office was Lady Margaret Stewart, who was also his girlfriend. She was a good journalist, too. But the ordinary rules weren't for Eric. He used Margaret's flat for other assignations, according to Ken, when he sent her to Europe on jobs.

Ken had left his family in Sydney to ensure that the *Herald* would keep its promise to release him from exile in a year. One weekend he and Eric went off to the country with a couple of women Eric knew. 'There's one thing I want to tell you, Ken,' said Eric. 'On no account while you're here get involved in anything serious, otherwise everything starts falling apart, the next thing you know your marriage is finished, you've lost your family, everything's a mess. I know. So there's one thing you've got to remember here, Ken: never look above the cunt. Never forget it, never look above the cunt, Ken, never look above the cunt,' he repeated helpfully. Ken didn't need the advice. His marriage and family were not in danger.

It was a few months before I had any opportunity to do much beyond working on the daily news service. I used to go up to Australia House for a weekly press conference given by the high comissioner, Jack Beasley, a former Federal Labor minister known in politics as Stabber Jack. But the high commissioner's job in London was regarded as the Australian politician's greatest perk, and once in it Beasley seemed perfectly benign and showed none of the characteristics that earned him his nickname. I cultivated Stabber Jack to get the London news on matters of special interest to Australia.

Our office was busy, sometimes frantically, buying books for serialising. The serials were one of many features being flung at readers in a contest for circulation in Sydney between the *Herald* and *Telegraph*. We also had special country pages, new magazine inserts, an ambitious children's magazine and competitions of all kinds. The *Herald* bought freight planes to get ahead in country circulation, dropping bundles of papers from the air in low-flying runs near a series of country towns and, incidentally, killing some pilots. We bought our serials in London from publishers offering new books by well-known authors. One of us had to hurriedly read each of these and make an immediate recommendation to Sydney.

We also bought a feature service from the London *Daily Express*. This also gave us access to books which the *Express* itself had bought; by buying them from the *Express* we were saved the work of editing them into serial form. But the pressure for material soon became so great that a telex arrived from Sydney one morning saying that that publication of one of the *Express*'s books would start the next day although we hadn't even bought it. It was too late to stop them. The book was a biography by Alec Waugh of Sir Thomas Lipton, the tea man, famous for his costly attempts to win the America's Cup.

In those days before computers and photocopiers there were no spare copies of unpublished manuscripts, so we had to get each episode of the book in proof form from the *Express* building in Fleet Street as soon as it was set in type. There was as much haste in the *Express* office as in ours, and they were rushing to edit and typeset their serials day to day, just ahead of their needs. Sydney had only just received the first airmailed sample episodes of the still unpublished Lipton book when they decided to start immediate publication and required instant follow-up instalments to keep going. These did not exist. We finally had to send the whole book in daily instalments by telex.

Telex messages were translated from English into cablese, a language developed partly for clarity and partly for economy, as messages were charged for by the word. If you were sending a Shakespeare sonnet in cablese, for instance, you would begin like this: SHALL EYE COMPARE THEE TO A SUMMERS DAY QUERY. This was the clarity mode. There was also the economy mode. The only example that comes readily to mind after all these years is, I regret to say, a crude imprecation used by an angry journalist: UPSTICK ARSEWISE. But it illustrates the style.

Each day after finishing work on the news service I edited the latest episode of Lipton into cablese and our teleprinter operator stayed back to type it up and send it. Near the end we received a telex saying that Sydney intended to finish publication of the book the next day. Luckily the *Express* was able to send us the final two or three episodes in one bundle. I immediately cut them down to a single instalment. It went off the same day, and thus ended the only book—as far as I know—ever telexed from Britain to Australia.

Among the people in the London office Colin Bingham was always going to international conferences but Harry Kippax was doing something that I envied much more. He had been sent to report on the civil war in Greece, where the communists' challenge to the government was reaching its climax. It was a bitter campaign engaging deep concern in other countries, for Greece was at the very edge of the conflict between the communist and non-communist worlds. The communists couldn't seize power there through political means with Russian support as they had done in East Germany, Poland, Hungary, Czechoslovakia and Bulgaria. Unlike those countries, Greece had not been 'liberated' by the Russians at the end of World War II. So here the local communists could win power in one way only—with the gun.

The countries of Europe were bound to Greece by twentieth-century alliances and two thousand years of culture. Britain especially was giving active support to the government, but the fighting was fierce and the outcome unpredictable. Harry bypassed the foreign correspondents who by then were reporting the conflict from Athens. Using what I would still call traditional Australian initiative, he went straight to the front and wrote the story of the war there. He was an eloquent writer, with power to evoke scene and mood. The *Herald* was doubly pleased with his series on Greece because it sold the material to *Life*; publication in this American magazine was probably the best billing that Harry's report could have achieved. And *Life* paid. The *Herald* got the money and Harry got a rise.

Then *Life* asked if he could do a piece on Andorra. He went there and wrote a marvellous article on this tiny, other-worldly principality hiding in the Pyrénées between France and Spain. When I read it I not only wanted to get some assignments like this, but also to see Andorra for myself. Years later I did, with results far different from expectation: in fact they were one of the disillusionments of my life. By 1961 Andorra's tiny ancient capital, Andorra la Vieja (population, approximately one thousand), was overrun with French cars, holiday crowds and shoddy new concrete hotels, cracked and old before their time. Andorra la Vieja had become a jerry-built monument to duty-free. But at the end of the '40s Harry's assignments in the old hidden Andorra and in Greece showed me that life in the *Herald*'s London office was not confined to mass production of news or the editing of serials.

Harry got his rise because the chairman, Warwick Fairfax, was in London. Warwick's mission had nothing to do with the office; he was there on holiday with his new wife Hanne, his secondary purpose being to buy a Bristol car. There could be only one reason to want a Bristol, and that was because nobody else in Australia had one. Bristol sports saloons were the Bristol aircraft company's folly. It produced hardly any of them, and the production of each was as personal and individual as in-vitro fertilisation. Ken Hacket spent days discussing Warwick's needs and queries with the Bristol people and relaying their answers to Warwick. He tried to persuade Warwick not to buy the car at all. Who would know how to look after it? Warwick was immoveable, and Ken's next task was to arrange the car's transport to Australia. He told me that it spent most of its time there in the garage, as Warwick had constant trouble with it and finally lost interest. While he was in London for this acquisition I was introduced to Warwick for the first time. We both said 'How do you do', and perhaps he may even have remembered who I was on subsequent days when he sneaked into the office for consultations about the car.

Billie was moving closer to America. The Grafton Rotary overseas scholarship fund was established and Bill Tart, editor of the *Grafton Daily Examiner*, was backing it. The principal fundraising activity was Billie's recital tour of the area. The *Daily Examiner* promoted it, local committees organised concerts, and in June she set out from Grafton with Stred in his company car. At the end of a month she had a new feeling for her father, one which had begun to develop when we sat up talking with Stred the night Vera died. At the end of the month there was money in a trust fund which would be sent in instalments to Billie in America until it ran out. She also had a cheque from the Young Musicians' Group of the Musicians' Union, which arranged a ball on the Sydney Showboat for her benefit. With these funds, and a little she had saved from her earnings, it seemed that she would have enough money to live frugally in the United States for a year or two. She booked a passage on an American ship leaving Sydney at the end of July.

Transferring funds overseas at this time required government assent, and American dollars were especially hard to get. Just as Billie was preparing to leave, a new wave of foreign exchange problems arose and all dollar allowances which had been approved but not yet taken up were reviewed. It was said that Chifley, who was treasurer as well as prime minister, went through them personally. Suddenly Billie's dollar allocation was cancelled and our expectations were overturned. She was coming to England instead, and would sail soon on the P&O ship *Maloja*.

Just before Billie arrived in England I went to Paris with Freddy Lassalle. A close friendship was developing between us. We both had time for it.

Freddy had had an English girlfriend before I arrived, but that affair hadn't lasted. He had tried Doreen's Irish maid instead, and been rebuffed; she had a man in Ireland.

Freddy loved Paris and wanted me to see his city through Parisian eyes. From the perspective of today's traveller it is hard to imagine how a foreign city could seem no less than holy ground. Yet Paris did then, to me and others. Freddy and I caught a boat-train at night, and in the morning stood off Dieppe in an impenetrable autumn fog, listening in the cold and damp to the bells of other boats close by as they too waited, motionless and invisible in the mists that enveloped us.

I was unprepared for one difference between Paris and London: parts of London, the city saved from invasion, had been bombed to bits; Paris, defeated and occupied, had been spared. Apart from the boarding up of the huge rose window of Sainte-Chapelle, the great buildings of Paris were intact in their splendour; the clerestory windows of Notre Dame cast their grey light inwards onto the slender soaring columns as they had done for seven centuries. As I walked down the nave a shiver ran over my back. Some music did this to me. No-one had ever told me that stones could do it, too.

The visit to Paris was a distraction that I needed as the SS *Maloja* neared England. I left for London after a week. Freddy confided that his sister Ginette liked me very much, in fact had developed the most tender feelings towards me. What do you mean? I asked him. As tender as they could be, he replied. Freddy stayed on in Paris and I caught a freezing train back through the frost-bleached French countryside. I had to get down to Southampton to meet Billie.

CHAPTER 5

The Flat Finder

1948 to 1951

Billie arrived in London with her sister Maxine. Max had broken off with her boyfriend and it was still only a few months since their mother's death. She suddenly realised what it would mean to be left alone, and sailed for London at a few days' notice.

Billie and I had to overcome a strangeness that we must both have felt— I certainly did—after our time apart. We had both been living at an accelerated pace, and been changed by unshared experiences. A surge of wonder and discomfort struck me at the sight of this new person whom I didn't quite know. Had the spell been broken? A day or so later I was able to bury these misgivings.

Swiss Cottage was too expensive for Billie and Max, so they moved into rooms on the cramped first and second floors of a small terrace house in Elms Crescent, Clapham. It was a brown house with brown furniture in a brown street. The elms of Elms Crescent were amputated stumps which later, in spring, put on modest signs of life. Installed in this dreary environment, Billie began piano lessons with Harold Craxton, who had been known for years as the best teacher at the Royal Academy. Craxton had just retired from the academy and begun to teach privately. He seemed to be still the best teacher in London for advanced piano studies.

I now began to get the kind of writing opportunities I was looking for. I covered a Commonwealth Prime Ministers' Conference in London, travelled north to the coalfields to write the story of Britain's nationalised coal industry and visited Holland to see the first Dutch migrant ship leave for

Australia. I travelled through much of Holland and wrote on the single-mindedness of its people in those early post-war years. Farmers were still living in timber cottages which had been neglected for so long that they were falling down about their owners, yet the stores were kept and the cattle slept in large and splendid new barns of brick and tile. And the Dutch didn't cry as they farewelled their migrating friends and families at the quayside.

In January 1949 the *Herald* started publication of a Sunday newspaper, and the *Sunday Herald* had such big feature sections that our whole office was busy helping to fill them. I started writing feature articles each week, sometimes on places I had never seen, such as Palestine, Hungary and Finland; for these I still had to draw on information from the British newspapers and weeklies. But I could often go to my own sources in London, and began a series of interviews for profiles of writers, artists and public figures.

The British Ministry of Supply arranged frequent tours of industry for correspondents from Empire countries—yes, there was still a British Empire. Britain was trying to show that the spirit of wartime survived and was getting the country back to normal. There was, indeed, a good-humoured determination about, yet there was a kind of aimlessness in our tours. The organisers entertained us excessively, but made no effort to discover our interests. So I wrote very little afterwards about British industry. There was something seriously missing in the whole effort, and later, as we know, the sense of something missing in Britain grew, the fighting spirit declined and an affliction known as the English disease emerged. The early symptoms were probably there in 1949 but we couldn't make the diagnosis.

I followed up a story that fifty-five former Czech members of parliament had fled the country since the communist takeover, and I interviewed some Czech political refugees in London. The story had special significance for me. My old left-wing sympathies had left me with still an uneasy suspicion about current reports on the excesses of the communist regimes. But the Czechs' emotional accounts of their treatment and escapes left no room for doubting. The repertoire of cruelty which they described was not new; it was the experience of hearing it directly from them, fresh from the events, that struck home. This and the overriding feature of all their ordeals, the story behind all the stories: the conversion of whole countries like Czechoslovakia into armed compounds from which citizens might escape only at the risk of death.

One of the refugees told me that near one escape point the regime in

Czechoslovakia had built a frontier within the frontier, and a guard post staffed with German-speaking guards in German uniforms to welcome escapees. By the time they discovered that they were still in Czechoslovakia, he claimed, some of those who were fleeing had incriminated people who had tried to help them escape.

So soon after World War II something near panic had overtaken the world. The USSR had brought under its control every country that its armies had liberated, and had turned international negotiation on its head; every step towards a more peaceful relationship was being blocked at the conference table. The West's wartime alliance with Russia had fallen apart. One could understand suspicion on both sides but the Russians were going beyond suspicion into a crescendo of hostility. Just before mid-1948 they had taken a very sinister step—in Berlin.

Germany was still divided into four occupation zones controlled by Americans, Russians, British and French. The old capital, Berlin, the centre of power and culture in pre-war Germany, was now under its own four-power control but was isolated deep within the Russian occupation zone. In mid-1948, when the Russians cut off all road and rail access to Berlin, the Berlin blockade became the focus and symbol of the east–west conflict. The Western powers were determined to supply Berlin by air and to do so as long as the blockade continued.

We were writing about the Berlin blockade and the Berlin airlift all through the second half of 1948 and the early months of 1949. Then, after almost a year, suddenly and without explanation, the Russians called it off. Had they accepted that the airlift had beaten the blockade? Or would they renege at the last minute? Irvine Douglas gave me the opportunity to go to Germany and find out, and to get to Berlin on the first transport through the Russian sector. A day or two later I was in Hamburg. It was the nearest major centre to Helmstedt, a small town on the border between the British and Russian zones. For me, coming from London, this was the only border point I could get to in time.

Midnight on 11 May 1949 was the hour for the lifting of the blockade. My first news story, filed the next morning from Berlin, was a descriptive piece 'From our Staff Correspondent, who Travelled to Berlin on the First Train'. I wrote of the wild scenes at the road border near Helmstedt as journalists, photographers and radio reporters from all over the world waited for the Russians to let the first car through. Scores of shouting photographers swarmed past the Russian barrier as midnight passed, jostling the German police and climbing on top of the Russian sentry boxes to get their shots as cars came through crammed to the roof with supplies for Berlin. Half an hour later, when the excitement had cooled, I rushed back to Helmstedt to be on the first train.

At the road border there had been a big crowd of Germans; all day long German families pushing prams, children in tattered and dusty clothes and young men on crutches, wearing old German Army uniforms, had been trudging up the three-mile road from Helmstedt to watch the preparations at the frontier. But in the early hours of the morning the first train left almost in silence from a nearly empty station. Soon afterwards we stopped at Marienborn, where Russians with rifles and automatics paced the platform and a few German civilians made faces at them behind their backs; then on to Berlin. When we reached the Charlottenburg station in Berlin in the morning there was a desultory search for the mayor, who failed to arrive for the ceremonial welcome, and after a few minutes everyone dispersed. The historic moment had ended in anticlimax, but the events of the night were tumbling through my mind as I typed out my first despatch from Germany.

When I got to my hotel in Berlin it was *verboten* to use the lift. It had been *verboten* for months, and I went up four or five floors by the stairs. At lunchtime the lift was working again; the liftman ran his hands over the walls for the pleasure of feeling again their lining of red plush. But he was disappointed: the first day was too much for his lift, and an hour later it had broken down. I mentioned the liftman in my big piece for the *Sunday Herald* the next day, feeling that he and his lift were somehow symbolic of the time and place, but I didn't write about the Foreign Press Club. The club had kept going through the blockade, and in near-starving Berlin its members still enjoyed the best of food and wine. We all got somewhat drunk there. Afterwards some of us staggered through the garden in the dark to listen to a nightingale. An enraptured BBC man was out there, too, recording the nightingale's song against the sound of a transport aircraft on the airlift run, breaking into the silence of the night. He was obviously finding it difficult to stay upright, but for a BBC man the show must go on.

The broken shell of Berlin lay almost as it had been after the last bomb fell. Along the wide highway that swept eastward through the city all was dead—government buildings, theatres, a university, huge office blocks all open to the sky. The outer walls of many of the great buildings were torn open but still standing; inside, the rest had crashed down, held in by the walls like rubbish in a bin. There were miles of streets like that. Plants growing wild in the ruins were in leaf and blossom. Under them were bodies trapped since 1945. Nothing in the worst damaged parts of London had prepared me for the huge desolation of the German cities.

There was little traffic along the highway into the Russian sector. You simply passed a notice, 'You are now leaving the British sector', and went straight on, no Berlin Wall, no sentry boxes, no guards. You were in Berlin's most famous street, the Unter den Linden—under the linden trees— the old romantic name resonating grotesquely with this relic of death and destruction. The ruin here was even worse. In the western sector they had at least cleared the roadways. In the Russian sector, buildings that had collapsed on to side streets still lay there. But I was in a madhouse. Loudspeakers on the pavements were broadcasting cheerful music, red flags were flying, poles on the footpaths were garlanded. All this to mark a 'free democratic election' in which the only missing element was a democratic opposition. The ballot paper required the citizens to vote for candidates from approved parties and to declare whether or not they stood for a united Germany and a just peace settlement. It was a nonsensical question.

I went back again to the Soviet sector to do an article on voting day. Technically, the elections weren't rigged: the restricted choice of candidates ensured control to the communists, operating there under the name of the Social Unity Party. When I tried to talk about the elections to people outside the polling booths or in the street they were suddenly in a hurry. 'You don't know whether you're being spied on,' said one. 'You can't say what you want to say here.' I went back out of the Soviet sector past a huge red banner across the street which translated as: Sector of Freedom.

I came back from Germany through Düsseldorf, in the state of North Rhine-Westphalia, the richest state in Germany. Even amid incredible destruction Koenigs-Allee, the main street of Düsseldorf, had hastily reopened shops full of luxuries, elegant glassware, china, fashionable clothes, jewellery, silverware, objets d'art. It was a callous street of opportunists, not haunted by thoughts of the homeless still living in the air-raid shelters. The British, newly conditioned to the welfare state at home, were fearful of the direction this recovery was taking and the seeming indifference of the German authorities to their homeless. The attitude of the British was understandable. How could they dream that in twenty years the living standards of the West Germans would surpass those of Britain, for the first time since the Industrial Revolution?

My final article from Germany was about the politicians likely to emerge in the new federal government of Germany. I had written copiously during my much-desired foreign assignment in Germany and felt happy with the result. But the *Herald* was, unfortunately, entering a period in which such assignments would be rare. It had sent correspondents all over the world during the war. For a few years after that, *Herald* staff still travelled fairly widely, reporting on the transition to peace. But gradually foreign assignments became a rarity, and *Herald* journalists had to find their opportunities in other ways.

Harold Craxton, recently retired from the Royal Academy, told Billie that it was pointless for her to study there. 'You've done all that at the Conservatorium in Sydney,' he said. 'What you want now is to concentrate on repertoire.' This was almost the worst advice she ever received. By going to Craxton's home in Hampstead for private lessons she missed all the opportunities that the academy offered, and missed the company of other young musicians. She bought an old Broadwood piano, practised on it in isolation at Clapham, and cried every day. Craxton had acted with good intention. He had taught at the Royal Academy for so many years that he took its advantages for granted and didn't realise what they could mean to a twenty-year-old stranger.

Early in 1949 Billie, Max and I picked up Freddy Lassalle in Paris and took a coach to the Mediterranean. At our hotel in Nice, Freddy and I shared a room. Billie and Max had a single room each. Each night I waited till Freddy was asleep, then crept into the room next door. When we got back to Paris Billie and I abandoned our discretion and took a hotel room together. We decided that when we got back to London Billie and Max would move to Hampstead and I would move in with them.

There were changes in the *Herald* office. Irvine Douglas went back to Sydney as news editor following Angus McLachlan's appointment as general manager. They wanted Ken Hacket to take Douglas' place in London as he knew they would, but he refused, so Harry Kippax took over as London editor. My own work didn't change, and it was a long time before I got another assignment outside England, but I did get a boost to my self-esteem: Harry as London editor made me his deputy. Stan Monks, who had returned to England and joined the London staff, challenged his decision. Stan was the British journalist who had taken over my spare-time role as a music critic in Sydney. Harry somewhat speciously explained that he was sure the management would want the responsibility of acting as his deputy to go to someone from the Australian staff. This was my first executive function, and when Harry was absent I exercised it. Stan Monks's objections were an extra attraction—not that I had anything against him. I understood exactly how he felt. He was ten years older than me, and ambitious.

There were other movements between London and Sydney, and the *Herald* recruited a number of British journalists for the Sydney office, but the most productive of our local recruits stayed on in London. He was Les Swainson, an unpretentious, likeable fellow who would write on anything, but came to specialise in the arts and entertainment. It took Les to demonstrate to us Australians the full potential for milking the British press. He had no time to leave the office to report on anything, and I suspect that he never saw or heard any of the performances he wrote about, for in his spare time he was busy writing pulp fiction for a publisher of cheap paperbacks. Les was worth two normal people to the *Herald*.

Warwick Fairfax's son James visited London during Harry Kippax's term. He didn't have anything to do with the London office but was being prepared in some way for his dynastic role in the Fairfax organisation. Harry went to the airport to meet him and was dismayed when James dropped his cabin bag and left it on the ground for Harry to pick up and carry. I am glad to know of the public-spirited things he has done subsequently, unwittingly making amends for his youthful behaviour. He must have had a lot of Fairfax upbringing to overcome.

We found a flat in an old building on the top floor of a four-storey building at 19 Hampstead Hill Gardens, a broad side street off Pond Street near a corner of Hampstead Heath. Hampstead Hill Gardens is not far from the Hampstead shops and Underground and Belsize Park station— exactly in the area where we wanted to live.

The owner of our new establishment, Miss Fiddler, didn't mind Billie's piano or her practice. The rent-collector was her nephew, Mr Smyrk, whose name was not a totally accurate description but had a sufficiently unfortunate tone to be appropriate. We found the flat through a man who called himself the Flat Finder, in Pond Street. It was really he who should have been called Mr Smyrk. He had an unctuously offensive manner which was on immediate display, even in giving such mundane information as the name of the laundry which collected and delivered in the area ('but you Australians do your own washing, don't you?') and the story on milk deliveries. Two dairy companies delivered milk in the area, one of them a cooperative.

'That's the socialist milkman,' he said with contempt. 'Of course not many people use the socialist milkman *here*.' After that I would have patronised the co-op even if its milk had been poisoned.

Our flat on the fourth floor was a sort of attic with sagging ceilings. The three bedrooms provided our new domestic arrangement with some air of respectability, and the largest bedroom was big enough to double as a practice studio. The illusion of respectability was useful in a way which it would be difficult for people of the same age, today, to understand. The convention allowed you to do what you wanted—with discretion. Openly living together would have unnecessarily defied the convention, and few people went so far. If they did they would arouse dismay in their families and other people's disapproval. We told the locals that I was Billie's and Maxie's cousin, and most people believed it. But—as it emerged later—not the Flat Finder.

A Norwegian pianist named Lars Larsson was one of Billie's fellow students. He was musically most gifted and was trying to make up for inadequate training earlier, the result of the war and of living in a small city, Bergen, where he didn't have access to a good piano teacher. Lars was liked by everyone, especially girls. He was tall and good-looking and had age and experience on his side, being already about thirty although he didn't want to be, pretending to be younger. His visits to our flat became more and more frequent, and soon he and Max were having a romance which was looking increasingly serious.

At the end of 1949 one of Australia's most significant federal elections had been held, the one which brought the return of Menzies to power after eight years of wartime and post-war Labor rule. Because elections are held on Saturdays the *Sydney Morning Herald* had no experience of election-night reporting, but now that there was a *Sunday Herald* everything was changed. The *Sunday Herald* mishandled the story completely, reporting a 'photo-finish' election when the opposition papers, the *Sunday Sun* and *Sunday Telegraph*, correctly identified a landslide to the Liberals. Irvine Douglas, as news editor of the *Herald*, had overall charge of the election arrangements and was held responsible. He was dismissed from the news editorship and sent to Canberra, displacing Guy Harriott as federal political correspondent. Harry Kippax returned to Sydney to take over as news editor. These changes had a great influence on my subsequent moves at the *Herald*.

I knew little of Harry's successor in London, Harry Williams, but from what I did know I thought that the good times had come to an end. The decision to move the two Harrys must have been taken quickly, for there was a gap of some weeks between Harry Kippax's departure and Harry Williams' arrival, and for that time the London office was left in my hands. My self-importance grew.

The new Harry was a tough-looking little man who, though balding already, still looked the part that he must have longed to relive, that of a hard Australian soldier, most at home in a comradely group of other strong, dependable men. He lived as much as possible in the past, dwelling on his stories of the war. He hadn't much imagination, had no new ideas for the office and was content to let me and others get on with our jobs as long as things went without trouble. But he turned out to be a first-class colleague and a man to be trusted. He was much more complex than I realised at first, for Harry was an only son and had a Mother. Phil Palmer, the secretary of the company, used to dread her calls and imperious demands after Harry left for London. And then she broke her hip. She was patched up, or so it seemed, but later that year she died. For Harry this was not only an occasion for regret: shortly afterwards he told me that his girlfriend Helen was coming to London to marry him. It was the wedding day that gave Harry away, though no-one knew what to make of it, exactly.

It was a middle-aged marriage, the first for both of them, and John Reading, a journalist I knew from Sydney days, said that for years Harry's friends had been asking him why he didn't make Helen an honest woman. So it had been going on all that time! I had always imagined Harry as sexless. He'd rather have been out in the desert with his slouch hat on, fighting Germans or Italians, I believed, than home in bed with a woman. At any rate Harry and Helen were married one lunchtime in a small church behind Fleet Street. It was undergoing repairs, full of planks, pews piled up, dust and dustsheets. The clergyman gave such a sombre and dreary oration that it seemed more appropriate to the last rites for a prisoner about to hang. He made me think of the Quivering Brethren in *Cold Comfort Farm*, and their preacher crying: 'You're all damned!' There was not even music, and we heard Harry's new shoes squeaking as he walked down the aisle in the otherwise silent church.

Were these the best church and preacher that Harry could find? Or did he choose them for some special qualities? Whatever, we kissed the bride and left the two of them and stumbled out over the builders' debris to get a late counter lunch near Fleet Street. The guests would reassemble that night for the wedding reception in a West End restaurant. Meantime it was back to the office for an afternoon's work.

And whom did we find waiting there when we got back? Harry Williams, the bridegroom. Not back to work, just there to pass the time until dinner. Just standing around looking at his shoes. Another journalist friend, Tom Flower, has claimed that Harry had a shoe fetish. He knew every type and brand, he collected unnecessary shoes, studied the art of shoe polishing and looked at his feet. At least it was something to do that afternoon.

Billie and I went to France again when I got my holidays in 1950. It was April, a time to go south to Provence and the Mediterranean. But under British currency regulations we could take only £30 sterling a year each out of the country, so we decided to hitchhike. Hitchhikers weren't popular in France, as some had been attacking drivers, so there were often long gaps between lifts. But these provided part of the joy of the journey as we walked on, sometimes for hours, absorbed in the landscape. We bought cheese and bread and fruit and red wine in the towns and ate them in the fields by the way, sleeping off the red in the long grass after lunch.

As we hitchhiked towards the south we were dropped off near the Roman ruins of Orange and the bridge of Avignon, and were picked up in a thunderstorm by a man taking cheeses to Nice. There we walked down to the waterfront and read a sign about a night sailing to Corsica. Despite our £30 budget we could afford this one, as it offered a fourth-class fare for almost nothing.

Fourth-class travel was either down in the airless bottom of the ship or on a stairway landing. We chose to hire deckchairs, again for almost nothing, and sat on the landing—a good move, as everyone downstairs was sick in a storm that night, even the dogs. Then we stepped ashore in Ajaccio in sunshine. The unexpected scent of gum trees hung in the air and we found Australian flannel flowers in bloom along the roadsides.

After a few days we tried to set off by bus for the other side of the island without seeing Napoleon's birthplace in Ajaccio, but the waiter in our hotel wouldn't let us—he took us there himself. Napoleon had had a favourable start in what was clearly the house of a family of influence. But once you saw the countryside of Corsica you could see where the toughness of the little self-made emperor came from. It was harsh and beautiful, and its feeling was of isolation. So I don't want to go back there. I don't want to know what the age of tourism has done to it.

Jimmy Trainer, a Scot, was a Church of England clergyman. His wife, Ailsa, was a cousin of Maxie's old boyfriend, Bob Spooner. The Spooners were a political family. Bob's father Bill was a minister in the Menzies Government. Bill Spooner's brother Eric was a state minister in New South Wales in the '30s who achieved fame by banning anything shorter than neck-to-knee bathing costumes for both men and women on Sydney beaches. Eric Spooner and family came to London while we were there, and we visited them in an elegant terrace house near Bayswater. His family didn't tell him when they discovered that they were in a street of brothels.

Jimmy and Ailsa invited us to their house in Eastbourne one weekend. Having had no association with the church except for the Franciscans of Waverley during my childhood, I was surprised at his reaction when we excused ourselves from his Sunday service. He merely arranged to meet us at the pub afterwards. I was surprised again when he arrived at the pub on his bicycle with his black cassock hitched up with a baby's nappy pin, dismounted, took off the cassock, strode into the bar and ordered a pint of mild and bitter. Then another.

The subject of Billie's and my future arose during this weekend, and we were both in the mood now to make an instant decision. We consulted diaries. 'The first time I can be in London is December the sixteenth,' said Jimmy. We two agnostics fell in with a church wedding because we liked Jimmy.

The first thing Billie did after the weekend was to book the Wigmore Hall for a recital. Partly for self-discipline and partly because a recital at Wigmore was virtually essential for a serious London debut. I asked the *Herald* to extend my term in London, as the date of the recital would be almost exactly three years after I left Sydney, and that was when I expected the *Herald* to recall me. They agreed to let me stay on.

Two major family events occurred at this time. Dad was in hospital after a heart attack, and as he was in his seventies the prognosis wasn't good. The other family news was Stred's remarriage to Jean Loane, whom Billie and Max had scarcely even heard of. They took it as good news, for Stred on his own was bad news.

Billie had started getting engagements in England. She had auditioned successfully for the Arts Council, which sponsored concerts throughout the country; she broadcast for the BBC; and she was invited to represent Australia in a music Festival of Empire Youth, sponsored by an organisation known as the Overseas League. During her first appearance at the festival Lord Louis Mountbatten, sitting in the front row, a few feet from her, noisily struck a match and lit a cigar as she played. At a reception afterwards Lady Mountbatten showed more interest, complimenting Billie on her dress.

'That's nice!' she said, fingering the material. 'Where did you get it?' The final concert of the festival got Billie her first critical mention in the London newspapers. The *Daily Express* critic Arthur Jacobs said he would now 'keep his ears open' for her.

With Mike Hutcheson as my best man, Harold Craxton gave the bride away and Doreen gave us the reception at 37 Eton Avenue. If Doreen had made any profit out of me at Eton Avenue—which is doubtful—she disposed of it then. She didn't have much money, despite her style of life, and couldn't have made her feelings towards us clearer.

It snowed that day. The wedding photographs were done by a Fleet Street photographer, and his picture of Harold and the bride in the snow somehow made the front page of the London *Evening Standard*—it was a Saturday, and there wasn't much news. The newspaper photograph was the end of anonymity. Billie ran into the Flat Finder coming back from the shops just after we returned from our honeymoon. He had seen the picture in the paper and had the ideal opportunity for his oily sarcasm. 'And how,' he asked, 'is the blushing bride?' The blushing bride and I had moved into a smaller apartment downstairs in our old building.

The Bonneys were in London soon afterwards. Garnet Bonney had organised a three-year post-retirement contract as Australian Director of Information in New York; now they were on their way home again via Europe. Mr Bonney was always attracted to progress, and had recently sent me, as a present, a product so new that you couldn't even buy one in London. It was a nylon shirt.

I became very unsettled at this time, disoriented by nearly three years in London. The same thing had happened to countless other young Australians. And, wondering where my future lay—in England or Australia—I wasn't conscious of the decay in British society, the weaknesses that undermined Britain, the slow decline that eventually had the country turning for help to the unlovable Margaret Thatcher. One of the people I wrote about then was C. E. M. Joad, the academic and popular philosopher. Joad was a cynical iconoclast who had become rich from his books and articles and his appearances on the BBC Brains Trust. He took shots, admittedly, at easy marks. Typical Joadisms were 'money doesn't make you happy but at least it enables you to be miserable in comfort' and 'if love is a disease, marriage is the best sanitorium that has yet been devised for the cure of it'.

This intellectual entertainer was in his heyday, and I went to talk to him in his house in Hampstead. He churlishly complained that I was trying to get his opinions for nothing. But I remembered his parting words. As I left to go he asked what on earth I was doing in London. After a brief explanation I walked to the door. 'Young, vigorous colonials, corrupted by our decadent civilisation!' he muttered, half to me, half to himself. I thought about these words but didn't accept them. I was blind if not corrupted.

Lars Larsson's time with Craxton came to an end. He went back to Bergen just before our marriage, and Maxie moved away from Hampstead. Lars talked of doing some concerts in Norway and going to Australia the next year. For Billie and me in our new flat in Hampstead Hill Gardens the early charms of married life had to compete with preparations for Wigmore Hall. The recital when it came was a turning point for her. To Harold Craxton and her musical peers, she had passed her professional test. *The Times* called the recital an 'excellent start to her career'. She was a very nervous performer and made me an equally nervous listener, and I was deeply relieved when the ordeal was over.

We should then have been able to settle into a less harassed life in London, but Dad's illness intervened. He was in hospital with heart trouble for the third time, and unlikely to come out. If I went home then, I realised, that would be the end of life in Europe for the next few years. The things I would have to attend to when he died ruled out a short trip home. So did money. But Harry Williams advised me not to expect the *Herald* to pay for my wife's return—after all, they hadn't sent me to London as a married man. So Billie and I decided that if she couldn't fly back with me she would go back later by sea. This would give her some extra time to learn and do more in London, a chance to return better equipped to pick up her career at home. These were hard decisions for both of us. At a time when I had least expected it I left my wife, and London, near the end of May 1951, wondering what Australia would look like to one who had become almost an expatriate.

PART III

Rewriting the Past

CHAPTER 6

Home Truths

1951 and 1952

Flying in to Sydney in the sunshine I feel the thump behind the ribs that the Sydneysider knows as the remembered harbour focuses into reality. But the effect does not last. June can be a bad time here, and it is now. The sun has soon gone, and my real life seems to have gone with it. This isn't the Sydney I have dreamed of. It feels like the time when I came home from the army, sleeping alone in my old bed in Mum's flat in Sydney.

I go to see Dad in a ward in the War Memorial Hospital in Waverley. He knows he is dying. 'Third time proves it,' he says conclusively. He is not one to protest.

But something else is happening, another change. My destination is not Sydney, as I have assumed. Harry Kippax tells me that the management isn't satisfied with the job Irvine Douglas is doing in Canberra, and they have decided that I should take his place. I am unprepared for such news. It is only three years since I arrived in London as the most junior member of Douglas's staff. Doug (as his colleagues know him) is a man in his fifties who quite literally was a newspaper executive when I was in short pants. Even in exile (as he now is, since the debacle of the *Sunday Herald*'s 'photo-finish' election) he runs the Canberra office where, as federal political correspondent, he has probably the most senior writing position on the paper. The possibility that I might replace him now would have seemed so remote that it hasn't even occurred to me.

I have never done a job like this. My experience in Canberra as a junior reporter has never taken me into the heart of politics or challenged me to win the confidence of political leaders, interpret national affairs or fight in the most competitive news game there is. So I am to go to Canberra and work for a time with Doug—who knows nothing of this plan—to catch up with what is happening there until they judge that I am ready to take over.

I am immature enough to think nearly as much about the style in which the Canberra representative lives as the job he does. I remember Ray Maley and his family in that two-storey house as I first saw it with the big garden, the big trees, the driveway circling past the front door. I think of its street, Mugga Way, the street of ambassadors and the most influential journalists of the press gallery. It was Ray Maley who said: 'One day this may be yours.' But he didn't mean now.

The Canberra job, I tell myself, is probably the riskiest one on the paper. The *Herald* is intent on politics and watches everything in Canberra that could affect its interests. If I take over there in the next few months I shall be the sixth person in the job in six years. Three of my five predecessors in this time will have been tried and soon rejected. But I am not discouraged by the statistics.

Looking back now, I am uncomfortably aware that I accepted this job without hesitation or consultation although I had a wife with a career of her own; and Canberra, as I knew, was hardly the place from which to pursue it. It was no more than a country town, and an artificial one at that. The entire population of Canberra was less than twenty-three thousand in 1951, and musical activity scarcely existed there, but I was being given an opportunity that was better than anything I'd hoped for. I figured that we would have reason and opportunity to go to Sydney often, and Billie could get there easily for engagements. She was still well known in musical circles in Sydney, and it wasn't as if she lacked professional contacts there. With such thoughts I justified my move. Had Billie and I made a decision together at this time it might have been to go to Canberra anyway, accepting an unwelcome compromise. But it was my decision, not ours. An act of selfish presumption on my part that I now find it difficult to understand.

These were times of conflict and confusion in Australia, full of significance for the political journalist. Menzies was prime minister again and had just won control of both houses of parliament in a double dissolution. The Korean War, nearing its end, had left a legacy of high inflation that was out of control, driving up the price of wool, our major export, to unheard-of heights. People who had a few sheep in the suburbs to keep the grass down were ringing Dalgetys to have them shorn and sell the wool. The

Dalgetys man was inquiring: 'And what are their names?' It was said that real graziers rounded up their sheep in Jaguars.

Chifley, now leader of the opposition, would soon die. Menzies would hold an unsuccessful referendum on his proposal to ban the Communist Party and would call a national conference on inflation. State governments were reinstating some wartime price controls. Strikes continued. Sydney was having rostered blackouts. Australia's population was eight and a half million, a little more than when I was a boy. The immigration scheme was just starting to drive it up and the baby boom was beginning.

I had been home about three weeks when Dad died in the hospital without fuss or further warning. He was seventy-three, a 'good innings', no doubt, in his terminology. I would be insincere to claim that his death was a momentous event in my life—we had lived apart for years now, and had so little in common—but he was a good man, and if you knew him you could not fail to have an affection for him.

After his funeral I went to Newcastle to see Stred and his new wife, Jean. I confess that Stred had become more of a father to me. A dangerous one, though. Much alcohol went into our exhaustive reviews of life, family, the world, the past and the future. Jean liked her whisky and sat up late with us. She was a sturdy character, without airs, dependable. Physical pain was one reason why talks with a bottle of whisky attracted her, though she wasn't a drinker the way Stred was. She was just determined to enjoy life with Stred as long as her enemy, rheumatoid arthritis, would allow.

Before I went to Canberra other staff moves had to be organised, so for a time I did fill-in jobs in Sydney. But then the move, and the old Hotel Canberra became my home again. As I vividly remembered, it was a lively enough place when parliament was sitting but a graveyard at weekends. Then the dining tables and the dark lounge outside the dining room were almost empty, and contemptuous waiters averted their eyes in case any guest might disturb them with some request. The licensee wasn't interested. He and his establishment were typical of the bad side of Australia in 1951, and I was a victim.

Irvine Douglas seemed glad enough to have me as his offsider. My predecessor, Ted O'Loghlin, was to stay on for two or three weeks until I settled in. Ted was the perfect Irish Catholic Labor man, whose style and inclinations would have been a greater asset in the time of a Labor government. They still had value, for the Catholic ascendency in the Labor Party was at its height.

The most Catholic member of the press gallery, though, was Kevin Power, head of the Sydney *Daily Mirror* office. Kevin was a plump little man with frizzy ginger hair—Irish hair—nicknamed Kewpie by the young journalists. He and his wife Jean were a good Catholic production unit. Jean was so ill after frequent pregancies that Kevin went to the priest with a doctor's certificate to gain a dispensation for the use of contraceptives on medical grounds. When the priest refused, Jean's pleas couldn't persuade Kevin to ignore the edict of his church, and another baby Power was born. I mention this because the Catholic certainties which it revealed had a political significance. They put Kevin at one with the Catholic Labor MPs. When parliament was sitting, the Labor caucus met each Tuesday morning and broke up about one o'clock. Kevin could get the story of its confidential proceedings within minutes and have it in the last edition of the *Mirror* that afternoon. Other afternoon newspapers were well represented in the press gallery but couldn't compete with the *Mirror* on caucus days.

Ted O'Loghlin normally wrote the *Herald*'s stories from caucus meetings. Doug—more at home in the Royal Canberra Golf Club or out in the hills behind Canberra fly-fishing—would have been hard put to get a story from the Labor Party even after the *Mirror* had broken it. His patrician style wasn't suited to the Labor politicians of the '50s. Ted, however, exuding goodwill, promised to pass on his caucus contacts to me. If there were any that he wasn't able to introduce me to, he said, he'd point them out in parliament from the gallery so that I could identify the people to cultivate. Ted's sonorous voice flowed with confidence and reassurance. Lucky that he was still there to give me a good start! But my sceptical friend in Sydney, Jack Colless, who had succeeded Ted as our state political correspondent, warned me not to expect too much.

Soon O'Loghlin was in partying mood, farewelling his friends and contacts all over Parliament House. He said no more about helping me, and his Labor contacts remained as much a mystery as the sources of Kevin Power's wonderful caucus stories, even though Ted was on our side and Kevin's paper was the opposition. 'That's exactly what happened to me,' said Colless afterwards. Fortunately O'Loghlin's help could be dispensed with, for it was government contacts that I needed immediately. There were people like Alan Reid of the Sydney *Sun* who specialised in stories from the Labor Party which were often fascinating, but seemed to be side issues at that time. In this period of economic turmoil it was the government that made the news.

Journalists in the press gallery formed defensive alliances, not necessarily known to their head offices. We had one with the morning papers in the Melbourne Herald group, and exchanged stories with Frank Chamberlain and Stan Hutchinson of the Melbourne *Sun News-Pictorial*, Elgin Reid of the Brisbane *Courier-Mail* and Stan Stephens of the *Adelaide Advertiser*. We showed each other 'blacks'—carbon copies—of all our stories. The arrangement was deficient from my viewpoint because the *Sun-Pic*'s political coverage was lightweight and the *Advertiser*'s interests were too parochial for our needs. But the relationship which developed between Elgin Reid and me made up for the shortcomings of the others.

Elgin was about my age. He was a thinker with a first-rate analytical mind for politics. My attention was directed to him in an unintended way by Kevin Power's assistant, Les Love. Les shared Kevin's allegiances to church and party. He was a person who spoke with great emphasis, seeming to masticate his words as if preparing them for his audience's consumption like a parent bird disgorging food for its young. He was determined to tell me about the *peculiar* people in the press gallery, savouring the word.

I drank with Les sometimes because he was young and unmarried, so we both had time on our hands when family men had gone home. There are some very *peculiar* people in the gallery, he told me in his declamatory style. People like Harold Cox, whom I knew, and Elgin Reid. What is so *peculiar* about Elgin? I asked. He supports the Liberals. He's a Menzies supporter. He's one of those *Young Nats*. Young Nats represented the most extreme, the most unthinkable conservatives. Allowing for the hyperbole, I gathered that Elgin was *peculiar* because—unlike most of the press gallery—he wasn't a Labor supporter. But I am attracted to heretics, and decided that Elgin Reid might be at least as interesting as some of his less *peculiar* colleagues. He proved to be so. The Reid–Myers alliance became a competitive news-gathering force and, overall, was probably second to none in the gallery in our time. Elgin also became my friend. And wasn't a Young Nat.

Elgin and the other heads of service in the press gallery had just returned from Chifley's funeral when I reached Canberra. Menzies' attendance as Prime Minister had been more than duty: he had genuine respect for Chifley. Also at the funeral was the next Labor leader, Dr H. V. Evatt, 'the Doc'. As I soon came to see for myself, Evatt was a man of almost Faustian ambition who must, at the least, have had mixed feelings on Chifley's death, which brought him within reach of the prime ministership.

Elgin said that at the funeral he was observing the two men. Evatt was silently weeping, Menzies was looking at him. Then Menzies turned and glanced across to some of the press party. Unable to communicate in words, he signalled his comment in the only other way possible. Menzies winked.

If anyone but Elgin had recounted this story I might not have believed it, but Elgin was not a witness to be doubted. I have savoured this incident, one which meant more to me each time it came to mind as I watched the subsequent contest between Menzies and Evatt. It cast an unexpected light on the two men who would absorb my attention for the next few years.

At the Hotel Canberra I shared a table with another permanent guest, Jim Plimsoll, a senior official from the Department of External Affairs. Being a bachelor, immersed in his work, he chose hotel life close to his office. Jim was a literate man with a wide-ranging mind, quiet but conversational. For me, our mealtime talks took some of the unpleasant edge off life at the Canberra.

Several weeks after I arrived the manager of the hotel resigned and the lessees, Tooheys brewery, sent a completely different type to replace him. The new man, Thornley Thorpe, quickly made life impossible for the more unbearable members of the staff and more possible for guests. Few journalists ever stayed at the Canberra but another who came now was Massey Stanley, one of the best-known newspapermen in Australia. Massey was a mumbling, moody, brilliant man who came down from Sydney each week during parliamentary sittings to write a political feature for the *Sunday Telegraph*. I'd never seen him inside the Hotel Canberra before, and Tony Innes, who had a long acquaintance with the press gallery, told me why.

Massey had once stayed regularly at the Canberra. He was one of the hard-drinking school of journalists, and came back to the hotel one night in worse condition than usual. He stripped off his clothes, lay down and went to sleep until the driver of the early bus past the Hotel Canberra in the morning found him in the bus shelter outside. There on the bench in the shelter lay the no-doubt repulsive body of the unconscious Massey Stanley, soft and white. He had mistaken the roadside cubicle for his room. The manager of the Canberra threw him out and banned him from the hotel. Now, with Thornley Thorpe's arrival, here was Massey Stanley once more, perhaps back in his spiritual home. But no, that cannot be right. He had once studied for the church.

There was another failed divine in the Canberra press gallery—Ken Schapel of the Sydney *Daily Telegraph*. If I describe some of the other journalists as the opposition, I can only describe Schapel at that time as the enemy. Known to the gallery as the Crow, he was a fairly tall, spare, black-haired man who had prepared for the church and finished up here instead. He had a deceptively benign manner, and addressed almost everyone as 'Biscuit' (but not his wife Betty, who was 'Lizard'). I myself wouldn't have chosen to name him the Crow, although with his colouring, his dark moustache and his penetrating features he was a striking figure that you might well have looked up in a bird book. I'd have searched for a wading bird instead, because of the way he stalked unobtrusively through the gallery trying to pick up any indications of what anyone else was writing. He would come quietly into your office and stand poised before you, ritually flicking the ash from his cigarette with a long, stiffened forefinger, fossicking for information like a bird after food in the shallows. 'Are you chaps writing anything about so-and-so?' he would ask, or 'I don't think there's anything in the such-and-such report, do you?'. If you had any sense you didn't cooperate. It was rumoured that Schapel was so inquisitive that he sometimes returned to the press gallery late at night to go through the carbon copies of other people's stories in their wastepaper baskets.

The pressure on political journalists at that time may have been no more intense than it is now but it was certainly different. The focus was almost entirely on a few newspaper offices, for there was no television. There was ABC radio news, but in those days it stuck essentially to the official facts. The real players in the newspaper offices lived by the scoop, the exclusive story, and had to be constantly vigilant to avoid being scooped by their opposition.

There were some experts in writing stories that looked like scoops but weren't. Journalists call these stories beat-ups, and Ken Schapel was the master of them. He used them to such effect that one of them eventually brought on Doug's dismissal from Canberra and my accession to his job.

An early-model example of the unnerving beat-up in my time was Schapel's front-page story revealing that the federal government would sell the Commonwealth Shipping Line to the major Australian shipping companies for £10 million. Howard Beale, who was Minister for Supply, told me later that the line would never be sold because no shipping company was interested in it at an acceptable price, so then I stopped worrying about the possibility of being scooped on this story by Schapel. Despite that, during my time in Canberra Schapel periodically recycled it. His story's weakness was also its strength. The fact that the government still wanted to sell the line, but couldn't, gave it a durability that most beat-ups lacked, since the policy itself was never abandoned—it merely faded away while Schapel's phantom scoop lived on. The sale of the Commonwealth Shipping Line was always front-page in the *Telegraph*, and always exclusive.

I got my own first noticeable scoop soon after I arrived. In July 1951, just before I left Sydney, Menzies had instructed the Public Service Board to report on action to reduce the size of the Commonwealth public service by ten thousand employees. This was an unprecedented decision, reversing years of growth in the size of government. But when I arrived in Canberra some weeks later no more had been heard of the plan, so I rang the chairman of the Public Service Board to ask how the cuts would be implemented.

The chairman of the Board, Bill Dunk, was a government auditor who had gone on to one of the most powerful positions in the public service. I remember Garnet Bonney hating him—a clerk on a high stool, he called him. How fair the description was I can't be sure, but Dunk certainly matched the conventional picture of an auditor as one who would never break a rule. Nor would he ever divulge confidential information or compromise sensitive situations by discussing them with the press. In the press gallery Dunk was on no-one's contact list. The established members of the gallery didn't waste their time with him.

'I'm calling you about the decision to reduce the public service,' I told him, oblivious of all this. 'Could you tell me how it is going to be implemented?' 'Certainly,' replied Dunk cordially. 'Come down to my office and I'll be happy to give you the details.' That afternoon he gave me a breakdown of the staff cuts not merely department by department but, in some, section by section. It was such a detailed story that I took it back to him in draft to ensure its complete accuracy. He made one minor correction and the story was published in full as he had approved it, without attribution.

This story was bound to arouse protests, and did. For one thing, it revealed retrenchments of four thousand in the Postmaster General's Department, which administered posts and telegraphs. It brought protests from the unions and from all the threatened sections of the public service. I have assumed, since, that Dunk must have been unhappy about the cabinet decision and wanting to stir things up. But the next day, when I rang him again to discuss reactions to the story, his demeanour had changed. 'I'm sorry, I can't say anything more about it,' he said, and I never spoke to him after that except when someone tried to introduce us at the Royal Canberra Golf Club. 'We have met before,' I said. He showed no reaction.

The press gallery was impressed by the *Herald*'s story, especially when they knew that I had written it. If I had just arrived in Canberra and got a scoop like this in the first few days, what would I do next? The answer was: not much. I had to learn more. But I'd had a reminder of two obvious principles. One, don't assume that something won't work until you try it.

Two, there is a right moment for everything. Afterwards, in situations of hesitancy, I sometimes thought of Bill Dunk and the staff cuts. But I confess ... sometimes I forgot them, too.

Another change in my life. In September a letter from Billie tells me that she has a passage home on the *Strathnaver*, one of the well-known liners on the UK–Australia run from pre-war days. It leaves on 22 November and will reach Sydney on Boxing Day. Billie has spent the time since I left London doing much as before—living in our old flat, taking a few more lessons with Harold, giving concerts, going with friends to concerts and to our haunt, the Everyman cinema in Hampstead, seeing A *Midsummer Night's Dream* on midsummer night in Regent's Park. She has made a short trip to Bergen for Maxie's marriage to Lars. Now this phase of both our lives— our time of coming to maturity in London, as I see it—is to end.

Accommodation in Canberra is hard to get. The *Herald* decides to transfer another member of the staff back to Sydney and let us have the cottage they have leased for him at Telopea Park. But there will be a period between Billie's arrival and this man's departure, and the Bonneys solve this problem. They have been allotted a small government flat in a new development near Mount Ainslie. But they will be at their house at Emerald, in the Dandenongs near Melbourne, in the new year and we shall be able to use this flat until we move into the house.

My memories of the weeks of waiting that follow are comfortingly swallowed up by time. I recall nothing until I am at the dockside in Melbourne, then aboard the ship sailing to Sydney with Billie. So we have already been reunited and have privately celebrated when she steps off the *Strathnaver* in Sydney to meet family and friends. We do not have long there. Doug is on holidays and I have to write his column for the next three weeks. That is how, at the very beginning of January 1952, we come to be sitting in this new, small, characterless government flat looking out across a dusty expanse to the shops and offices of Civic Centre, which, despite that name, is at this time Canberra's last outpost. From London to this.

Canberra, 1952. Burley Griffin's plan for the capital has placed everything where it should be when the concept is realised and exactly where it shouldn't be in the meantime, if human considerations were to reign. The modest, temporary Parliament House faces the distant War Memorial across the open spaces. Near Parliament House are small government offices and, a stroll away, the Hotel Canberra. Canberra's few suburbs, separated by miles of dry summer grass and weeds, cluster around meagre shopping centres or stand further away under Red Hill and Mount Ainslie. Each living area is a village with its own identity and insularity. And if you allow for a few outcrops around the edges—Duntroon military college, the first uncompleted buildings of the Australian National University and the community hospital, set apart—that is Canberra, with the empty miles beyond. Even across Flinders Way opposite the *Herald* house under Red Hill you are in sheep country.

You get around this extraordinary capital by car or with difficulty. Doing her shopping as a Canberra housewife, Billie finds that we are off the bus routes. She does the long walk to the shops at the so-called Civic Centre and back across the rutted red-clay paddocks, under a midsummer sun that blazes down at full strength through the dry air from an inland sky that, at this time of year, knows no cloud. She is carrying two armfuls of shopping and can't even brush away Canberra's little sticky bush flies as she walks.

She has been to see the ABC in Sydney and already has some broadcasts and concerto performances with the Sydney Symphony Orchestra, but back in the Bonneys' flat in Ainslie we have no piano, and she has to organise access to one in the local ABC studio. The main artistic activity in Canberra at this time is talking about the lack of it. There is one cinema, no art gallery, one amateur repertory theatre that plays in a hut, but is a delight, and a few ABC concerts. The ABC sends two or three of its visiting recitalists to Canberra each year and has no more than fifty regular subscribers to its concerts in the small, usually half-empty Albert Hall. It's another matter if political conversation is your interest. Canberra seems to be in world class for that.

We move into the cottage in Telopea Park. The Bonneys arrive to stay in their flat. He is driving the last of his long, chromium-striped Pontiacs, which he has sent home from New York, new and gleaming, a retirement fund in metal. Such cars are unprocurable in Australia, and as soon as he has owned it long enough for it to be free of duty when he sells it, he will get more for it than the price of a new car, and will buy something small and boring. He takes us for a Sunday drive to see some of the countryside we haven't seen before, up to Brindabella in a lovely valley in the lower ranges near the snow country.

Billie observes him with sudden surprise, seeing physical characteristics that she has never noticed before. As soon as we get home that night she asks if I have ever thought that Garnet Bonney could be my father. It isn't a question that really surprises me. I know that my mother has known him for many years, that I don't look anything like Dad but am much more like Garnet Bonney physically, mentally and temperamentally. He has taken such a personal interest in me that I am like a substitute son for the Bonneys, with no children of their own.

'Yes,' I say. 'I've often thought about that, and I think it's more than likely true.'

'Next time we go to Sydney I'm going to find out,' Billie replies. And she does.

The acquisition of a father at such a stage of life overturns one's understanding. For me it establishes a logic that I have half known but never fully recognised. It sorts out relationships with the Myers family that have had to be distorted to fit into a picture to which they don't belong. The incompatible members of the family mean nothing. Those who are compatible, whom I can admire, like, or even love, are there for what they are and not for what they are supposed to be.

I can now piece together the earlier part of my personal story as far as I know it from the only sources I shall ever have: old memories and conversations, my mother's intimate revelations to Billie, and some records. Of these, the most productive is an autobiography which Garnet began in retirement. It stops short of his inner life and his secrets. The avoidance is deliberate, but the story of his later years as an editor and his government jobs is also missing, simply because he stopped writing. As far as it goes, though, it has the genuine flavour of an earlier time, of a hard life in the bush, of old-time journalism, and a young man's passage from the bush to the city. A typical story of its time, with its familiar theme of success against adversity. There is a feeling of history about it, too. And some of this touches on the history of journalism in Australia, the world into which I have moved.

The following chapter is the story of Garnet and my mother, which I have told because it is also my own story. It is the missing part of my Chapter I—the part that I did not understand at the time.

CHAPTER 7

Family Secrets

1884 to 1939

Garnet Bonney—Edmund Garnet—met my mother in Grafton. She had grown up there; for him, there was nowhere that he could call his home.

He was the youngest of four children, born in Sydney on 24 November 1883, although later he fudged the date and gave it as 1885. His father, William Henry Bonney, remains an almost unknown figure. The name is Scottish. He was American, a draughtsman from New York. His wife Annie was a Sydney girl, and they obviously lived together for some years, but Garnet says that his only memory of his father was of their parting 'on the deck of a huge steamer' when Garnet was about five. His mother told him afterwards that he would never see his father again, and she was right. Unable to keep her children, she sent them to live with her parents in Newcastle and went off to earn money to support them. Garnet and his sisters spent the next five years with their grandparents; his grandmother, he says, brought them up without affection.

Garnet was eleven when his grandmother told him that he was to rejoin his mother, who had recently gone to Wyalong with a new husband named Fielding. Less than four years earlier Wyalong—about three hundred miles inland from Sydney—had been nothing but a sheep run. Now Garnet's new stepfather had joined thousands of prospectors who had rushed there after the discovery of gold. Garnet made his journey alone, by train and coach, to be reunited with his mother. His new stepfather was 'not a bad man' but completely uninteresting and without brains, and Garnet wondered how his intelligent and refined mother could have married him. She told him much later that Fielding had seemed genuinely fond of her, she had thought he had money, and she had decided to accept him for the sake of her children.

Within a few months two of Garnet's three sisters followed him to Wyalong. But Fielding's savings were already running out. By the time the family began to go short of even essential food Garnet, just turned thirteen, left school and got his first job. It was on *The Argus*, a newspaper that had recently started up in the town, but his own start in newspapers was in the most menial job they had—as type monkey, the typesetter's assistant. Garnet worked at the paper from six in the morning till four in the afternoon, then spent the remaining hours of daylight helping his stepfather cut wood to sell to neighbours.

After two years of struggle *The Argus* closed, and Garnet, out of work at fifteen, saw that action was needed. He persuaded his now defeated stepfather to appeal for help from relatives in Coonamble on the north-western plains of New South Wales. Soon afterwards enough money arrived for Fielding to buy a wagonette and horses to go to Coonamble with his new family. Fielding had once been a drover, and knew the country well. They were six weeks on the journey, camping by the roadside, cooking dampers in a camp oven and sitting around the fire at night. They shot wild pig, duck and bronze-wing pigeons for food, and Garnet afterwards recalled the journey to Coonamble as the highlight of his many travels.

After they reached Coonamble he went droving for eighteen months, but by then he was cured of the bush. He found a job as a typesetter on another struggling newspaper in Forbes. When after a few months it, like *The Argus*, failed, he headed for Sydney and settled into a steady job in a printery there. But two years later his life took another of its unmapped turns when he was offered a job on a ship as a purser's clerk. He spent two years at sea, never doing two voyages on the same ship and never visiting the same port twice. He 'left Sydney an over-sensitive lad of nineteen' and 'returned with all the diffidence knocked out of me, ready to take on anything'. He signed off from the sea in New Zealand, and that was his last move before Grafton.

He had chosen to go to Dunedin because one of his sisters was now living there with an aunt, their father's sister, and had written to him about the beauty of the country. He found his aunt wise and cultured, and always remembered her benign influence and support for him during his years in New Zealand. Her home was a haven such as he had never known before. His days as a wanderer were over.

Garnet was a reader, and though he left school at thirteen his self-education continued through books. At sea he started writing short stories, mailing them off to publications which did not use them, and never getting his manuscripts back. In Dunedin he started writing short stories again; this time they were published and paid for. He had found a job as foreman of the job-printing department of the Dunedin *Evening Star*; he studied at night at a shorthand and typing school, and did an English course at the technical college. His aunt introduced him to Shakespeare.

I have found it tantalising to reflect, as so little can be gathered about Garnet's father, what Garnet's own writings may suggest about the man, and it is perhaps the character of the aunt in Dunedin that gives a clue. Garnet says in the never-finished book that he eventually met some relatives who told him that his father had remarried and had died at forty-seven, 'a broken and unhappy man'. Yet, having a sister who was cultured and kind, William Henry Bonney must also have had some culture and quality. Adding this evidence to Garnet's feelings about his mother, his origins take some shape and his character and his success in life are easier to understand.

But there is something more to the story of Garnet's time in New Zealand, an event concealed in the unfinished autobiography—yet one which shaped his life. It was a shotgun marriage to a girl named Elizabeth Johnson in the registry office in Dunedin. They had a daughter, Dorothy, who was somewhat backward, and I know that fifty years later, in his retirement, Garnet was still sending money for her support. He did not love or much respect Elizabeth, and their eventual separation and divorce seem to have been inevitable from the start.

Garnet lived in Dunedin for three years and would have stayed longer but for the unexplained advice of a doctor that he should give up indoor work. So he tried to become a journalist. But he could not get a job in New Zealand, and returned to Sydney. It was when he failed to break into journalism in Sydney that he became a reporter on the Grafton *Argus*. Elizabeth, I surmise, must have stayed behind in New Zealand with Dorothy until he could provide them with a settled existence in Australia. It was at this time that he met my mother.

Grafton was a simple town then, just past the first pioneering stage, pushing back the age-old stands of black bean, eucalypts and casuarinas that ran down to the edge of the Clarence River. Tall, forest-straight cedars still stood in undisturbed profusion at the edge of the town square. Among the townspeople were the real pioneers—English, Scottish and Irish migrants and their children, with a strong mixture of German families and Italians, Schwinghammers, Schaeffers, Zietches, Bassettis, Giovanellis and other names

well known around the North Coast of New South Wales. Small, newly
built timber houses with a certain elegant simplicity were the first instalments
of homes which would expand over the years to hold the large families yet
to be born there. Local transport was horse-powered, whipping up mini-
duststorms over unsealed roads. Journeys to Sydney, Brisbane or Newcastle
were made in coastal steamers which left the coast at Yamba and navigated
up-river as far as Grafton itself. I know the scene well, some of it from my
own childhood memories, some from old photographs of much earlier times.

Garnet's arrival must have been noticeable in such a community. His time
in New Zealand, softening the effects of his early struggles and his years at
sea, must have given him a degree of social command. He had, he says, a
'fairly good' baritone voice which would have been a social asset in what
was then a very musical town. Garnet was just over six feet tall, well built,
and strong from his droving and wood-chopping days. As a journalist he
was ideally placed to meet people and make an impression.

My mother, Olive Beryl Walker, would have been twenty when he came
to town. In the old photographs it is perhaps her femininity that is the
pervasive quality. She is of no more than medium height, the figure slim
but womanly. Her attractions for Garnet and other young men of Grafton
are not hard to imagine.

Whereas Garnet was complex and could provoke hostility in some people,
she was almost completely the opposite. Once she was voted the most
popular girl in her school, though why a school should conduct such an
election I cannot imagine. At twenty she would have been as she was later,
a warm, affectionate and emotional woman, absorbed in personal relationships.
She had as much intelligence as she needed, but intellectual interests were
of no account to her. Being the eldest of a large family, she had left school
after a modest convent education in order to help her mother at home. She
played the piano and was a good sightreader, and so was in demand in the
musical life of Grafton—hence my picture of her at the age of about twenty
with the Grafton orchestra, for which she was the orchestral pianist. I have
never heard how she and Garnet met, but I suspect that it was a story of
a 'fairly good baritone' encountering one of the local beauties, who played
the piano, at a musical function.

The Grafton chapter of Garnet's book says nothing of his personal life:
it is almost entirely about his experiences as a reporter, his on-the-job crash
course in journalism. Working sixty to seventy hours a week without
complaint—in fact with enthusiasm—he covered courts, sports, churches,
carnivals, school break-ups, council meetings and a hot local issue at the

time—prohibition. He tells a story which reflects a resourcefulness which got him through tricky situations throughout his life. Assigned to cover a Saturday race meeting and unwilling to admit that he knew nothing about racing in those days, he attended the meeting and was entirely unable to describe what had happened in any of the races. But that night in his boarding house he heard a conversation between two city bookmakers who obviously remembered every incident. He asked if they could say it all again, and took it down in the shorthand he had learned in Dunedin.

'This is pretty good, Bonney,' said his boss when he turned in his copy on the Monday. 'I didn't know you were a turf expert.' 'I won't admit I'm an expert,' replied Garnet guardedly, 'but I'm glad you like the report.'

After a few months he was offered a job on the other Grafton newspaper, the *Examiner*, with a rise of ten shillings a week on the £2 15s. he had been earning. Attracted by prospects rather than money, he took the job. And as a reporter on the *Examiner* he saw two city journalists at work when they accompanied a state government minister to the town. He decided that one day he, too, should have telegraph boys standing beside him, ready to rush his copy to the post office for transmission to his newspaper.

He worked at the *Examiner* for a few more months, but then a strange thing happened. The editor, who had previously been very encouraging, called him in to his office and told him he feared that Garnet was not cut out for newspaper work. When the editor went on to say that he didn't seem to be wholehearted about his work Garnet was sure that the man wasn't being honest with him, and immediately resigned.

He was forced to take almost any work he could get. He opened a school for shorthand and typing, sang illustrated songs at the Grafton cinema—these were the early days of the silent film—travelled the Northern Rivers as organising secretary for the Grafton eisteddfod, published a book of short stories (without much success, he says) and worked as a travelling salesman for typewriters. Finally, realising that the life of the commercial traveller was not for him, he booked his passage by coastal steamship to Sydney, and three days later got a job as manager and sub-editor of the *Shire and Municipal Record*.

In Grafton Garnet, separated from the wife he did not love, had proposed to Beryl that they become lovers. But with her convent education and sheltered Catholic family upbringing she did not even know what he meant. And when he left, their relationship had gone no further, and he left without any expectations in her mind. But it was the day when he got his job on the *Record* that must be counted as the real parting between them. Nothing that Garnet has written, and nothing that I have heard, reveals anything more about their interrupted romance at this time.

Beryl's father, Alex Walker, my grandfather, was manager of the ironmongery department at Gerrard's general store in Grafton. The family regarded him as very intelligent, and the reason why he never got beyond the ironmongery department was his drinking. It kept the household poor and at one stage lost him his job, which Nanna saved by pleading with Mr Gerrard to keep him on for the sake of their children. The drinking habits of Alex Walker, remote as they may seem, are of deep importance in my story because of their effects on my mother. It is no exaggeration to say that they determined the course of her life and therefore, to some extent, mine. Through her teenage years, especially, her problems at home were always in the background. Perhaps worst of all in her eyes was the shame she felt when her father proudly arrived at some of the musical functions at which she performed, swaying drunkenly at the back of the room for all to see.

Into this scene came Alf Myers, commercial traveller, some fifteen years older than Beryl. A gentlemanly, self-effacing man from a good family in Sydney. Thinning and probably greying hair would have given him an air of maturity, seeming to offer the practical and emotional security that she needed.

Quite likely he met her through music. In a family divided between the money-makers and those to whom culture and the arts were important, he was certainly on the non-commercial side. His aspirations had been in music. He was an amateur violinist of limited attainment but genuine enthusiasm, and had played in Henri Verbrugghen's orchestra in Sydney. There was nothing like a professional Sydney Symphony Orchestra then, and though Verbrugghen's group would have fallen far short of such standards it was probably the nearest thing that existed at the time. Verbrugghen became the first director of the Sydney Conservatorium of Music.

As a commercial traveller on the North Coast of New South Wales it is easy to imagine Alf going to any musical events in Grafton and other towns, probably taking his violin and offering to help out if he could. Nothing about him was exceptional. He was short but not very short; pleasant-looking but no more; Jewish by race and culture yet lacking the Jewish faith and tribal loyalty; serious-minded but not very bright. He excelled in other ways, though, notably in a certain generosity of mind towards others, and in his integrity and dependability.

Alf Myers wanted to marry Beryl Walker. Beryl wanted to escape. She could not have the man she would have wanted, and marriage to Alf seemed the best alternative. He had nearly £1000 in the bank. Even wanted her to look at his bank book to see for herself. She wouldn't.

The year was 1912 and Garnet was rising twenty-seven when he came back from a country assignment for the *Shire and Municipal Record* realising that he had a good daily newspaper story. As the *Record*'s next issue would not be published for another three weeks, he sold the news story to the *Sydney Morning Herald*. Typically, instead of just going back to collect his cheque he interviewed C. T. Harris, the assistant to the general manager, and asked for a job. Harris gave him no encouragement. 'A year earlier Mr Harris's polite but formal manner would have chilled me,' he recalled. 'But I had watched a man sell an office system to a business man who did not want it, and knew that one must never acknowledge defeat.' He finished up with a job as a travelling representative for the *Herald*, with a territory stretching from the southern Sydney suburb of Hurstville down to Eden on the South Coast of New South Wales and inland to Cooma, Queanbeyan and Canberra. The job paid well, and from a cryptic reference in his writing it appears that Elizabeth had come to Sydney. After three years covering the southern district he was transferred to a city news round as a general reporter, and late in 1916 he was sent to cover the summer session of federal parliament, which then sat in Melbourne.

It was during this assignment that Garnet became involved in a hearing, before Justice Isaac Isaacs, of the Australian Journalists' Association's application for its first industrial award. He had strolled into court one day while W. G. Conley, general manager of the *Sydney Morning Herald*, was cross-examining Teddy Clegg, secretary of the New South Wales District of the Australian Journalists' Association. Clegg was not a good witness, and Conley had him rattled. Garnet turned to Cam Pratt, a fellow employee on the *Sydney Morning Herald* who had been brought to Melbourne as a witness. 'What's wrong with Clegg?' he asked. 'I could turn every question Conley has asked against him.' The AJA put him up as a witness.

'I had a true story to tell of the *Herald*'s inconsiderate treatment of its literary staff,' he says, 'and Conley's attempts in cross-examination to lead me up the garden path ended in his own embarrassment.' Isaacs accepted the AJA's log of claims, and Garnet got a note from a Sydney colleague telling him that Cam Pratt and he were not likely to be forgiven for their role in the case. He found a job on the Melbourne *Argus* and resigned from the *Sydney Morning Herald*.

It seems the strangest of coincidences that I, too, should have worked for the *Herald*, regarded it as a sometimes parsimonious organisation and left it as Garnet did, as a direct consequence of an industrial dispute and an AJA award hearing. We made our moves, too, at a similar age. But we moved in very different directions.

Garnet's account of his role in the 1917 case might seem boastful, but later developments suggest otherwise. In 1920–21, while still a general reporter on *The Argus*, he became Federal President of the AJA. He conducted negotiations for the union at a special conference on salaries, journalists' conditions having been badly affected by inflation after World War I. The proceedings were so successful that members of the AJA presented him with a wallet of notes and the Federal Council awarded him its gold honour badge.

At *The Argus* he went on to become deputy chief of staff, then leader writer—a position he didn't enjoy because the paper's politics were so much in conflict with his own. 'I wrote hundreds of sub-leaders,' he says, 'designed to prevent the people of Melbourne from adopting new-fangled ideas.' An escape came with the offer of a position as news editor of the *Evening Sun* (where, incidentally, the chief sub was Syd Deamer, whom he remembered for his 'brilliant treatment and display'). Fairly soon the *Sun* was bought by the Herald and Weekly Times and Garnet began a long association with its managing director, Keith Murdoch. His next jobs under Murdoch were as chief of staff of the *Sun News-Pictorial* and then of the Melbourne *Herald*.

Alf and Beryl had gone to live in Lismore, a hundred miles or so from Grafton, after their marriage. They stayed there, I believe, until Dad went to Sydney to join Myers and Solomon in about 1922, two years before I was born.

The marriage of Alf and Beryl Myers would have seemed a successful one. They must have been comfortable financially, though I don't know exactly what Alf did for a living, that is to say who employed him as a commercial traveller or what he sold. The two of them took an active part in the musical and social life of Lismore, and Alf bought Beryl a fine new Bechstein upright piano. He also bought a motorbike with sidecar and took her around in it until the day when the wheel fell off the sidecar, after which she refused to have anything to do with it. So he bought a car, a Chicago-built two-seater Partin-Palmer convertible. Life went on smoothly, it seemed, except that after some years they still had no children. But for Beryl it was not a satisfactory marriage, though perhaps it was all she expected. She had feelings of affection and respect for Alf but not sexual love. It was fortunate that the marriage worked as well as it did, never the disaster that such marriages so often are. Alf was devoted to Beryl, and she was a good wife to him. When World War I came, his inclination was to join up. She wouldn't let him.

Garnet and Beryl did not entirely lose touch after he left Grafton. They corresponded, perhaps rarely, over the years. The backwardness of Garnet's daughter, Dorothy, may have been the reason his marriage continued, as he was not a man to evade responsibility. He and Elizabeth had a second child, a son named Nelson, soon after the *Herald* transferred Garnet to Melbourne, but when he was three Garnet wrote to tell Beryl that the boy was desperately ill in New Zealand with an epidemic disease, and could die. 'Surely,' he wrote, 'fate could not deal me this blow.' To his dismay, it did.

A cartoonist on one of his newspapers designed a bookmark for Garnet, showing him as a devil, with horns and a long tail, sitting at a typewriter. 'It's because you're a devil for work,' the artist explained. The worse his life outside the newspaper office, the more he drove himself in his job.

He and Beryl met again and eventually, when she went to Melbourne for some reason, they became lovers. He now had the opportunity, the excuses and the money to visit Sydney, where I was unintentionally conceived just before Christmas, 1923. Beryl had been married for ten years. How Alf succumbed to the deception that must have been woven for him I have never understood. I believe absolutely that he did so.

As soon as Garnet knew about the pregnancy he pleaded with Beryl to leave Alf and join him. They would go away together, he proposed, and come back married. But such a step would have involved a long period of openly adulterous living, since divorces for the two of them under the old law would have taken a long time. Garnet had no hesitation in contemplating this step but for Beryl it must have posed enormous difficulties. Cutting herself off from friends and family, and living a life which many of her acquaintances would have rejected, she would have had to act completely out of character. She would have greatly wounded Alf, who was at least a kind and faithful husband. Above all she would have been conscious of the blow it would be to her mother, a devout woman unswervingly guided by the Ten Commandments. She told Garnet that she could not make this move.

After he pleaded fruitlessly with her to go away with him, communication between them ceased for a time. She did not contact him when I was born.

This was because she was in a state of confusion, not because she was putting him out of her life, but he did not know. Waiting in vain to hear from her for some time before my birth, knowing that the date of the birth had come and gone without a word, he took her silence as final.

I was born on 16 September 1924. Three months later my mother found an excuse to go to Melbourne. Her visit was intended as a surprise, to show Garnet his new son, but the way it turned out was anything but as she expected. Being rejected, as he saw it, he had moved in for sex and consolation with his Melbourne landlady, Minnie Hester, who darned his socks. Minnie was one of those people who look after injured birds and animals. She had taken to looking after the injured Garnet; he married her after his divorce in 1928 and lived with her till he died.

My mother was stunned to discover that Garnet was no longer alone. He asked what she had expected from him: did she think he was going to live the rest of his life in a monastery? There was nothing that either of them could do under the circumstances. Beryl returned to Sydney, still bound to Alf and her own family relationships.

In this year, 1924, Garnet left *The Argus*. After that he had several moves within the Melbourne Herald group, finally going to Adelaide in 1932 as editor-in-chief of the evening paper, *The News*, and *The Mail*.

By this time his relationship with my mother had resumed. I do not know exactly when it did, but I have learned that he watched me leaving home on one of my first days at school at the beginning of 1930. His affair with my mother continued for the rest of his life. It was a way of life that he would not have chosen, for I believe that Garnet was not by nature an unfaithful man. But from then on he had two women to be faithful to.

It was while he was still in the Adelaide job that I first remember Garnet. He turned up at our house in Bronte one day—a jaunty figure, I thought. An old friend of the family. He made occasional visits through the '30s. The one which occurred when he was on his way to the United States was part of what would have been diplomatically called an 'extended holiday'. He was sent away by his newspapers' proprietors on what must have been intended as a cooling-off period for both sides. Adelaide, like *The Argus* in Melbourne, had been too conservative for him. It was probably Australia's stodgiest capital city at the time—ruled, he complained, from the Adelaide Club. The Adelaide establishment could hardly have taken to this outsider with working-class sympathies that traced back to his early life in the bush and at sea. Getting away from it all, he and Minnie crossed the Pacific by sea, as every traveller to the United States did, and spent three months making a leisurely motor tour across North America by one route and back by another.

He reappeared at our place on his way back to Adelaide from the United States, wearing a straw boater. This was when he brought back one of his big American cars, a Pontiac. He drove Pontiacs until after he retired. He obviously liked their rakish appearance, with their band of narrow stripes, made of five thin parallel chromium-plated strips which swept up in line from the centre of the front bumper-bar over the whole length of the long, streamlined bonnet to the windscreen, and started again under the rear window, running down over the boot lid to the back. Members of the Adelaide Club, I suspect, would never have driven a car like that. Theirs would have been strictly Made in Britain.

This was the time when Garnet began to make a greater impression on me. I knew no-one else who dashed around like this. Over the next few years he would turn up once or twice each year and, whatever else he may have organised with my mother that I didn't know about, he would take the two of us for a day's drive in his latest Pontiac. He sent me a book every year for my birthday, inscribed: 'To Hal, from EGB.'

Once I remember his staying to dinner at our place with Alf, Mum and me. Usually he disappeared before Alf arrived home from work. Alf, it seemed, accepted the 'old friend from the early days in Grafton' story with reasonable equanimity but didn't seem to want to know him any better. Minnie Bonney was a figure in the background, to be imagined. She and Mum never met during Garnet's lifetime, to Mum's relief.

Garnet left Adelaide and ended a fourteen-year association with Murdoch in 1938 when he became editor of *The Argus* in Melbourne. It was from this position that the first Menzies Government recruited him as Chief Publicity Censor in the early years of the war.

Garnet's entry in *Who's Who in Australia* omits any mention of his first marriage or his children. There is nothing about his parents. His autobiographical writings say nothing of these things or about his inner self or the darker side of his life, except for a few cryptic words: 'Ours has been an ill-starred family. Misfortune has pursued us unrelentingly ... We were foredestined to a greater share of trouble than ordinarily falls to the lot of human beings.' From the loss of his father, the years of separation from his mother, his unhappy first marriage, the death of his son Nelson and the debacle with my mother after I was born, I can understand what he was moved to write.

Billie's discoveries did not lead me to confront Mum or Garnet about my parentage and they, too, never brought it into the open. Billie was never asked, and never said, whether she had told me what she knew. Garnet placed too much value on the relationship that he and I already had to endanger it with new revelations. I on my part did not know what emotional pressures might be put on me if we all confronted, at this time of our lives, the truth that had been so long hidden. And so we said nothing. Whether this was the best way of handling our strange situation I do not know.

But since then, reflecting on this whole story, I have naturally asked myself one question: what might have happened if I had grown up with Garnet, not Alf, in the role of a father? If Mum had married Garnet my life and opportunities would have been less determined by shortage of money. For whatever Garnet lost at the races could always be replaced in his next pay cheque. I would have grown up among more interesting people. But getting to know him as I did, supposedly as a friend of the family, I was able to choose whether to make a friend of him myself, and did so of my own accord. Any questions about different lives that might have existed, but didn't, are meaningless in the end.

Garnet would have been a much stronger influence than the uninterfering Alf Myers, and for me that might have been both good and bad. At least I was saved from the hazards of growing up with a powerful father.

Alex Walker, my maternal grandfather.

Mary Walker, my grandmother, born
Mary Sweeny.

Beryl Walker, my mother, shortly before her
marriage.

Alf Myers, my dad, around the time of
World War I.

The Grafton orchestra, about 1912. Next to the drummer in the front row, l. to r., are Meldrum (Mel) and her younger sister Vera Giovanelli, Mr Stone (conductor) and Beryl Walker. Beryl, then twenty or twenty-one, is the orchestra's pianist. Vera, in her very early teens, is the leader. Vera married Roger Stredwick and but for her untimely death would have become my mother-in-law.

Roger Stredwick, my father-in-law, in fancy dress. In reality he wore army uniform, fighting with the AIF on Gallipoli.

Stred's second daughter Leone (Billie) at sixteen, when I first met her—a publicity shot for one of her first ABC broadcasts.

In the snow outside the church in Belsize Park, London, where Billie and I were married in December 1950.

Above left: Garnet Bonney, whose part in my story is told in these pages.
Above right: Billie with the conductor Eugene Goossens before a concerto performance. (*Australian Consolidated Press*)

Above: Old Parliament House (subsequently extended) as it was in the '40s not long before I first worked in Canberra The sheep are absolutely genuine. (*National Library, R.C. Strangman Collection*)
Below: At these once-shabby farm buildings we bought a Christmas goose, beheaded and plucked for us on the spot. In a transformed scene the farmland is now Lake Burley Griffin and the farmhouse (Blundell's Cottage) a tourist stop on its foreshores. (*National Capital Planning Authority*)

As it was: the *Sydney Morning Herald* residence at 29 Mugga Way, Canberra, and a small part of its big garden. Subsequently extended by new owners in the original style, it survives as a historic Canberra house. (*Courtesy of E. and R. Digweed*)

quatting on a cracked and worn-out artificial ather chair and clutching the day's stories torn off e teleprinter, Elgin Reid relaxes in the cramped risbane *Courier-Mail* office in Parliament House.

Malcolm McColm, Queensland Liberal MP, my closest friend among the politicians.

The press gallery, 1951–52. Back row, l. to r.: Peter Wheeler, Melbourne *Herald*; Ian Reid, ditto; Ian Stewart, *Sydney Morning Herald*; Paul Ormonde, Sydney *Daily Telegraph*; Kevin Bridger, Sydney *Daily Mirror*; Gavin Handsley, *SMH*. Middle row: Stan Stephens, *Adelaide Advertiser*; Michael McGeorge, Melbourne *Age*; Bill Bissell, Aust. Broadcasting Commission; Tony Innes, SMH-AAP gallery service; Oliver Hogue, Sydney *Sunday Sun*; Farmer Whyte, Federal News Service; Bernie Freedman, Melbourne *Argus*; Keith Madden, *SMH*. Front row, seated: Ken Murchison, Sydney *Sun*; Les Teece, Aust. United Press; Ron McCauley, AUP; Stan Hutchinson, Melbourne *Sun News-Pictorial* ('Sun-Pic'). Front, kneeling: Kevin Power, *Daily Mirror*; Les Love, *Mirror*.

More press gallery, 1951–52. Back row: Frank Ryland, AUP; John Farquharson, AUP; Hal Myers; Rob Chalmers, Sydney *Sun*; Bruce Lunn, *Daily Mirror*; Bob Dempsey, *Aust. Financial Review*; Brian Wright, *Argus*. Middle row: Jack Commins, ABC; Gordon Burgoyne, ABC; Lew Yardley, AUP; Bill Slade, *Adelaide Advertiser*; Bill Price, *Sun-Pic*; John Bennetts, Melbourne *Herald*; Alan Reid, Sydney *Sun*. Front row, seated: Fergan O'Sullivan, *SMH*; George Kerr, *Daily Telegraph*; Hec Sholl, *SMH*; Ian Fitchett, *The Age*. Front, kneeling: Leo McDonnell, Brisbane *Telegraph*; Roy Hanson, ditto; Rex Banks, *Sun-Pic*.

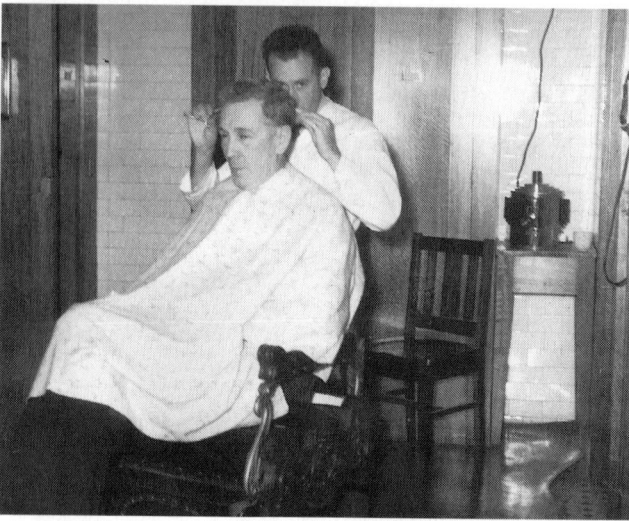

Above left: The only picture of a prime minister having a haircut? The Parliament House barber (and SP bookie) Cec Bainbrigge is giving a short back and sides to Ben Chifley, who was PM when I worked in the gallery in the '40s. (*Courtesy of the Manuka Photographic centre; photograph believed taken by Canberra commercial photographer Les Dwyer*). Above right: Bill Bourke, a personal friend who was my best informant in the Labor Party. (*National Library, from the* 11th Parliamentary Handbook).

Below: Dr H.V. ('Bert' or 'Doc') Evatt, Chifley's successor as leader of the opposition. He looks what he was: a cunning, single-minded intellectual who at times unexpectedly displayed a kind of homespun charm. (*Australian Archives, CRSA1200, L10375*)

A Menzies press conference in 1951 or early 1952. The journalists from l. to r. are Elgin Reid, Bris. *Courier-Mail*; Frank Chamberlain, Melb. *Sun News-Pictorial* ('*Sun-Pic*'); Hal Myers; Ian Fitchett (partly obsc.), Melb. *Age*; Kevin Power, Sydney *Daily Mirror*; Jack Allsop, Aust. United Press; Gavin Handsley, *Sydney Morning Herald*; Les Teece, AUP; Irvine Douglas (partly obsc.), *SMH*; Stan Hutchinson, *Sun-Pic*; John Bennetts (partly obsc.), Melb. *Herald*; Fred Coleman, Melb. *Argus*; Ray Maley (partly obsc.), *Argus*; Brian Wright, *Argus*; Jack Kenny, Sydney *Daily Telegraph*; Jack Commins, Aust. Broadcasting Commission; Harold Cox, Melb. *Herald*; Bob Logue, *Daily Mirror*; Gordon Burgoyne (partly obsc.), ABC; and the nose of Alan Reid, Sydney *Sun*.

Harold Holt (l.) with Sir Arthur Fadden (r.) march down a parliamentary corridor as Fadden arrives to deliver a budget speech. The tie slightly askew and tucked into the pants is a typical Fadden touch. (*National Library, negative no. 00003916*)

Menzies' press secretary Stewart Cockburn arrives in London with Heather Menzies (l and Menzies' secretary Hazel Craig (r.) in May 1953 for the coronation of Queen Elizabeth II. (*Courtesy of Stewart Cockburn*)

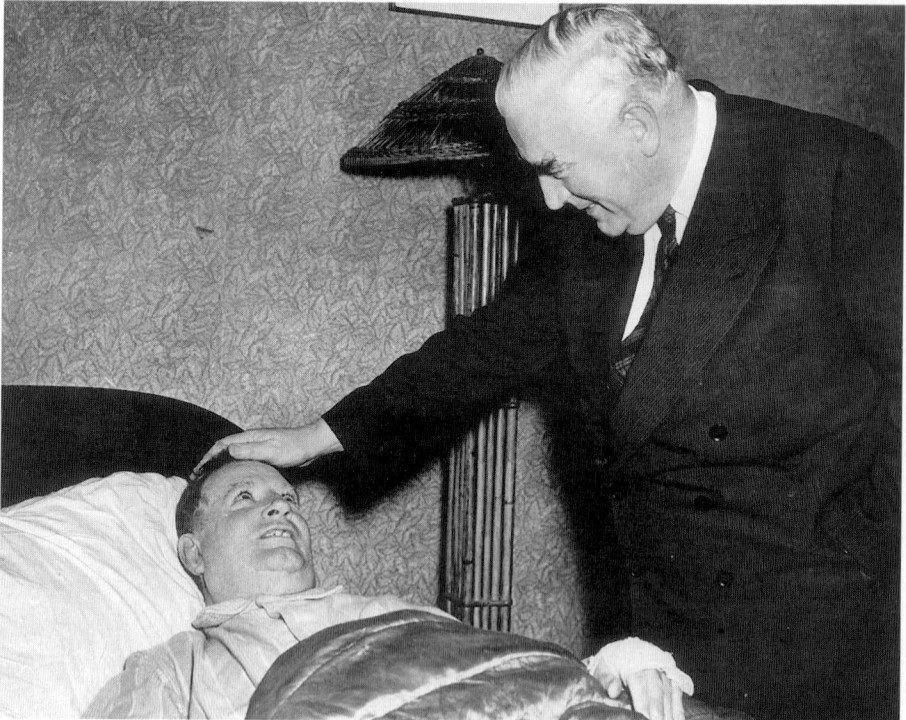

Menzies comforting Fadden in his sickbed after a car accident during an election campaign. The benign smile and gesture didn't represent Menzies' constant feelings about his treasurer, whom he found something of a trial. (*National Library, from MS4936*)

Above: The famous picture of the distraught Mrs Petrov, wife of the Russian spy and defector, being dragged aboard an aircraft by two Russian security men, bound for Moscow. On a stopover in Darwin she defected after being reassured by a telephone call to her husband. (*Australian Archives [ACT], Series CRS A6201/1 Item 62*)

Left: My former colleague Fergan O'Sullivan, who became a key figure in the Petrov inquiry. The photograph, taken at the Russian Embassy, was an exhibit at the Royal Commission on Espionage. (*Australian Archives [ACT] Series CRS A6201/1 Item 77*)

Billie and I at the journalists' ball, Canberra, in the early '50s.

Allen Fairhall, whose leaked story caused Menzies 'witch hunt' when I wrote it. Allen was later seen as a possible successor to Holt as PM. (*National Archives [ACT], from the* 11th Parliamentary Handbook)

John Gorton at the time of our last encounter. Betty Gorton sits with pressmen as her husband addresses a journalists' luncheon at the Hotel Canberra during the 1969 election campaign—the campaign which gave rise to my embarrassment over a speech writer. (*National Library photograph no. NL9154*)

PART IV

In the Gallery

CHAPTER 8

Flying with the Crow

1952

Canberra, January 1952. With Doug on holidays, I fed his cat and wrote his column. Of the *Herald*'s political correspondents in my time Ross Gollan, in the later stages of the war and the early post-war years, was the best. His commentaries were incisive and influential. Doug's didn't have the same bite or flair; they were sedate, like their author. But now I was under challenge to do better, and there couldn't have been a worse time than early January, when nothing was happening in Canberra. The major issue was a sterling-area currency crisis, on which the main action was taking place in London. And that's where the Australian Treasurer, Sir Arthur Fadden, would be, as I sat in Canberra wondering what to write about.

I picked up one idea from Jeff Bate, one of the farmers in the Liberal Party, and—for want of a better subject—wrote a column reflecting his views. It debunked current talk about government plans to stimulate food production. Jeff was my first informant on the issues that were agitating Liberal backbenchers. Some government members were interested only in talking to the heads of the newspaper offices, but Jeff was keen to talk to anyone. (He was an unconventional character. One night while parliament was sitting he parked a large truckload of young cattle outside the front of Parliament House and let them out for a comfort stop. The animals showed no respect for the shrine of democracy, gratefully using the grand front steps of the building as a public toilet while, inside, politicians filled the chambers of parliament with words.)

I managed to write one moderately provocative column while Doug was away. The thought behind it came from a conversation with Fergan

O'Sullivan when Fergan commented on the Menzies Government's strange decision to increase its investment in Commonwealth Oil Refineries, although the public thought it had been elected to get out of activities like that. I developed this theme, as ministers and Liberal MPs were also having second thoughts about the expected sale of the government airline, Trans Australia Airlines, and the shipping line. 'If any politician had tried to stand on the Government parties' 1949 election platform last week he would have risked falling through the holes where some of the planks used to be,' I wrote. It was a somewhat cliché-ridden statement but it gave me a theme.

Fergan O'Sullivan, whose comment provoked the thought, was a young journalist, born in Australia and raised in Ireland, whom the *Herald* had just sent to Canberra to replace the man who had been living in the Telopea Park house. He was much more politically minded than the man he replaced. Just how much so I discovered later, when a document he wrote during this period became a major exhibit in the Petrov Royal Commission.

The furnished house provided for us in Telopea Park belonged to a public servant who had been posted away from Canberra. It was a small, sparsely equipped government-built bungalow built to one of a short list of early standard Canberra designs. Inside, it was carpeted with a cheap product called Feltex—felt with a pattern printed on it—which was wearing into holes. Outside, it had a brown lawn in front and a small, dusty backyard with malnourished fruit trees and the remains of a vegetable garden. But we wouldn't be there for long, and the house had one great advantage. This was that the next-door neighbours were the *peculiar* Elgin Reid and his family, a lovable though disconcerting group.

Elgin was eccentric in a restrained, unflamboyant way. He was long and thin with ropey fair hair which hung in a disarranged way over his forehead. He had a disregard for appearance, and while I knew him in Canberra he bought one pair of black zebu-hide shoes each year and wore them all day and every day—at work, at diplomatic parties, gardening, chopping logs for the fire or on picnics in the bush. After twelve months he replaced them with a similar pair and threw the old ones away. Driving the kids to school one morning when they were a little older he ran out of petrol near the shops at Manuka. So he walked off for help to the nearest service station wearing the clothes he was driving in: an old woollen dressing gown, long winter pyjamas, football socks and the latest black zebu hides.

Drinking in bars with pressmen or politicians, Elgin talked or listened intently, standing with a characteristic backward lean, always oblivious of the angle of his glass; some beer would usually spill onto his tie or suit or both, but his concentration was not disturbed. Soon after we moved to Telopea Park Billie found him sitting on the side of his kitchen stove in the same old pyjamas and dressing-gown, stirring on the stove top some jam which he was making from plums from the *Courier-Mail*'s fruit trees. Knowing nothing about jam-making, he carried out research on the subject in the Australian National Library. Now, stirring the mixture with one arm, he was holding and feeding his youngest child with the other—but his mind was on his book, *War and Peace*, which was open beside him on the kitchen sink as on a lectern.

Elgin's wife Thea could not be described as eccentric but, like Elgin, was remarkably vague in practical matters. She had been a journalist on the *Courier-Mail* but became pregnant as soon as they were married, and left her job. Thea was knowledgeable and well-read. She was sweet and tolerant too, and, in her words, 'incapable of imposing my will on another human being'. As a result the Reid children were a cause of wonder in Canberra. They cut up an eiderdown one morning and the hose another day, put sand in Elgin's petrol tank, tried to paint his new green car yellow, and pulled up the gladioli bulbs in our sparsely planted garden. Elgin and Thea did not flinch. When we called at the Reids' after we had moved from Telopea Park, and the kids started throwing mud at our car, Elgin's solution was simple. 'Well, Myers,' he declared, 'I think you'd better go.'

It was no ordinary family, this. But the Reids were to do more than anyone else to make our life tolerable in Canberra. And since I am not writing a mystery story I can report now that the five Reid children grew up to prove that sparing the rod may not spoil the child. Not that I'd recommend the Reids' method to everyone.

Billie's first major engagement after her return to Australia came as soon as we got to Canberra. It was a series of three performances of Rachmaninov's *First Piano Concerto* with the Sydney Symphony Orchestra conducted by Eugene Goossens. So, while I went off to Parliament House with Elgin, she practised.

Not having children or thoughts of any at this stage, we acquired a pup. I mention this because of the person who found him for us, Frank Green, clerk of the House of Representatives—the most senior officer of the parliament. Frank, a well-worn sixty-two-year-old, was another appealing oddity. He had a dog, too, an ugly mongrel which threatened all callers. When the post office refused to deliver his mail unless he got rid of the dog, Frank got rid of the mail instead and had his private letters sent to Parliament House. When a young police constable, new to Canberra, tried to knock on the Greens' door one night to inquire about someone's whereabouts the dog instantly attacked. The constable returned to the station to lay a charge against Frank Clifton Green, of 54 National Circuit, ACT, but was advised against this course by his sergeant, who also knew Frank as a special magistrate of the Australian Capital Territory.

The most touching story about Frank's relationship with his dog, which gave us faith in his affinity with the species and therefore his ability to find a suitable dog for us, related to the time when this animal went missing for several days. He was merely chasing bitches on heat and getting into fights, and a few days of these efforts left him wounded and exhausted, but not short of his mental resources and cunning. When his adventures were over, and he couldn't stand the pain and effort involved in getting home again, he went to Parliament House instead, lay under Frank's car there and waited for a lift. So our little mongrel pup, based on a beagle and other unknown breeds—whom we called Paddy in memory of an old Stredwick dog— came with the recommendation of no less an authority than Frank Green. But our Paddy had nothing in common with the Green dog. He was neither savage nor intelligent, just a friendly little roller-over.

Family members and friends came to stay with us in Telopea Park. On one of Mum's visits Billie found her trying to dig up the soil in the backyard with a kitchen fork. She was looking to see whether the owner had ever planted potatoes which might be surviving underground. Mum, with her Irish background, carried her own potato famine with her. It would break out after any brief period of deprivation, but Billie had never been aware of the complaint or the symptoms.

Elgin and I left Parliament House together one night and arrived home at Telopea Park simultaneously. 'What about a rum before we go to bed?' he suggested. Queenslanders often had rum on the mind—a patriotic gesture towards a by-product of the Queensland sugar refineries. Elgin and I had already had a few drinks together in the Non-Members' bar at the House, and these made his suggestion especially attractive, so much so that as I left his house afterwards I attempted to leap over the hedge of daisy bushes that separated our drives. What I had never seen there was the strand of wire fencing hidden among the flowers. And when my foot caught it I came in for a crash landing and ruined a disc—my old drinking injury, I called it. I have to mention the event as it happened, for the disc reappears in my story on a more significant occasion.

Economic issues continued to dominate after Doug's return from holidays. At the beginning of March, federal cabinet began a review of Australia's balance of payments problems, which were so serious that ministers had set aside six full days over two weeks for their discussions. Restrictions on practically all imports were inescapable, virtually taking the country back to a wartime condition. Specific action was also needed on imports from the dollar area, and although dollar imports were already confined to essentials such as agricultural equipment, more cuts were inescapable. As cabinet began its meetings the question was not whether imports would be reduced but when the decisions would be made. I could not foresee how fateful these decisions would be for me.

There was a long meeting on the first day, but no news. The next day's sitting went even longer, all day and into the night. Occasions like this were nervous times in the press gallery. No matter how late a cabinet meeting continued, you had to sit around in case there was an announcement. And if there was no announcement you tried to pick up an unofficial indication of what had happened—if you didn't, your competitors might.

The old Parliament House was an extraordinarily informal place, with little security at any time, and sometimes none at all. Journalists could lurk freely in the corridors near the Cabinet room and in those that led to the ministers' offices, including the prime minister's. You could watch to see when ministers left the Cabinet room, or station yourself in a position to see your favourite minister go back to his office ('his': there was no woman in Menzies' ministry at that time). If you were friendly with a minister's staff you could go down and talk to them in one of the minister's outer offices while you waited for the man himself to return. You could loiter in King's Hall, between the two chambers of parliament, reading a copy of the Magna Carta under glass for the thousandth time while you waited for ministers who were in the Senate to cross over to their quarters there, and stop them on the way. More discreetly, when cabinet rose you could try ringing ministers in their offices. If it wasn't too late you could finally try ringing them back at the Hotel Canberra. There were so many ways in which you or your competitors might pick up a story from cabinet that you couldn't relax until all the lights went off in the press rooms.

The press gallery looked relaxed that night, though. We were all lounging around smoking and chatting until cabinet rose and we could go home. The routine stories of the day had been sent off long before, and now the teleprinters were silent throughout the gallery. It was becoming increasingly obvious that no announcement would be coming that night, and we would probably have to wait until cabinet returned for more discussions the following week. And as it got later, the possibility of anyone getting a story unofficially from a minister that night was rapidly diminishing. This was the picture shortly before eleven o'clock when Schapel came into our office and said to Doug: 'I don't think I'm going to write any more tonight, are you?' 'No, I don't think there'll be anything more now,' Doug replied. 'Well, I won't be writing any more if you're not,' said Schapel. 'Are we agreed?' 'Yes,' said Doug. 'We won't send anything more unless there's an announcement.' Cabinet rose at eleven-fifteen and the teleprinters remained silent. But Schapel's story of the cabinet decision to impose drastic cuts in imports from 1 July was all over the front page of the *Telegraph* the next morning.

The import cuts, the *Telegraph* said, would allow only the bare essentials to come to Australia in the next year. These were the most extensive cuts any Australian government had ever introduced, and would cover the entire field of imports. Schapel listed many products that would be affected, and quoted plenty of figures. He said that the full details of the drift in Australia's balance of payments had shocked many of the ministers and created a 'grave note of urgency in the Cabinet'.

Schapel's scoop was a beat-up prepared with exquisite skill. His figures were drawn from common knowledge and informed speculation, the 'shock' to ministers from his imagination. The statement that cabinet had made its decision had no foundation in fact when Schapel wrote it earlier in the day, but could not be denied. Everyone knew that import cuts were coming, and it would have been unpractical for Menzies to issue a denial and then announce the cuts, as he would have to, immediately afterwards. And as Schapel's story was a beat-up he didn't have to wait till late at night to write it. He would have written it in the afternoon and sent it early that night in time for the first edition, as soon as he knew that cabinet would be resuming its meeting after dinner. So when he came and talked to Doug later that night he could truthfully say 'I'm not going to write any more' and bamboozle Doug with this cunning ambiguity. He was even able to satisfy himself that there would be no story in the *Herald* to match his own.

Doug received a terse demand for an explanation from Sydney, and tried to brand the *Telegraph*'s story for what it was—a fake. But whatever the truth might have been, the government announced the import restrictions immediately, as it had to, and made any possible explanations from Doug meaningless. He could never even say that the Crow had fooled him or admit that the two of them had agreed to a truce.

Latham Withall, director of the Associated Chambers of Manufactures of Australia, put me on to the counter-scoop which, as it turned out, finished Doug in Canberra. The restrictions which Schapel wrote about, and Menzies announced, related to imports from the sterling area, but imports from other areas, especially the dollar area, had yet to be considered. Imports from North America were especially sensitive because they were already confined to goods classified as essential. Further restrictions on these would therefore be very significant for the Australian economy.

Withall was the doyen of Canberra lobbyists, a man in his sixties with a background in economics and nearly ten years in the job. I'd known and liked him since my first time in Canberra. It was at the end of another week of cabinet discussions that he told me that the decision on dollar imports had already been made but not yet announced. He had learned this from a trade official in the Indian High Commission who had been alerted by some steps already taken by the public service to begin implementing the new cuts. I rang the Indian, checked the story and wrote it.

My story revealed that the dollar restrictions would be much more severe than expected. Some ministers had urged that there be only a token cut, but most of the cabinet had recognised the need for something much more substantial. The cuts would not only affect future dollar licences: the government was also considering freezing credit on many licences already granted. Importers who had not obtained irrevocable letters of credit for goods they had ordered could find their licences recalled and reduced. I listed the items which would be affected: not only North American tobacco, but also such essential goods as timber, motor-vehicle chassis and parts, tinplate, aluminium, mining machinery, electricity-generating equipment, lubricating oils, drugs and chemicals, iron and steel, aircraft, aircraft parts and American agricultural machinery, which was specially suitable for Australian outback conditions. My story forced the government to move immediately. It recalled all dollar licences that day and the Commonwealth Bank temporarily froze all dollar finance.

These moves had major repercussions in Australian industry and my scoop had major repercussions in the *Sydney Morning Herald*. I had been back in Canberra for about six months and still the *Herald* had not decided when to move Doug on. Angus McLachlan had even become somewhat equivocal on the matter, I'd learned to my annoyance, as he had recently asked Harry Kippax whether he thought I was really ready and able to take over. Import restrictions changed all that, and Harry was on the phone. 'We're bringing Doug back as soon as possible and you will take over,' he told me now. I felt sorry for Doug at the end. Although he couldn't have lasted much longer in Canberra, the event which triggered his departure was set up by Schapel's deviousness, which he had no hope of matching. He was too much the gentleman.

I had already decided that I would never, never come to any arrangement with the Crow.

Between the two series of cabinet meetings which led to the the scoop and counter-scoop, I had gone to Sydney to hear one of Billie's performances with the Sydney Symphony Orchestra. They were her first appearances in Australia in the role of a rising young professional rather than successful student. There was something deeply personal for me in this concert. I had heard her play part of the same Rachmaninov concerto before we went to London, and the music brought back the feelings of that earlier time. It is a slight work, probably not a good choice by the ABC for her first appearance back in her home town. But I didn't hear it with critical detachment, this music of our first days together; it had emanations for which the composer was not responsible. During 1952 the Rachmaninov concerto also took Billie on tour with the orchestra to a number of centres outside Sydney which included three of special significance to us—Grafton, Newcastle and Canberra, starting with Canberra almost immediately after the Sydney performances.

Billie also booked the Conservatorium hall in Sydney for a recital later in the year. For performers this was the local equivalent of Wigmore Hall, and a solo recital there would complete her return to the Sydney musical scene. Her practice studio for these and any other performances would be the living room of the *Herald* mansion in Mugga Way, to which we would shortly move. It wasn't a mansion, really, but it seemed so when viewed from our temporary quarters in Telopea Park.

George Romans, the head of *Hansard*—the official parliamentary report— built this house for himself and his family. He designed and planted a garden worthy of the size and position of the land. It had its formal elements, notably the tree-lined front drive which circled past the front door. Beyond the drive were soft grassy areas rather than lawns, one of which was the setting for a large formal stone fishpond overhung by a graceful drooping Chinese elm. There were a large formal rose garden, an orchard of sixty fruit trees behind the house, a wild part dominated by huge snow gums, and a hidden vegetable garden which would be wasted on me. The garden was bordered on its three streetfronts—on Mugga Way, Flinders Way and Vancouver Street—by an enormous length of hedge, which was the required form of fencing under the Canberra plan; the Department of the Interior employed crews of men to clip the hedges which it compelled residents to grow at their street frontages. On the fourth side this estate adjoined two large houses, one of them the Brazilian Embassy; it was walled off entirely from the Brazilians by a cascading hedge of Kentish cherry which Billie later attempted to convert into jam. The street trees of Mugga Way, big white gums and candle barks, added to the sense of scale, as did the open spaces beyond, on the opposite side of Flinders Way, where Canberra at that time ended.

The house was a two-storeyed cream stucco building with large entertaining rooms downstairs and a kitchen with twenty-seven cupboards to provide for the entertaining, and a bedroom which could have been a maid's room. Upstairs under a steep roof were three bedrooms and a study. The main bedroom looked across the rose gardens to two massive snow gums, one of which in spring was half-hidden in the pink of a climbing dog rose which grew up through it, the other half-swamped by a tidal wave of wisteria, the two joining overhead in a great coloured arch. It was a romantic house to look on but hardly a practical setting for an undomesticated young journalist with a wife interested in music, not housework. It was impractical in other ways, too. Our neighbour Harold White said he thought that George Romans had taken the design out of an American magazine. The house was so badly oriented, and in most parts so inadequately equipped with windows, and so much overshadowed by the big gums, that in the frosty Canberra winters the sun never penetrated.

We owned nothing more than a piano and a radio to put into this substantial residence. Each of my predecessors had been long enough married to own a house-full of furniture and equipment. We had neither. Angus McLachlan gave me a budget to overcome this problem but we had to spend it in accordance with the taste of Rupert Henderson. This created the illusion that we were living in another century in the formality of carved rosewood and Regency stripes. It wasn't our idea of Australian living but we were thankful to be accommodated in any style.

The Douglases left Canberra quickly. Doug went gracefully although he must have felt humiliated and under great pressure, especially at home. His wife Winnie was an unhappy woman who was well known for belittling him in public; life must have been equally difficult for them in private. Tony Innes, who was kindly towards other people, had known Doug in their earlier days in Tasmania and spoke of him as 'a good man ruined by marriage'. Doug's professional standing and their social position were essential compensations for Winnie, and their sudden eviction from the job and house must have been hard to bear. She would not have made life easier for herself or for Doug at that time.

The first political event of moment after I took over from Doug was a Premiers' Conference. My friend Jack Colless, who came down for it, warned me about the man who had been selected as my number two, a thirty-year-old named Dick Cross. 'He's quiet, ambitious and only out for Cross,' said Jack. Remembering his well-justified caution about Doug's previous offsider, Ted O'Loghlin, I took his warning seriously. I didn't know Dick Cross; he was a New Zealander who had joined the paper only recently. I wasn't in a position to choose my staff, though, so I could only hope that the two of us could get on. But this time Jack was wrong. I soon found that the *Herald* could not have sent me a better colleague.

Meanwhile Schapel set out to welcome me as his new competitor in his own way. As I shuffled down the drive to pick up the newspapers first thing each morning I became used to wondering what revelations he would have on page one of the *Telegraph*. For a time it was as if he had been granted almost exclusive use of the front page to test my nerve. Today, some of these stories sound trivial, almost ridiculous, but the *Telegraph* thought they were worth front-page headlines. And each morning the first reading gave me a slight shock. Each time, I had to establish whether I had been scooped, whether Schapel had merely resuscitated the contents of the files once more, or whether his latest story was nothing but a furphy.

One day the controlled prices of butter and cheese were to rise, then the federal government expected the coronation date to be in June the next year (a serious matter!), then the government was going to reconstitute the Australian Shipbuilding Board—but this was all stale, reheated information. A few days' respite during the Premiers' Conference and a meeting of the Loan Council, then Schapel was back with a new series: federal cabinet would consider abolishing or restructuring the trading section of the Commonwealth Bank; the government was considering sacking communists in the public service; more tax cuts coming; Menzies to report to cabinet on a grave new financial crisis in the sterling area, to which Australia belonged. And then suddenly, except for the budget speculation, the onslaught stopped. Schapel must have run out of old stories to rewrite, or perhaps he was tired of the pace he had been setting for himself. I was confident that I had won this battle. The Crow's efforts had failed to produce one genuinely exclusive story, and I never worried much about him again. But I wanted to scoop him properly in return.

CHAPTER 9

The Leak in the Corridor

1952

I had seen quite a lot of Menzies by this time, as his recently appointed press secretary, Stewart Cockburn, had persuaded him to hold regular press conferences, usually twice a week when he was in Canberra. The press conferences were revealing of Menzies. There was something of the Byzantine emperor about him as he presided over them from his desk in the Prime Minister's office overlooking the lawns in front of the old Parliament House. His performances had the flavour of a historical role staged in modern dress: his attire, invariably a double-breasted suit, gave added substance to his large form. He comfortably played the herd leader, dominant in appearance as well as manner.

The journalists stood in a huddle around his desk, asking questions and taking notes. All present were free to ask questions, but Menzies never lost control of the proceedings. Once when I asked him about some fractious behaviour by the Public Accounts Committee of the House of Representatives which he did not want to hear about, he tossed off the question, saying: 'Oh, we'll meet that problem when it arises.' 'It *has* arisen,' I complained, but he had already seized on the next question and changed the subject.

There were contradictions in Menzies. Most obviously there was his aloof side, with the seeming disdain for lesser people which many had seen and resented before he was driven out of office in 1941 to spend eight years in opposition. The experience of Garnet Bonney was an illustration of this quality in Menzies. The two of them had been quite friendly in Melbourne in the '30s before Menzies became prime minister for the first time—friendly enough to sit up late at weekends playing poker or some such game—and it was the first Menzies Government which appointed Garnet as Chief Publicity Censor early in the war. Yet as prime minister Menzies would walk past him without recognition, and only once did Garnet see him officially. But after Menzies lost office his memory was restored. He knew and greeted Garnet again.

On the other hand Menzies could exercise a charm which, while you were subject to it, was hard to resist. When not being purely political, or not roused to anger, he was an extremely reasonable man. And he won loyalty from people close to him, who saw the apparent aloofness as merely the deceptive outward sign of a natural and, often, benign reserve.

The *Sydney Morning Herald* had never liked him. There were rumours, possibly false and some of them quite scurrilous, which linked its attitude back to old and very personal jealousies between Warwick Fairfax and Menzies. The paper had temporarily abandoned its conservative tradition in the wartime election campaign of 1943, when Fairfax wrote a series of penetrating articles on politicians and issues. His piece on Menzies ('the Opposition's Hamlet') was unsparing, labelling him as greatly gifted but vain and indecisive. Menzies lost those elections. Although the paper returned to its traditional politics and supported Menzies in subsequent elections, it was a niggling critic at other times. Thus, as political correspondent, I felt no inhibition in criticising or embarrassing Menzies or the government whenever I thought that criticism was justified.

The *Herald*'s feud with Menzies was just one element in the cool relations that existed between him and the press gallery. Other proprietors were undeviating supporters of the Liberal cause, but Menzies knew that most of their representatives in Canberra were pro-Labor. The exception was the Melbourne *Herald*'s man, Harold Cox, a fully qualified conservative. And when other ministers began to urge Menzies to do something about his public relations as the goverment's popularity dwindled, not surprisingly he sought help from Keith Murdoch, who by then had been knighted and had become chairman of the Melbourne Herald group. Murdoch responded by sending one of his most senior executives, Reg Leonard, to Canberra for three months to observe and advise. Leonard said that Menzies should appoint a press secretary without delay.

It was a strange feature of Menzies' approach that he had used a press secretary as leader of the opposition yet felt no need for one when he became prime minister for the second time in 1949. Labor ministers had all had press secretaries, and the Liberals and the Country Party had made them a political issue, complaining that they were there only to manipulate the press. Back in office, Menzies abolished the role of ministerial press secretary entirely. (Pursuing a similar policy he also downgraded Garnet

Bonney's Department of Information to the status of a bureau.) Instead of having press secretaries for individual ministers the government appointed Fadden's old press secretary, Mick Byrne, as Government Public Relations Director; and all ministers, including Fadden and Menzies, had to go through Mick's office for their announcements.

Mick was a drinking mate of Artie's, a short, pudgy figure, who murmured and mumbled almost inaudibly. To me he was notably unhelpful and uncommunicative. He and his assistant Jack Hewitt, with an office staff of one, were the government's whole public relations establishment, and couldn't do much more than keep their copying machine at work throughout the day and often into the night, rolling out statements and announcements for the ministry.

This was the way Menzies liked things. He knew what he wanted to say to the press and public, and wasn't looking for advice from any Mick Byrnes. But when Reg Leonard reported that this would not do, Menzies remembered young Stewart Cockburn. Stewart was a Melbourne *Herald* journalist who had interviewed him in London in 1947 and 1948. Menzies invited him to Canberra and gave him the job as his press secretary. Then other ministers began to get press secretaries, too. Stewart was twenty-nine, keen, and ambitious to make the job worthwhile and to do it well. But his Melbourne *Herald* background caused problems.

Trying to make things run more smoothly between a sceptical prime minister and a sceptical press, Stewart went to Washington in 1952 and attended a Truman press conference. He came back with a discovery. Press conferences recorded! Recordings transcribed immediately! Transcripts distributed to the press! After a summit conference in the Prime Minister's office Stewart was allowed to acquire one recording machine—though tape recorders were so new that they couldn't be bought in Australia, and he had to make do with a more primitive wire recorder instead. The senior members of the press gallery were invited into the PM's office to see it and hear about the proposal to record future prime ministerial press conferences and give them transcripts later in the day. Many of the journalists were incensed: the transcripts might find their way into the hands of their editors and proprietors. They would be a breach of the political correspondents' special, private and sometimes confidential relationship with the prime minister. There was also an offensive implication that transcripts might improve the accuracy of their reporting—or expose its inadequacy.

A special meeting of the Canberra division of the Australian Journalists' Association was called, and even considered a protest strike. Stewart's proposal was eventually agreed to, but on the say-so of the editors and proprietors, who welcomed an opportunity to read what actually happened at the press conferences. It was some weeks before the press gallery accepted the service as useful. Then they conceded not in words but in action, queuing up for the transcripts and complaining if they were late.

One of the most hostile journalists was the Melbourne *Age* correspondent, Ian Fitchett. To him Stewart Cockburn's background was a special provocation, for to Fitchett the Melbourne *Herald* was a direct and serious opponent. Cockburn had persuaded Menzies that whenever he was able to hold two press conferences a week one of them should be in morning-newspaper time and the other in afternoon-paper time, and this even-handed concern for the afternoons could be seen as further evidence of favours to the Melbourne *Herald*. Everyone knew that, except in Melbourne, the morning newspapers vastly outweighed the afternoon papers in influence and responsibility, and the afternoons seemed to be getting too much consideration.

Fitchett was in many ways the most noticeable personality in the press gallery. He was a bachelor in his forties, a big man, full of good living, well scrubbed and well trimmed, with disciplined ginger hair and moustache. He was always immaculately turned out. He was related to an older Fitchett, William Henry, an English-born churchman with the improbable record of having been principal of the Methodist Ladies' College in Melbourne for more than forty years. William Henry was a successful writer, too, author of a most popular book of the turn of the century, *Deeds that Won the Empire*. Ian Fitchett had a certain pomposity of manner, accentuated by a booming baritone voice, which went well with this family association. But that was the limit to any conformity with the world of William Henry Fitchett.

Ian was the wit of the press gallery, and used his gift to the discomfort of many. When Harold Cox was reported to be going overseas with Menzies, Fitchett asked in disbelief: 'Which suit are you going to take, Harold? The blue one with the hole in the arse or the brown one with the piss stains down the front?' It was a perfect shot. Cox was socially conscious and was judged a snob by the rest of the gallery, but his manner of dress hardly fitted the part.

Fitchett was good at nicknames, too. When my friend Rodger Rea as a young man worked in a junior position in Harold Cox's office Fitchett named him Childe Harold. Frank Chamberlain of the *Sun-Pictorial* was sleek and chubby; Fitchett called him the Greaseball. But his best inspiration was his name for Stewart Cockburn. It was Frizzledick, and it stuck to Stewart through his time in Canberra.

Exercising the freedom that I knew I would have to write about Menzies as I saw him, I started mildly and worked up. One thing that irritated me in Menzies was what I saw as the legalistic approach which he took when it suited him. It came out especially in ambiguous forms of words which appeared to mean one thing but, on closer examination, didn't necessarily do so. So I tweaked him after a series of cabinet meetings for saying that the cabinet had had 'no discussions whatever on the Budget' although it had held substantial economic discussions, and the budget had shortly to be finalised. 'Cabinet,' I wrote, 'has apparently considered all round the budget and even peeped underneath for unsuspected trouble but has succeeded with great intellectual dexterity in avoiding the subject itself.'

While the 1952 budget was being framed, and just as inflation in Australia was seemingly being brought under control, the Commonwealth Arbitration Court granted a relatively massive increase—approximately 10 per cent—in the 'basic wage'. This was widely seen as a major new threat to economic stability, and when Treasurer Fadden spoke glowingly, immediately afterwards, of a 'greatly increased' purchasing power of the pound, I described him as 'one who can actually see the silver lining without the cloud'. 'My god, that Myers is cynical,' was Angus McLachlan's comment to Harry Kippax. 'If he's like that at his age,' he said, 'what'll he be like later?'

Until I took over from Doug, most of my political contacts were among the younger New South Wales Liberal backbenchers who could only indirectly influence government decisions, usually by applying pressure in party meetings or by influencing the press. Jeff Bate was one of these. Another was Bruce Graham, an ex-soldier who had lost a leg during the war but retained a fierce military manner and outlook. The one with whom I was most at home was Allen Fairhall. Many of these Liberals who came into parliament in 1949 had served in the forces and had not had much time for other careers, but Fairhall had done well in business. He was also, I judged, a political thinker as well as a politician. I found him personally appealing, and stimulating company.

The issue which was burning Allen Fairhall and the others was the threat which they saw the Commonwealth Bank posing to the private banks. They were critical of their government's inertia on this issue, wanting quick amendments to the banking legislation to protect the private banking industry. Banking had been a great crusading issue before the 1949 elections until Chifley's attempt to nationalise the private banks foundered in the High Court and the Privy Council. Chifley's move was a call to arms, not only for Liberals and the banks but also for bank employees everywhere, and the Bank Officers' Association rose up as one of the most effective fighting groups yet seen in Australian politics. In defending the banking system as they knew it they gave immense support to the Liberal Party. Now the young Liberals, swept into office by public reaction, wanted their government to demonstrate its commitment to those who had put them there. They had no patience with the measured approach of Menzies. They wanted action, not technicalities and delays.

Their complaint was that the Commonwealth Bank's trading division—the Commonwealth Bank that the public knew—was not subject to the same restraints or taxes as the private banks. Liberal politicians saw this situation as one which a Labor government could use to crush the private banking system competitively without any of the constitutional obstacles encountered by Chifley.

Debate on this issue was at its height when I ran into Allen Fairhall in the corridor outside the government party room just after a party meeting had finished. 'Anything interesting happen at to-day's meeting?' I asked automatically. For all our friendly relationship I'd learned that Allen did not breach the confidentiality of the party room, and I wasn't expecting an answer. 'There certainly was,' he replied to my surprise. 'I'll tell you all about it.' He did so, indiscreetly standing in a spot where any of his colleagues passing by could see us in discussion.

The New South Wales Liberal backbenchers had launched a revolt on banking policy and Menzies had sat on them. Fairhall and another colleague, Roy Wheeler, had gone into the meeting with a detailed resolution which they planned to move and second, one which demanded legislation to separate the Commonwealth Bank from the Central Bank and deprive it of its protected status. Menzies had refused to accept the motion, declaring imperiously that 'cabinet does not accept direction from the party meeting'. Allen was still so worked up about the meeting that he gave me a full account of it, abandoning his normal discretion.

'I'd like to see this resolution,' I said. 'Would I be able to get a copy?'

'Yes, I've got it with me,' said Fairhall, pulling some paper out of his pocket. 'Here, you can take it.' It was a precise, four-part proposition for reform.

The next day, after publication of my detailed account of the row in the party room, which included the verbatim text of the resolution, he was on the telephone. 'Have you still got that piece of paper with the resolution on it?' he asked. I told him I had. 'I must get it back,' he said. 'Menzies is furious. He's told Joe Gullett [the government whip] to find out who leaked the story, and there are only two copies of that resolution in existence. Roy Wheeler has one and you've got the other.'

Allen suggested that I go down to the parliamentary library and read something in the newspaper files. He would go over and consult the file next to mine. He asked me to leave the document under the front page of my paper, and when I left he would retrieve it. So I went down, we staged a furtive handover, and I returned to my desk in the press gallery. Later that afternoon I wanted to write a follow-up to my party room story, and rang him. 'I don't want to say any more about it,' he said with finality. After that we remained as friendly as before, but I knew that I had had my last as well as my first party room story from him.

If he hadn't normally taken a strict view on the confidentiality of party meetings, the reaction of Menzies would no doubt have persuaded him to do so in future. Menzies, as is well known, dominated most of his ministers and party members, and threatened drastic consequences for any serious breach of party discipline. I do not know whether Allen Fairhall's career was checked at all by this incident, but if it was he certainly overcame any setback and reached high office later. But Roy Wheeler gradually became obsessed with the idea that it had ruined his political chances. He lost his seat in the 1954 elections and returned to stockbroking. After that I ran into him somewhere in the financial end of Sydney. 'You bastard!' he said the first time, when someone tried to introduce us. 'You put me in the shit with Menzies. He thought I gave you that story about the party meeting and you didn't have the guts to put me in the clear.' I tried to reason with him, disclaiming any knowledge of what had gone on with Menzies afterwards. He seemed to relax a little but his bitterness was still there. I felt that there was something wrong with Roy which had nothing to do with me or with what had happened in Canberra. He began to look disorganised and dishevelled, more so each time I saw him. He had the demeanour of a man in the grip of some serious disorder. I do not know what it was, but he died prematurely, a sad figure in my memory.

As soon as we moved to Mugga Way, Dick Cross moved into the Telopea Park house with his wife Clare and their infant son Glen. Clare was in her early twenties with the silhouette of someone older, thin and slightly stooped; and a rather high, girlish, expressionless voice gave her an air of vulnerable immaturity. The appearance was deceptive. We learned that she was indeed weak in some ways physically but not in character. She was destined to need strength, and had it.

Dick was physically the opposite—compact but strongly-built, square-shouldered and good-looking. He was a quiet and undemonstrative young man who smiled slightly but often. He was also a capable journalist, and if he was ambitious, as Jack Colless claimed, he certainly was not the one to attempt to pursue his ambition at my expense. I valued his company on and off the job.

Our permanent staff at first were Dick, Fergan O'Sullivan and me; in addition the *Herald* rotated its bright young journalists through Canberra, reporting parliamentary debates and working with me on non-sitting days. John Valder and Craig McGregor were two of them. My office was concerned with everything but the debates. A separate staff came down to cover parliament when it was in session. Tony Innes was often the man who supervised them, and that was how I came to know Tony well and favourably after my first disconcerting experience with him.

It was my office at Parliament House that covered the press conferences, investigated the current issues, wrote stories from the multitude of reports that were tabled in parliament, analysed statistics, interviewed ministers and contacted public servants for information. We interpreted developments in Canberra, followed up queries from the office in Sydney and searched for information that no-one else in the press gallery might get. One of my difficulties was to decide whether to give priority to news-gathering or to my political column.

As a reporter on the political scene and as a commentator and columnist you were in danger of offending two different sets of politicians, and possibly not having any political friends left. But you couldn't get good political stories without political friends. Bill McMahon unwittingly made me conscious of the problem very early. He was a junior minister, for Navy and Air, when I became political correspondent, and each of us at first was trying to ingratiate himself with the other. 'There's no doubt about it,' he told me, 'your stuff is much better than Irvine Douglas's. Even your worst enemies would say that.' *Worst* enemies? What enemies? Did I have enemies? Was Billy McMahon trying to warn me? His unexpected observation remained a puzzle. But I decided that my priority would be to build up my news sources, for the practical reason that the news had been Doug's undoing. The same thing was not going to happen to me.

The result of this decision was that my weekly column took second place. Sometimes it read that way. I somewhat reluctantly put aside the news for a day each week, often with little preparation and little idea of what I should write about, straining to find an opening thought. At other times I was more than ready with something to say, but these were usually the times when I did make a new enemy or irritated an old one. Probably the one who liked these writings least was the prime minister.

CHAPTER 10

The King Hit

1952 and 1953

Out behind the press gallery in Parliament House were some of the MPs' rooms. Two Queensland Liberals, Malcolm McColm and Reg Swartz, shared one of them. Reg was likeable and unobtrusive, Malcolm an independent, cantankerous rebel, probably something of an irritant to more tractable colleagues. Malcolm was Elgin's closest friend among the politicians and became mine. His room in Parliament House, U65, known as 'the submarine', provided a threatening supply of bottled beer, political stories and late nights.

Malcolm was about ten years older than Elgin and me, son of a Scottish sea captain who sailed clippers on the Australian run and skippered the last sailing ship to reach Sydney Harbour before World War II. As a boy Malcolm rounded Cape Horn under sail with his father. He was an adventurer, strong and stocky, with that stubborn mouth and resolute jaw that I associate with his Scottish origins. He grew up on the Darling Downs. While still a teenager he was a champion buckjumper and bullock rider. In the mid-1930s he worked his passage to England and joined the RAF. He was a squadron leader during the war, flew in a bomber squadron and was shot down over Germany. He spent nearly four and a half years as a POW and escaped several times. Once he even managed to get aboard a Swedish ship in a German port, but the Germans searched the ship before it sailed. Then they sent him to Colditz, where they put the persistent escapers.

Back in Australia after the war he made a living growing mushrooms in tunnels under the old fort and penal colony on St Helena, a small island in Moreton Bay. These crops needed large supplies of manure, and he contracted to buy so much of it that he had to set up a secondary business to dispose of the surplus. Malcolm was selling bags of manure door-to-door in Brisbane from the back of his truck. He dropped some off one night on his way to a formal function in tails and his pre-war English opera cloak.

Malcolm captured the traditionally Labor seat of Bowman in Brisbane in the 1949 elections. He took impulsive risks in politics, and was never promoted. He had a series of public differences with Menzies, and soon after I took over in the *Sydney Morning Herald* office in Canberra he was crossing the floor of the House to vote against the government over the sale of its shares in Commonwealth Oil Refineries. His political attitudes were sometimes hard to follow but always fervent.

Malcolm McColm in a sense marked one end of the spectrum of my government contacts. The bands of this spectrum were made up of senior ministers, up-and-coming ministers, ministers who were getting nowhere, backbenchers who were getting somewhere and would finish in the ministry, backbenchers who might get somewhere, backbenchers who mistakenly thought that they might get somewhere and those who, for various reasons, would sit on the back benches for the whole of their parliamentary lives. Malcolm was in this last band. He was also part of the broader, disorganised group of discontented Liberals who had seen the government's support collapsing and their own political careers slipping away in the economic upheavals of 1951 and 1952. It had been a quick and spectacular change from the high point of Liberalism which had put Menzies back in office in 1949 and put many of the government members in parliament for the first time.

Billie's first recital after London went with all the usual preliminaries of practice runs and nerves. Lindsey Browne in the *Herald* praised most of it but thought that a little more of her old 'cloudy, youthful romanticism' would have profited her in the major work, the Schumann *Fantasia*. The cloudy romanticism of her student days was indeed gone, but a more womanly depth of feeling was beginning to emerge.

The Rachmaninov concerto was programmed again when the orchestra lost another soloist for a concert in Newcastle. Billie's return to her old town, Grafton, with Goossens and the orchestra took place later in the year. I couldn't get away from Canberra for it—regrettably, as it would have been an event to savour. 'Leone's return to her home town was truly magnificent,' sang the *Daily Examiner*. 'She is a great source of pride and happiness.'

We saw much of other musicians on our many visits to Sydney, and a Hungarian pianist of Billie's age, Marta Zalan, came to have a special place in our lives. Marta came from a background of wealth and culture in Budapest and had studied with Leo Weiner, the leading piano teacher at the Franz Liszt Academy, an institution at the centre of the great Hungarian musical tradition. But during the war her family had known what it was like to live in hiding in a cellar, going out at night for food when people were cutting flesh off the frozen bodies of horses in the snow-covered streets. And for the duration of the war they had used false papers to conceal their Jewish identity. After the war and the communist takeover Marta was allowed out of the country to attend an international music competition. Once out, she rang her husband Charles and told him that she was not coming back, and that he should escape and join her.

Charles was well equipped for whatever risks and subterfuge might be necessary. He was a dashing character in his way, son of the owner of a timber-veneer factory which the communists had seized. In wartime, while Marta's family were hiding in their cellar, Charles was pretending to be a soldier invalided home to Budapest because of war injuries. For a year or more he feigned a stiff leg, secretly going for walks late at night to unflex it. After the war, being too independent to work for his father, he went to Persia and found a job managing a veneer factory there. Back in Budapest later he married the beautiful Marta Gardon. The communists arrived at the factory. They went through his father's office and seized some packets of cigarettes which they considered weren't there for his father's use but to offer in a capitalistic way to customers. Then they put Charles and his father on wages and told them to get on with managing the factory.

Charles didn't hesitate to try to escape when Marta's call came, but was captured on his way to the border, brought back to Budapest and gaoled. The Hungarian guards were worse than the Germans had been in Hungary during the war, he said. To discipline one of his fellow political prisoners they made this man, every morning, drink the contents of a public spittoon. After three months Charles was released, and told his father that he was going to try again. His father said that if Charles was killed escaping he would rather be dead himself; so this time the family went together. They paid someone to take them across an unguarded part of the border at night, and this attempt succeeded. Charles and Marta went to Paris and a year later to Australia. We spent a lot of time with them in Sydney. Marta became the closest friend Billie had ever had, and the musical soulmate she badly needed, though as musicians they were quite different.

Life in Mugga Way was greatly improved by the arrival of the Reids. The *Courier-Mail* had bought a house in another large garden at 23 Mugga Way. Between us were the Chancery of the French Embassy at no. 25 and the Commonwealth Librarian, Harold White, and his family at no. 27. Harold and his wife Elizabeth were entertainers on a big scale, and Elizabeth was devoted to good works. She once found herself producing a surplus of breast milk and donated the excess to the Canberra Community Hospital, which fed it to babies whose mothers were not so gifted. She used to leave her donation in a jar by the kitchen window; someone from the hospital picked it up without ceremony each day. Until the day when someone had served it to guests at one of her tea parties. But Elizabeth was by no means only a social do-gooder. She used to do our washing in her washing machine—the *Herald* house didn't have one—on condition that Billie practised the piano at her place so that she could listen.

We would have hated Mugga Way, however, if we had disliked visitors. Everyone wanted to stay there. Charles and Marta came, Mum, Stred and Jean, Billie's aunt Emmie from Grafton, and other friends. But we were not at home to visitors when Christmas, 1952 came; we spent it at Emerald with the Bonneys. It was the first time we had stayed with them. Garnet had acquired the house cheaply in the Depression and had clung to it above most other possessions. It was a European or North American-style building with attic bedrooms set in its steeply pitched roof. Emerald was the pick spot in the Dandenongs and the house itself was next to the grounds of the Emerald Country Club, with a stream running through the garden. It could be a cool place even in summer, and we sat around a fire in a big stone fireplace on Christmas Day. It was a cosy, friendly end to the year.

Hugh McClure-Smith resigned as editor of the *Herald* at the end of 1952 and was replaced by John Pringle. As Rupert Henderson had deprived McClure-Smith of most of the functions of an editor, he had meant nothing to me. I had spent some time with him once or twice during his rare visits to Canberra. But Pringle immediately wanted to meet the *Herald*'s political correspondent. A Scot, fresh from London, he was avidly absorbing the new country he was in—its politics, its arts, its scandals, its gossip, its discomforts and pleasures. He was burrowing into the internal workings of the *Sydney Morning Herald*, too; on these he was indiscreetly informative.

The Canberra office was running smoothly until I heard the news about Dick Cross. He had told me about his problem six weeks earlier but had gone to his local doctor and been reassured. When the trouble didn't disappear he went to a specialist in Sydney. 'I've got to have an operation,' he told me as soon as he got back. 'I'm going to lose a testicle.' I made a fatuous comment to the effect that it had happened to other people without ruining their sex lives. 'It's not losing the testicle that's worrying me,' he said, 'it's the reason why. Cancer.'

He went to Sydney and had the operation. I was in Sydney when he was ready to go home, and we arranged that he would come back with me in the car. We met at the *Herald* staff's old pub, the Grand Hotel in Hunter Street. His shirt was open. 'I see you've been getting a bit sunburned on the chest,' I said innocently. 'No, I've been having some radiation treatment. They found that I had a bit of a secondary cancer. It should be all right.' Medical science has surged on since that time, but successful treatment of cancer then was rare, and in my experience once you had a secondary you had no hope. There I was standing with a middy in my hand in the saloon bar of the Grand, suddenly talking to a dead man. I felt ill. I stood silent and couldn't finish my beer. Then we drove back to Canberra and Dick returned to a wife so early in another pregnancy that possibly they didn't even know about it yet.

The discontent and rebelliousness inside the government parties in 1952 had their origin in events both past and future. In the past, Artie Fadden's budget of 1951; in the future, the Senate elections due in 1953. The vote would be for only half the Senate, so the government's survival was not at issue. But the elections would determine whether the government would continue to control the Senate or have a hostile Senate working against it. Late in 1952 the swing against the government was enough to suggest that Labor would win this contest. Malcolm McColm and his friends in the House of Representatives, though not directly affected by the Senate elections, were not looking forward to them either. But I was: this would be my first election campaign.

Fadden's 1951 budget had been a drastic remedy for the worst inflation Australia had known. It can be measured by the movements at the time in the basic wage, a minimum wage set by the Arbitration Court and—by its decree—automatically adjusted for inflation each quarter. Over the year 1950–51 it increased by 36 per cent. Each quarterly wage rise fed back into the cost of living and caused another wage rise. Fadden's 1951 budget was designed to break this cycle. It included a 10-per cent income-tax levy and other anti-inflationary measures so unpopular that it became known as the horror budget. Fadden was attacked and jeered at wherever he went.

This was the time when he said he could have held a meeting of his supporters in a telephone box. His only consolation was in the bottle.

The next budget in 1952 removed some of the impositions of the horror budget, but a by-election in the Victorian electorate of Flinders showed that voters were still in revolt. There was a swing of 11 per cent against the government in Flinders, and in December a comparable swing put the Liberal state government out of office in Victoria.

Not long before this a strange event, to my mind, occurred. Fred Osborne, a Liberal member from Sydney, was one of the politicians I talked to. He refused to disclose anything that happened in government party meetings, but was quite frank about everything else. I found him one of the most agreeable of the politicians. Fred had been expected to get the cabinet post which went to McMahon in 1951. The position was due to go to a New South Wales member, and Fred, a lawyer by background, was rumoured to be Menzies' choice. Three other New South Wales Liberals—Jeff Bate, Bill Wentworth and Bill McMahon—then went to Eric Harrison, the most senior minister from New South Wales, to oppose Osborne's appointment, knowing that it was also opposed by the New South Wales Liberal Party organisation. Osborne heard about this after McMahon's elevation and said: 'I didn't know that you could walk around for two weeks with your throat cut.' And he waited another five years to become a minister, so when I first knew him he was just another restive backbencher.

I wasn't surprised when Billie and I were invited to dinner one Saturday night at the Osbornes' house in Strathfield. What surprised me was the company—Gough Whitlam and his wife Margaret. Whitlam had just been endorsed as Labor candidate in a by-election that was coming up in the seat of Werriwa, and Osborne was taking the trouble to have a look at him. It was a night of good conversation, though from my viewpoint it led nowhere. Whitlam's development as a politician was overshadowed by other events in the Labor Party during my time in Canberra, and I had almost no further contact with him. The Whitlams were just as bewildered as I was about Fred Osborne's dinner party, as I believe it was the only personal contact they ever had.

Reviewing the prospects for the Senate elections at that time one could say that the government's unpopularity in New South Wales, Victoria and South Australia was so great that its position there looked impossible. In both Western Australia and Tasmania the death of a senator since the last elections had complicated the voting pattern in a way which made a government majority virtually impossible there, too. Queensland seemingly remained the government's only hope. But Queensland was Fadden's territory, and except to the most immovable supporters of his Country Party he was now an object, literally, of hate. Everything depended on Menzies, and the outcome would be determined by the coming struggle between two men, Menzies and Evatt. That was what made the prospect of the campaign so attractive to me.

Bert Evatt, or Doc Evatt (I and most of the press gallery called him Doc) was a man whose mind never rested or wandered; it was focused entirely on pursuit of the prime ministership. He had begun to ring me most Sunday mornings, getting me out of bed to hear his weekly political analysis. The phone was set into the wall on the landing between the floors of 29 Mugga Way. None of my predecessors had thought of getting an extension downstairs, or upstairs by the bed; nor had I. So I stood on one leg in my pyjamas on cold Canberra mornings, cursing the Doc until he came to the end of his twenty-minute performance.

Evatt was a stout man with short, straight hair that stuck forward in no style at all. His glasses gave him an unfocused look as if he were vaguely searching for them and had probably forgotten that they were on his nose. He moved without exertion, like a man to whom unnecessary bodily movement was foreign. His clothes looked as if they belonged to another period of his life. One hears now that in his younger days he was a passionate, faithful lover but no-one who didn't know would have suspected this of the seemingly disembodied brain that we knew at this time, a missile-guidance system locked on to the Prime Minister's Lodge.

This was Evatt's first election campaign as leader of the opposition, and he set himself to outdo Menzies in electioneering as in everything else. He would give his policy speech a week earlier, campaign a week longer and visit every state once more than Menzies, going to Western Australia twice and every other state three times in four-and-a-half weeks of frenetic talk and travel. As to his election policy, it was one which he would never have to carry out, since the half-Senate election could not change the government. So he presented a prescription for Australia's economic recovery which was so extravagant in its promises to all sections of the electorate that it worried even his own party. A Labor government would ensure 'full use of Central Bank credit for home-building', he said, and would 'finance employment up to the limits of available men and resources', but despite the inflationary pressures that such a policy would unleash there would be no increase in interest rates. His only proposal for paying for anything was a vague review of the defence vote, yet he also promised unspecified increases in social service payments and pensions and a costly tax concession for industry.

I began travelling with Menzies the following week. He started in the crucial state, opening his campaign before a crowd of three thousand — three times as many as Evatt's opening meeting—in the Brisbane City Hall. He promised tax relief in the next budget which would go 'as far as we can or as far as any other responsible and honest Government could'. Then on to Bundaberg and Maryborough, where there were more good, attentive crowds. He was warming up by the time we got to Sydney at the end of the week. A Senate election vote for Labor, he told a suburban audience in Sydney, would mean that the communists would control Australia, 'yelping at the heels of a socialist government'. Menzies was far from finished with the communists as an electoral asset.

Within a week of joining Menzies on the election trail for the first time I wrote a column which finished me with him from then on. I think it was my occasional twitch of cynicism rather than the substance of what I wrote that struck a sensitive spot. Queensland, I wrote, was a politically old-fashioned state. It took Menzies at face value, while many of its respectable citizens regarded Evatt as probably a communist in disguise. I commented that Menzies was least in touch with politics on occasions like this when he was devoting his whole time to it, for he was then in the hands of his local Liberals, had to go to their functions wherever he went, and would have to 'look pleased at receptions even if he had a bee on his nose'.

Before the column was published I left Menzies and went to Western Australia to spend some time with Evatt. It was only when I picked up Menzies again in the west a week later that Ian Fitchett told me that Menzies took great exception to what I'd written. Menzies' attitude, he said, was that I'd written about private Liberal Party functions to which the travelling press were invited only as a courtesy, which in Menzies' view I had abused. I thought this reaction extreme: it wasn't as if I had told stories at his expense about incidents that I might have observed as a guest. But as Menzies saw it I had misbehaved in the officers' mess and would now be relegated to the other ranks. Our relationship from then on would be strictly formal. I wasn't worried, for I felt sure that Menzies had always disliked me and would have disliked any twenty-seven-year-old—as I was when I started this job—who was presumptuous enough to criticise and sometimes even ridicule him. The other reason why I wasn't worried was that my most direct competitor, Schapel, got a more amicable reception from Menzies but there was no sign that he got any worthwhile help. Menzies had often had bad treatment from the press and, in return, didn't have a high opinion of it.

I was making my first trip to Perth since the end of the war. I searched for my old girlfriend Joy's married name in the telephone book but found nothing. As I discovered afterwards, she had gone to live in a country town with her husband. I saw some of my wartime friends and acquaintances in Perth, but most had disappeared.

I went for a drive around Fremantle with Evatt on the Sunday morning before my week of political meetings. He had taken on my former *Herald* colleague, Fergan O'Sullivan, as his press secretary in time for the campaign, but none of his staff came with us on this excursion. It was the Doc's idea. He knew a lot about the history of the place, and supplied an unusual commentary. This was an unexpected and, for once, apparently relaxed Evatt. Among the history he recounted was some of his own including the story, which I don't doubt, that in the early 1930s he had compered a jazz program on Sundays for a Sydney commercial radio station. A more unlikely person for the role I would have thought it hard to imagine, but nothing about Evatt fitted conventional patterns.

My *Herald* colleague Colin Bingham once wrote a magazine piece on Evatt's relentless pursuit of the presidency of the United Nations—which he achieved. Bingham told some good stories about the devices Evatt used to get votes at the UN. One was incredibly corny though apparently effective—a promise of a kangaroo for a delegate's hometown zoo.

I asked Evatt as we chatted in Fremantle what he thought of Menzies the lawyer, curious to see whether he could speak with any impartiality about such a rival. I knew that Menzies, KC, the brilliant advocate, had faced Mr Justice Evatt, the eminent jurist, on the High Court bench. Evatt made only one comment on my question. One thing about Menzies, he said, was his ability to sum up a bench of judges and quickly decide which of them he could dispense with so as to go for a majority decision. This for what it was worth was probably a genuine comment on the master politician as lawyer, but with Evatt you couldn't be sure.

For a man who was putting himself forward for the prime ministership, Evatt was almost unbelievably eccentric and disorganised. I discovered that he never caught a plane without nearly missing it, and was late everywhere. His plans changed constantly. While in the west he changed his packed schedule for Queensland the following week to squeeze in still more towns and speeches. He would have four of them one day, starting with a meeting at the wharves at half past seven in the morning. He was obsessive about safety and comfort, and when flying, if possible, took the first flight of the day even at the greatest inconvenience, to avoid turbulence. He usually wore his hat, incongruously, in aircraft as the air was always too cold or the light too bright for him, or there was some other problem which only a grey felt hat could solve.

My week with the Doc gave me the feeling that he might be consolidating his advantage in the elections, thwarting Menzies's effort to make up the margin that separated them. Evatt often spoke to relatively small meetings in places chosen mainly for their symbolism. It was the press coverage that counted, not the size of the audience. As well as doing the usual city and suburban meetings in Perth and Fremantle, Evatt in shirtsleeves was out addressing crowds of railway workers in Northam and Midland Junction. Menzies wouldn't have taken off his coat for anyone. But Evatt was positioning himself with the right wing of the union movement. He detached himself from conventional Labor positions, attacked bureaucrats, bureacracy and a 'silly strike' that was going on, and went out of his way to emphasise the importance of private enterprise. He was pointedly and publicly dissociating himself from the left wing of his party, trying to advance a new image of Labor as a party of the centre.

Evatt returned to Sydney and Menzies arrived in Perth. There I rejoined Menzies and was given his frigid treatment. His campaign theme was that the government had responsibly done what it had to do to fight inflation, its policies were working, and soon the whole community would benefit. Labor by now was struggling to keep the issue of unemployment alive. A few people in the audience booed as Menzies rose to speak at a meeting at the Fremantle Town Hall, and some were interjecting constantly. Menzies suddenly challenged them. 'Stand up,' he said, 'the person who is really unemployed and wanting a job!' There was silence, and all eyes searched the room as two men stood in the audience. 'Let me have your names afterwards,' Menzies told them. Then he turned on the hecklers. 'That shows you the difference between propaganda and fact,' he declared. 'There are about fifty people who are howling about unemployment and two who are unemployed in fact.'

Ian Fitchett came up to me the next day. 'Schapel got a big rocket from Sydney this morning over your story about the Fremantle meeting,' he told me. 'He didn't write anything about the two who stood up when Menzies asked if there was anyone unemployed there. It was a good story.' Schapel must have been asleep. Reporting the campaign you were always searching for something new, an unexpected event or a fresh argument—anything for a new point to an old story. This little dramatisation of the issue of unemployment in Fremantle was quite significant, for it brought to the surface a major feature emerging in the campaign. It showed that one of Evatt's big issues was no longer really running for him.

Menzies spoke in the Adelaide Town Hall on our way back from the west. Immediately before the meeting Stewart Cockburn was waiting by the stage, having arranged to pass a signal to an ABC technician as soon as Menzies arrived at the hall. Fitchett approached Cockburn and started asking him about the plans for a visit to the Woomera rocket range the next morning. Cockburn was preoccupied and Fitchett persistent. It was a nervy time, and everyone on the campaign tour was suffering from the non-stop day and night meetings and travel. Fitchett wouldn't be put off, and Cockburn lost his temper. 'Can't you see I'm busy?' he demanded. 'You'll have to wait.' 'Ah, you fucking Murdoch stooge!' replied Fitchett. 'You're holding it back for the *Herald* to-morrow.' Cockburn, who normally showed restraint, broke completely this time. In front of a thousand people he punched Fitchett in the face. The astonished Fitchett, a much bigger man, hit him in the jaw and nearly knocked him out. Cockburn reacted by sinking his fist into Fitchett's fleshy middle, then a police inspector and the slightly built Alan Reid got to the spot and stopped them. Stewart said afterwards that his main memory was of seeing the amazement on the face of Sir Roland Jacobs, a prominent businessman, sitting nearby. Jacobs happened to be the father of one of Stewart's old Adelaide schoolfriends. The police inspector said it was the first time he had ever broken up a brawl at a political meeting before it started.

None in the press party knew why Cockburn had hit Fitchett. I didn't hear the full story for years: at the time we all assumed that Fitchett must have said something so insulting about Menzies that Stewart had been provoked to an absurd act of loyalty. And Fitchett explained nothing, just went around repeating: 'Would you believe it? He king-hit me.'

The episode in Adelaide took over the conversation in the press party until an unscheduled event occurred the next day on our visit to Woomera. We flew up from Adelaide in two converted RAAF freighters, one of which—the plane carrying the press party—nearly crashed on the way there. It reached Woomera on one spluttering engine after the pilot had been forced to cut the other. Then we spent the day at Woomera trying to concentrate on the rocket launch which we were there to see. But no-one in the party could think or talk for long of anything but the experience we had just gone through. Except for Fitchett, who was still making his little speech: 'Would you believe it? He king-hit me.' Now at least he had two subjects of conversation.

But except for the incident on the flight to Woomera, my first election campaign had been everything I had expected. I had looked forward to it as the high point of my political experiences so far, and was not disappointed. It was a rare opportunity to tour almost the whole continent, to scent the political atmosphere in the cities and in the country. You saw more of the political leaders on a campaign than you ever did at other times, saw them on their good days and bad, watched their reactions to issues as they developed in the campaign and to changing public moods as they read them. You had to make your own daily assessment of the political trend; opinion polls were rare, and had no day-do-day influence on the campaigns of the '50s. You had to go by your own feeling for what was happening.

Election campaigns were crude affairs at the same time, especially in the country. In country hotels we usually shared rooms and usually had to go wandering in the corridor to find a toilet or shower. The only facility in the rooms, except for the bed, was a handbasin. No man staying in the country ever went down the corridor in the middle of the night for a pee. Anyone would have been mad to use the washbasins in these rooms for washing.

I followed Menzies to Victoria and Queensland for the end of the campaign. 'The professional mourners have been going around Australia trying to prove that the country is in a terrible mess,' he told his audience in Ballarat. 'Well, ain't it?' asked an interjector. Menzies loved interjections and handled them by the experts' technique of ignoring all but those he could best score off. Then he didn't restrain his sarcasm or his arrogance; he was prepared to make one insignificant enemy for life if he could use him—or her—to sway the crowd. 'There are limits even to humour,' he told this man. 'I should think you are twice as well off as your father was.' 'I can't get a job,' the man complained. That might have stopped another politician, but Menzies attacked. 'I wonder why!' he said. 'I should think at a quick glance that you talked yourself out of the last one.' The interjector wasn't bad. 'You talked yourself into this one,' he retorted. But Menzies had used him enough. 'You have only to open a newspaper, even a borrowed one, and you'll find columns and columns of jobs,' he said, and resumed his speech.

I should probably have interpreted Menzies' mood. He was an acute judge of political situations, and behaviour like this must have indicated that he was becoming confident of victory. If he really did expect it then, he was right and I was wrong. My final pre-election column, admittedly written a week before polling day, said that Labor still seemed to have a slight advantage. But the result was clear on election night. The government still controlled the Senate, thirty-one seats to twenty-nine. The following week Menzies left for London with his wife Pattie and daughter Heather for the coronation of Queen Elizabeth II.

I wrote on election night that the voting showed that the government had passed the depth of its unpopularity. Back in Canberra Elgin and I analysed the figures and agreed that on this result the government could easily win the following year's general election. We were probably the only political journalists in Canberra to say so. On the Senate voting figures the government couldn't have won an election for the House of Representatives, but Elgin and I were looking at the trend. The swing against the Liberal and Country Parties in the Senate election was less than in any federal by-elections since 1951 and in recent state elections. We concluded that it would now take only a small improvement in the government's position for Menzies to win the House of Representatives once more in 1954. But it was hard to get support for this view in Canberra.

Mischief Making of a Deplorable Kind

1953

Billie was broadcasting for the ABC in 1953, and gave another recital at the Con to maintain pressure on herself and a presence in the Sydney music scene. As a warm-up she played the program at the Albert Hall in Canberra the night before. She had an audience of about fifty, and that was a good one—almost exactly the same as the number of ABC subscribers, a measure of the almost complete lack of music in Canberra. The Sydney recital attracted more attention than the previous year's. 'Leone Stredwick,' wrote Lin Browne, 'chose a rich and delightful programme for her piano recital at the Conservatorium last night, and met a good many of the considerable challenges that she thereby offered herself.'

There were good reviews in some of the other papers, though the most gratifying comment came from an entirely unexpected quarter at an entirely unexpected time. In 1994, more than forty years after this recital, Billie had a telephone call from an older pianist, Muriel Cohen, whom she had never met. After so long, Muriel Cohen was ringing to tell her that she had never forgotten her playing of one of the works on that program. (For anyone familiar with the repertoire, it was Ravel's *Gaspard de la Nuit*, a magical but also demanding and revealing work for the pianist, both technically and musically.) This call was a reminder, I reflected, that one should never be too much discouraged by a critic, or for that matter too much encouraged.

Billie also began to build up a teaching practice in Canberra. One of her pupils there went on to an international career. Another, who would have made a better typist than pianist, was Madame Chen, wife of the diplomatic representative of China—which meant the old Nationalist government which had fled to Taiwan with Chiang Kai-shek's army in 1949. Mme Chen may have lacked talent in music, but she invited us to dinner and was the first person to introduce us to the artistic sensations of high-class Chinese banqueting.

We moved partly in a diplomatic circle anyway. You could almost have survived in Canberra on diplomatic and non-diplomatic cocktail party food, but especially the diplomatic; you would probably have got enough at the cocktail parties to stay alive until the next diplomatic (or non-diplomatic) party or dinner invitation arrived. The invitation lists were all much the same—a certain group of senior public servants and senior journalists, politicians, a few miscellaneous Canberra figures and the diplomats—and on national days it would have been easy to forget whose day you were celebrating.

The grandest and most lavish of all these occasions were the Fourth of July parties at the new American Embassy, a mansion created only recently from dreams of the past and the Deep South. Artie Fadden had a great time at the first American party we attended, as we discovered when we ran into him on the way out. A woman we didn't know arrived on the scene simultaneously. 'Hello, Artie darling!' she shrieked. 'Tell me, when are you going to make me a Dame?' 'My dear,' he replied gravely if not quite soberly, 'I'd much rather make you a mother.'

We had a special relationship with some neighbouring diplomats. Across the road in Mugga Way was General Cariappa, the Indian High Commissioner. One evening he invited us to a small dinner party with two other couples including the Haslucks. I never took to Paul Hasluck. No-one could deny his ability or his service to the government and country, but I found him heavy going. The night with Cariappa was the best opportunity I had had of seeing Hasluck at close range and I still didn't warm to him, although it was another occasion that turned me off. That was when he was guest of honour at the annual press gallery dinner. Hasluck had been a journalist on Perth's morning newspaper, the *West Australian*, in his early days. In his speech that night he made it clear not only that he didn't think much of the journalistic standards of our time, but that they compared badly with those of the good old days when *he* worked as a journalist. Knowing that the *West Australian* was not superior to the rest of the Australian press, I found his comments somewhat objectionable.

Cariappa himself was a fine man, full of contradictions. He was tall, with an aristocratic bearing, perfectly groomed. He smoked black Balkan Sobranie cigarettes with gold tips, and with black cigarette in hand spoke much of the folly of judging a man by the colour of his skin, pointing with one hand to the back of the other as if to make sure that you hadn't mistaken him for an albino. I believe that he performed great public service in India after he left Canberra and that the work he voluntarily undertook showed him as a man of great humanity. But I shall leave the subject of the Canberra diplomats; some others were unexpectedly interesting but they aren't very relevant to my story.

I have to acknowledge what happened, though, at the Coronation Banquet held in Parliament House, a great patriotic feast presided over by Fadden as Acting Prime Minister while Menzies was revelling in the celebrations in London. The cocktail party crowd was there but this was no cocktail party. I knew it would be a long and dangerous night and I wisely cautioned my wife, for someone had decided to seat couples apart, and she was to sit at a table on the opposite side of the room. 'You've never been to one of these big dinners,' I said, 'and you mightn't realise how easy it is to get drunk without knowing it. There'll be waiters refilling your glass every time you take a sip, and you lose track of what you've had. You have to go easy and make sure you know exactly what you're drinking.' She took this advice and, sitting next to my colleague Frank Chamberlain, transferred the problem to him. Whenever a new glass was poured she gave it to Frank. She had little to drink, and was a credit to the press gallery. Probably the only one there.

Sir Arthur Fadden was in some trouble, as was obvious when he stumbled over the loyal toast. 'God save the King!' he declaimed. 'Long may she reign!' But apart from his confusion over the sex of the monarch he got through. For others the Coronation Banquet was not going well, and at my table one of the drink waiters, who knew me from the Non-Members' bar, took it as his mission to see that I lacked nothing. What I had warned Billie of happened to me and many others. I sustained such damage that I drove home in first gear, stopped entirely whenever any vehicle approached in the opposite direction, paused to lie down for a few minutes beside the road in Flinders Way, lost my front-door key, and with extreme difficulty got into the house through a high window. I couldn't even remember whether I had had a good time.

Stalin died; Vice-President Richard Nixon visited Australia and impressed everyone; economic recovery favoured the government; the Labor Party favoured internal warfare; the Fairfax organisation bought Associated Newspapers and started the *Sun-Herald*; a gambling frenzy seized Australia after the country's first oil strike; one of Australia's biggest by-election campaigns was fought in the Gwydir electorate because history showed that as Gwydir voted, Australia voted; and, as 1953 closed, the Queen was on her way to Australia for the first visit by a reigning monarch. And Dick Cross died.

I had watched him dying day by day, and now I was helping to carry his coffin across the grass at the Canberra cemetery. He had worked until the last three weeks, and usually I saw him on our days off, too. He was grey. He crouched over a little radiator in the office. I walked into the house in Telopea Park one day and found him squatting right inside the big fireplace beside the flames, rubbing his hands for warmth. His doctor told me that there was nothing to be done for him, as I'd realised. 'This should resolve itself one way or the other in the next few weeks,' Dick said to me one day. Then he went into hospital in Sydney and did not come out alive. He was just over thirty years old.

The government continued to relax its import restrictions. Unemployment fell. Income tax was cut by twelve-and-a-half per cent, pensions and social service payments were increased and some sales taxes and company tax reduced—a well-timed set of measures in a pre-election budget. But although Menzies had claimed before the budget that cabinet had 'had the pruning knife at work', expenditure was marginally increased. I declared that what had been pruned was not expenditure, but dreams. 'It is really like pruning the air,' I wrote sarcastically. I thought my comment was pretty clever, and wondered how Angus McLachlan would rate that one for cynicism.

As growing hostilities between the Labor factions began to make things increasingly difficult for Evatt I fortuitously acquired a new informant in the Labor caucus. I had just been introduced to Bill Bourke, an unusual figure by Labor standards of the time. Bill was a well-to-do Melbourne lawyer with family money from a dry-cleaning business, and a substantial house in Toorak. I was having a casual drink with him in Parliament House when he suddenly began to tell me about a row in the caucus meeting that morning. 'I'm telling you this because I'm sick of the things Evatt has been getting away with,' he said. 'There's a lot of criticism in caucus and he wants it to be kept behind closed doors, but I don't think he should be allowed to get away with it any longer. As far as I'm concerned it's time the public knew what was going on.'

That day the Labor caucus had had its biggest showdown since Evatt became leader. Evatt got the fright of his life, Bill Bourke told me. A series of members had attacked his leadership, criticised his tactics in the budget debate, accused him of failure to consult, and objected because he had committed the party to policies which a future Labor government might never be able to carry out. The promise of Evatt's that they specially objected to was the abolition of the means test for pensioners, which they believed no government could then afford. Such irresponsible commitments would compromise Labor priorities if the party gained power.

Bill Bourke told me this in a characteristic pained monotone. He might have been reading a railway timetable, and it was hard to see him as a participant telling of political history as it was being made. But political history it was. Though this row in the party meeting was not in itself a major event it was the forerunner of greater ones yet to be played out. A medium-scale seismic shock that warned of the big one to come. Bourke's financial position and professional standing gave him a degree of independence, and his Catholic conscience gave him a political purpose, which were both threatening to Evatt.

Pat Kennelly, the other main critic of Evatt in the caucus meeting, was in a very different position. Kennelly was a prominent left-winger who had just been elected to the Senate. He was also federal secretary of the Labor Party and was clinging to this job as long as possible, as it gave him power over party funds—including the funding of the next election campaign. He was reputed to be manoeuvring to 'get Evatt'.

Then the Federal Executive came to Canberra with the appointment of a new federal secretary on its agenda. But Kennelly and his faction thwarted this move by a superb piece of organisation. His supporters had engineered a last-minute change of delegates from two states, and it wasn't until members of the executive assembled in Canberra that the right-wingers discovered that they had lost their majority. So the executive decided that Kennelly should continue as federal secretary until after the elections, and suddenly he looked like Evatt's worst problem.

Fred Coleman Brown, the *Herald*'s industrial roundsman, had come to Canberra to report this meeting. Fred lived union and Labor politics, and I sought some personal background on Kennelly from him for my weekly column. He left me some biographical notes. They included what I thought was a fascinating sidelight, which I used. 'From being a communist street demonstrator in the Depression,' I wrote, 'he had become a union secretary, rejoined Labor, reached the Presidency of the Party in Victoria, then become its first full-time Federal Secretary.' This was an unexpected background for a federal secretary of the ALP at the time when the most far-reaching issue in the party was the fight against communist power in the unions.

I don't know who got the greatest surprise when my column was published. For I soon learned that Kennelly had not been a communist street demonstrator at all. He had never been a communist. He had never been Victorian president of the party. He hadn't even been a union secretary. What I had written was not a description of Pat Kennelly but of the ALP's new federal president, Dinny Lovegrove. Alan Reid commented on my mistake with a sympathetic smirk when I passed him in the press gallery. He had a suitable face for smirking.

I was advised to go to see Kennelly, and I did so. For a hard little Labor fighter wrongly labelled as a communist he was unexpectedly reasonable. He wanted a retraction published, but was satisfied with a modest one. He clearly didn't want to draw undue attention to the fact that the former communist street demonstrator was Labor's new federal president.

The *Herald* disliked errors and hated publishing retractions, but on this occasion it had no choice. Fred Coleman Brown, though, denied any responsibility for the mistake. According to him he had merely given me what I asked for—some information about Lovegrove. Kennelly's name, he insisted, had never been mentioned.

I knew he was wrong. Even in discussion after the article appeared, I'd noticed, he had confused the two names. I hoped that he wasn't lying deliberately but was merely confused. Sitting at home going over this episode in my mind, I rang Colin Mann, a newcomer in the Canberra office, who was on duty at the time. 'Will you see if you can find Fred's notes in the office—and look everywhere, please—even in the wastepaper baskets?' I asked. He rang me back five minutes later. Fred's notes were indeed there among the waste paper, and the name in them was—Kennelly. I don't think Fred Coleman Brown liked me after that. He caused more trouble the next time we worked together.

With affairs in the Labor Party warming up rapidly, Elgin had a surprising suggestion. He'd heard that someone in the gallery was taking advantage of the fact that, from a window in the press gallery, you could hear the voices in the caucus room on the floor below during caucus meetings, and could even hear what some of them were saying. Elgin suggested conspiratorially that we put this story to the test.

I had often thought of the press gallery as the whispering gallery, a mental reference to the furtive conversations in parliamentary corridors in which confidences were revealed and stories were born. But if Elgin's report was correct the House of Representatives courtyard must in effect be a real whispering gallery, like the one in St Paul's Cathedral in London. There, by a trick of acoustics, words merely whispered close to the roof of that long gallery can be clearly heard by someone standing equally close to it on the other side. It is a telephone system in stone.

For this phenomenon to work, the whisperer and the listener must both stand in exactly the right positions. Could the courtyard outside some of the press gallery windows in Parliament House be like that? Had some of our competitors discovered a way to hear, which you wouldn't know about unless you tried from exactly the right spot? If so, we had better know about it. So Elgin and I went up to Parliament House on the next Tuesday morning. This was unusual. We didn't normally go there till two o'clock in the afternoon or, at the earliest, just before lunch.

The old parliament building in Canberra was never intended as more than a temporary Parliament House, but no part of it was more temporary-looking than the press gallery. From the small offices in which the *Herald* staff worked, with their shabby furniture and torn lino, we could push up a sash window and step straight out onto the flat bitumen-covered roof. The rooms occupied by the *Courier-Mail*, the *Sun-Pictorial* and the *Adelaide Advertiser* were just as cramped as ours but looked out over one of the courtyards. They were among the few offices in the gallery that were directly above the caucus room. And, as the building wasn't air-conditioned, you could be sure that the windows in the caucus room would be open, except in winter.

Elgin and I had to be careful. We would take it in turns to listen, for if we tried at the same time we would look too conspicuous. Fortunately Elgin's room was away from the only newsrooms which were normally at work in the mornings, so it should be possible for our activities to be carried out without attracting attention.

When I first took over the watch I began by sitting on the windowsill, trying to look casual, as if Elgin and I were merely chatting there, and I merely lounging by the window to get some fresh air. From time to time I could hear unintelligible sounds from below. But as eavesdropping this method was a failure. Then I tried standing in the room with my elbows on the windowsill and my head outside. I began to feel exposed but looked around, actively inspecting every visible part of the sky, the courtyard and the poplars in it as if my sole interest were in admiring the view. The occasional audible sound from the caucus room was slightly louder than before but unintelligible still. Perhaps this was a bad day. Perhaps the birds in the poplars in the courtyard were over-active, or maybe there was too much breeze rustling the leaves.

Elgin had no success. After half an hour we were ready to decide whether the idea was entirely a failure or whether we should try again another day. Suddenly Alan Reid thrust the door open with a warning, 'Quick! Archie Cameron has heard about you two and he's on his way up now', and disappeared down the corridor. Archie Cameron, the Speaker of the House of Representatives, with power to ban any journalist from the press gallery permanently! A cranky and unpredictable man who threw MPs out of their rooms to organise the parliament as he thought fit, and to whom only the prime minister could stand up—and only just!

Elgin and I knew that what we had been doing was indefensible. Without a word we took off, racing out through the back of the press gallery, past Malcolm McColm's room and down the flight of stairs furthest from the Speaker's suite. Then Elgin stopped. 'Alan Reid has just made fools of us,' he said. 'Archie Cameron doesn't know a thing about this. He won't be coming anywhere near the press gallery.' I knew he was right. I was angry with Reid, but mainly with myself for behaving like a schoolboy—I, the federal political correspondent of the *Sydney Morning Herald*! The worst thing was that Alan Reid knew.

When the Fairfax organisation took over Associated Newspapers—publishers of (among other things) the *Sun*, a Sydney afternoon newspaper, and the *Sunday Sun*—it merged the *Sunday Sun* and the *Sunday Herald*. The *Sun-Herald*, which replaced the two, combined the *Sunday Sun*'s popular approach with the more serious style of the *Sunday Herald*. That was how Colin Mann came to Canberra. The new paper wanted a change from pure politics in its Canberra coverage, so as Colin had no interest in politics at all he must have seemed the right choice for the job. He had been a police reporter. Now he was a misfit. Someone else wrote any essential political and economic stories for the Sunday paper, and Colin went in search of human interest, but for a time he couldn't find any in the national capital that was fit to publish.

His first published story from Canberra was about a well-known scientist there who found that a black rock which he had been using to prop open his door was radioactive. He and the man who gave it to him had set out to investigate its origin so that they could claim a £1000 reward which the government was offering for the discovery of a uranium deposit. But when they traced it back to a place near Batemans Bay they found that it was a piece of ballast from a pile once dumped there from an old sailing ship, and could have come from anywhere in the world. Colin could put together a well-turned story when something appealed to his whimsical taste. He must have got this gift from his father, Cecil, a writer whose short stories I knew. Colin chose the news medium for his own short stories. While politicians and political fortunes rose and fell, while the future of the Australian economy was being decided, he kept the balance with a note of mild insanity.

He moved into the Telopea Park house with his wife and family when Clare Cross went back to New Zealand with her young son Glen and her new baby, Penny. Colin was a delight to have in Canberra but I still needed a deputy. This time, despite the success of Dick Cross's appointment, I wanted to choose his successor, and approached my friend Rodger Rea. Rodger had had a period in London, then gone to Melbourne to work for the Melbourne *Herald*. Now he was spending part of his time in Canberra, coming up during the parliamentary sittings, but was intent on getting back there permanently. He was addicted to this city and to politics and the processes of government. And he had married Eldwyth Edgell, daughter of a senior Commonwealth public servant.

Rodger had been assured of the next vacancy in the Melbourne *Herald*'s Canberra office but this assurance had two weaknesses: nobody knew when the vacancy would occur, and when it did it would mean working with Harold Cox. None of Harold's staff was happy. His assistant, John Bennetts, a man of Rodger's and my age, hated Harold so much that he was building up a dossier in the hope of using it against him some day. Harold was unwittingly my main support in attracting Rodger to the *Sydney Morning Herald*. Rodger went to Sydney to meet Harry Kippax, and Harry offered him the job, but the terms bore the fingerprints of Angus McLachlan, a man of Scottish prudence. They offered him a rise of two shillings and sixpence a week on what he was getting from the Melbourne *Herald*. He was so keen to get back to Canberra that he accepted.

For Billie and me, unlike Rodger, Canberra itself still had little appeal, and for Billie it was musical exile. The *Herald* had equipped me with Rupert Henderson's cast-off Chevrolet, a big American sedan which easily absorbed the winding, bumpy, potholed highway to Sydney, and we used it as our escape vehicle for many weekends. We stayed in Mum's flat, saw our Sydney friends, heard some of the concerts and saw some of the plays that Canberra missed.

Menzies was angrier about my story on the Gwydir by-election than about anything else I wrote in Canberra. I heard that he told Stewart Cockburn: 'This has cost us the by-election.'

Gwydir was a contest that Menzies was determined to win. Of all federal electorates Gwydir was the one that most nearly mirrored the national vote, and a loss there would be seen as a signal that the government was on the way out. Earlier in 1953 the government would have lost it. Now the December by-election would show whether the government's marginal recovery since then was enough to give it any chance of surviving for another term after the House of Representatives elections in 1954.

There was another reason Menzies was disturbed. The Liberal and Country Parties, the parties of his coalition, were fighting between themselves. Gwydir had been a Country Party seat but the New South Wales executive of the Liberals had nominated a candidate in Gwydir in opposition to the Country Party nominee, despite Menzies' efforts to dissuade them. As Menzies saw it, they had endangered the government's whole campaign.

Parliament was about to rise till the New Year, and the Gwydir campaign would be the final political event of 1953. Liberal, Country Party and Labor leaders and MPs and the party organisations were preparing to rush the electorate. Malcolm McColm told me about the discussion in the government party room on this dispute between the Liberals and the Country Party.

'Canberra, Wednesday—The Prime Minister, Mr Menzies, today rebuked the New South Wales Executive of the Liberal Party for endorsing a candidate for the Gwydir by-election on December 19,' said my story the next morning. '"If the Liberal candidate wins Gwydir the seat will still be in the hands of the Government," said Mr Menzies. "If he loses, perhaps the New South Wales executive will have learned a lesson."' There was a lot more to the story, but these were the words that infuriated Menzies. The next day he issued a long denial, disowning any rebuke to the New South Wales executive of his Party. My report, he declared, was mischievous nonsense.

'That section which dealt with some alleged complaint by me directed against the Liberal Party executive was entirely and irresponsibly false,' he said. 'I say irresponsibly because the very suggestion that I should make such an utterance at a joint party meeting is utterly ludicrous.

'Meetings of the government parties are not open. No authoritative statement was issued after our perfectly amiable discussions on Gwydir. The report, which I have said was completely untrue, is mischief-making of a deplorable kind.' He concluded with the declaration that the only people who could be helped by 'the circulation of false rumours and the creation of irrelevant conflicts' were the Labor Party, who no doubt were promoting these statements 'to distract attention from their own internal miseries'.

I wasn't unhappy for my story to be paid so much attention by Menzies, and I assured the *Herald* that my account of the meeting had been accurate. I didn't mean that Menzies was lying. If you looked closely at what he said you found that he didn't specifically deny having said the words I had quoted, he really denied that they constituted a rebuke to the New South Wales Liberal Party, and that of course was a matter of interpretation. I knew he disagreed with what the state Liberal executive had done.

His statement also gave the impression of claiming that this 'entirely and irresponsibly false' story had come from Labor sources. But again, on more careful reading you could see that he hadn't said this at all. The Labor Party would certainly promote such statements, as he observed, but he did not claim that it had originated them. I would have described Menzies' press statement as a phantom denial, one that disappeared on closer examination. A lawyer's technique.

And there I was a week later out bush in Gunnedah listening to Artie Fadden opening the Country Party's campaign in Gwydir. I'd seen him the night before, sitting on the platform in the Inverell Town Hall in a staged display of unity as Menzies opened the government campaign. But the best hall in town wasn't for Artie. Tonight he was out in the streets, standing on a corner with amplifiers set up on the back of a truck. An audience of about seventy people, I calculated, lounged around to hear, and others sat listening from parked cars. Artie wasn't a pretty sight. Artie sweating in his shirtsleeves, with his protruding teeth and his dewlap, looked little like a national leader. But he was saying effective things about the last three years, the three saddest but proudest years of his life, he called them, and about the danger that a Labor victory in Gwydir 'could pave the way for a federal government similar to the New South Wales Labor Government'— a threat indeed in Gunnedah.

I went to the post office to file my story on Artie's meeting, then back to the old pub where we were staying. I didn't know Artie very well then. But he spotted me and came over as I was sitting with a couple of other journalists in a corner of a bare lounge room, having a drink. He sat next to me and pulled me aside. 'You don't want to worry about what Menzies said about that story of yours on the party meeting,' he told me.

'Oh, thanks, but I wasn't really worried,' I replied.

'As a matter of fact I wasn't at that meeting,' he said, 'but from what I've been told what you wrote was completely right.'

'Thanks!' I said again.

'You don't want to worry about what he said,' Artie insisted.

'No, I wasn't worrying, really!' I assured him once more.

Sir Arthur Fadden, leader of the Country Party, federal Treasurer and Deputy Prime Minister, got up to go, throwing me one final reassurance. 'You don't want to worry about that big prick.'

CHAPTER 12

The Rabbit, or Albatross

1953 and 1954

After my meeting with Fadden in Gunnedah I was very happy about the Gwydir campaign. But I didn't see Artie again. I spent the rest of the time with Menzies and Evatt as they worked their way through the huge north-western electorate, bigger than the state of Victoria. Menzies's campaign had been billed as a meet-the-people tour, Evatt said that his was a *real* meet-the-people tour, Menzies called him 'band-waggon Bert'. Evatt went everywhere. Breeza 11 a.m., Werris Creek 11.30 a.m., Wallabadah 2 p.m., Willow Tree 4.30 p.m., Quirindi 7.15 p.m.—that was one day's speaking schedule. The Country Party was so worried that it hired a city journalist, Bill Caldbeck Moore, as a publicity man for its candidate, Ian Allan, and what I described as a midget aircraft to take them around. These were measures of unprecedented sophistication for a bush campaign.

Back in empty Canberra, while the absent politicians and the political journalists roamed the Gwydir electorate and I was writing about a 'general election in miniature', Colin Mann was in full stride with a story about twin calves born six weeks apart—a 'near miracle' in Canberra—and another about some men from Tharwa, near Queanbeyan, who were preparing to compete in a bathing beauty contest in the new year. And Ian Allan won the Gwydir by-election for the government. The Liberal candidate came nowhere. There had even been a slight improvement in the government vote since the 1951 elections—a good result for Menzies and Fadden, since no government had ever recovered from a swing against it as great as the one they had experienced.

The Reids' new house in Mugga Way had been redecorated by Hilda Abbott, mother-in-law of the *Courier-Mail*'s managing director, Colin Bednall. Given a freer hand than most decorators, she left her mark in such touches as a living room with gold-painted exposed beams and a blue ceiling with stars, spinning an incongruous cocoon of fantasy around the domestic realities of the Reids' household. Stred was staying with us that Christmas. Migratory waves of Reids, Stredwicks and Myerses moved backwards and forwards between 29 and 23 Mugga Way. Now Stred had gone up to the Reids with his red dog named Red Dog for a drink with Elgin.

Stred and Elgin were sitting in the Hilda Abbott living room comparing the literary qualities of Shakespeare and the Bible. Red Dog, with his kelpie instinct, was circling the house rounding up Reid children. The Reids' border collie, Archie, slipped inside with one of them, then two yelping animals were catherine-wheeling around the room together, teeth in flesh and fur. At first Elgin didn't seem capable of seeing or hearing them, but eventually even he had to take notice. He backed out, still talking, returned with a bucket of water and resumed the conversation as he entered, offhandedly tipping the bucketful over the frantic pair. The fight came to an instant end. Red Dog and Archie got to their feet, shook themselves and flew out of Hilda Abbott's masterpiece through the closed flywire doors, which from then on could never keep out any fly smaller than a kelpie or border collie. The Reids had begun redecorating Hilda Abbott's redecoration.

Everyone was staying with us that Christmas. Not just Stred and Red, but Jean Stredwick, Mum, Jean's son Terry and his wife Maralyn, and a series of shorter-term stayers. New Year's Eve was the night we lost Stred in Harold White's yellow-flowering hedge. I don't know how Harold had prevented the Department of the Interior from trimming it, but he had, and it had grown into the biggest and wildest hedge in Canberra, falling all over his grassy garden on one side and the footpath on the other, hiding the Whites from the street.

We were all at the Reids' for new year and the party must have started early, for it was too much even for Stred, who set off alone for home just before midnight. But when Billie and I went to check on him he had disappeared. It was only during a second search that we saw the faint glow of Stred's cigarette from deep within Harold's jungle of jasmine, guiding rescuers to the spot. He was prostrate and speechless at that stage, and would have spent the night there but for the alarm signal from the cigarette. I had great trouble getting his bulk out of the undergrowth but we got him home, and long after midnight most of the rest of us—except Mum—went out to the Cotter River for a skinny dip.

The end of 1953 should have been a time for some reflection on my part. I had the job I wanted, but didn't want to make it my life. I was living in a city where I didn't much want to be, and my wife wanted even less to be, from which she could never properly pursue her music. The working hours and the way of life which my job dictated were not helpful in a marriage. At 29 Mugga Way, with the office Chev, the impressive accommodation and a reasonable expense account I was living much better than most journalists, but when we returned to Sydney it would be different. I was twenty-nine and three years married, but the £500 I had accumulated by the time of our marriage had gone, and I was living from payday to payday. I hadn't faced reality.

I could never have stayed in Canberra indefinitely because to do so would have been too destructive to Billie. But I didn't want to, anyway, and I knew just by looking at some of the old gallery hands. This was a fatuous reaction on my part, and I could just as realistically have taken the well-known political journalists of other countries as models, respected figures who had real influence in public affairs. But I didn't see things that way.

Despite my recognition that there was much wrong with this kind of life, it had its disturbing advantages, and as the holidaying visitors departed I threw myself back into politics. The first major story of 1954 began to emerge in the earliest weeks of the new year.

It would be hard for anyone who had not lived through World War II in Australia, or served in the Australian forces, to fully understand the emotions which this story would stir. It arose from an American defence plan to conduct a survey of the islands off New Guinea and New Britain. The Americans had pointed out that there were serious, potentially dangerous gaps in knowledge of this strategically important territory and had offered to carry out the survey. But they claimed that a shortage of specialists would compel them to include Japanese crewmen and survey teams. Despite opposition from some Commonwealth departments, the Defence Department was preparing to go ahead. But when the general in charge of the Australian army's northern command heard of the plan he was so incensed that he went secretly to the *Courier-Mail* in Brisbane to expose it. He was confident that there would be such public protest that the government would be forced to abandon the plan. When I heard about it I knew he was right.

The areas to be surveyed were the very ones where Australians and Japanese had fought so recently, and so close to Australia. Japan was the enemy at whose hands Australian prisoners had been starved, tortured and killed. And since the war there had been no forgetting and no forgiving. Not only that, but stories about Japanese spying were part of Australia's folklore. Since before World War II an indelible picture in Australian minds was that of the Japanese civilian with camera in hand, photographing everything. In retrospect the cameras of pre-war years took on a sinister meaning, and in wartime the Japanese propaganda machine was widely credited with having a frighteningly detailed knowledge of what was happening in Australia. Pre-war spies in the guise of tourists were assumed to have provided the basis for this knowledge. To most Australians the employment of Japanese surveyors in the islands where Australia's forward defences lay would be unthinkable.

The story of the planned survey was written in the *Courier-Mail* office, and Elgin had left it with Stewart Cockburn for a comment from Menzies. After a week there was no response. A week was long enough, Elgin and his office agreed, and the *Courier* was about to run the story. But I'd been unable to confirm it independently, and unless I could do so I would not write it as a hard news story. I wrote an anaemic version, full of 'it is believed' and other qualifications, and told Harry Kippax that we would have to be satisfied and publish it as the full story would be in the *Courier-Mail* the next morning. Then I took the night off to go to a big party which Cariappa was giving in his garden, opposite our house in Mugga Way.

It was one of Canberra's best parties. A large crowd of guests circulated over the lawns, enjoying plentiful food, drink and talk. At one stage I went back to the marquee where the food was set up and saw Jim Plimsoll, my old companion from Hotel Canberra days. Jim was now the number two in the Department of External Affairs and would know about the survey, but how could I get this discreet public servant to talk about a matter that was probably Top Secret, certainly Highly Confidential? 'Hullo, Jim!' I said, and after the briefest of social preliminaries I made my move in case I lost him. 'Jim, I really think the government is making a great mistake with this idea of letting the Americans use Japanese on this survey of the islands,' I said soberly. 'I'm sure there's going to be a huge controversy about it.'

'Oh, I don't know,' he replied. 'There are all sorts of safeguards, so there isn't really a problem.' Having unwittingly excited me by confirming the story, he went on to elaborate with a lot of significant detail about the plans for the survey that the *Courier-Mail* hadn't heard. I went home and rang through an entirely new story. Back at the party I found that Elgin had just arrived. He had to leave again immediately to give his office the rest of the story, too. Billie was sitting in the garden in semi-darkness with

Biddy Alderton, wife of the New Zealand High Commissioner, with whom we were friendly. 'Hal's just had to go to call his office about something very stupid that Menzies has done,' Billie told her, making conversation. 'Oh, Billie, have you met Dame Pattie?' said Biddy, nodding towards the prime minister's wife, who was sitting on her other side in the shadows.

By the second day the story was a front-page lead throughout Australia, and the protests were flowing. 'A betrayal of Australia's vital interests,' said Evatt, supporting the leaders of the Returned Servicemen's League, the Legion of Ex-Servicemen, the Air Force Association and various individuals including Lieutenant-General Gordon Bennett, wartime commander of the Eighth Division in Malaya. It was the kind of situation Menzies hated. 'You've only got to mention Japanese and it's enough for three headlines,' he said. 'I can't understand it. It's like uranium.'

Despite Menzies' blustering, this story was not just a matter of newspaper headlines. Elgin and I discovered that though the Defence Department seemed determined to accept the Americans' offer—which was conditional on the use of the Japanese—the Department of Territories and Paul Hasluck as its minister were strongly opposed. The next day, though parliament was not sitting, fifteen government members who were in Canberra went to Menzies about the survey and many of them believed that the government could lose the next elections over this issue. Fred Osborne, Malcolm McColm and John Gorton were among them. Some were as sarcastic with Menzies as he had been in his first public outburst. One asked whether the Americans had invited any Russians to take part in the survey. Another wondered whether President Eisenhower had been asked if he would accept a Japanese survey team on the Californian coast. The members also learned that some of their ministerial colleagues had known nothing about the plan. Others had heard about the survey but not about the Japanese.

The story rolled on until the weekend, when the US Eastern Command headquarters in Tokyo announced that the idea of using Japanese technicians had been abandoned for 'technical reasons'. But immediately the critics in Australia were back. The Americans still intended to use Japanese ships' crews, and that was not good enough. Finally, a week after the story had broken, cabinet decided to reject the American proposal.

This episode was one of the most extraordinary events of my time in Canberra. The arguments used to justify the plan had some merit, and thanks to Jim Plimsoll were published in my original story—one being that the Americans had used Japanese on similar surveys since the war, and operated under strict safeguards. But the failure of a small group of ministers to understand the feelings this plan would stir in the Australian community amazed me. I wrote of the indecisive attitude of ministers—mainly Menzies and McBride, Minister for Defence—and the way in which members of cabinet could lose touch with public thinking. 'If the government wanted to throw the next election away,' I commented, 'it could hardly find a more effective first step than to accept the American plan.' The elections were only a few months off. Elgin's story and mine, contrary to Menzies' comments made in pique, did not sensationalise the issue. Menzies was probably lucky that they were published. They stopped the government from committing a gross affront to public opinion at a crucial time politically.

The day after the cabinet decision, though, the angry controversies of the past week were erased. The Queen had arrived in Sydney, and loyal fervour swept the country. Stories about her arrival filled the first ten of the *Herald*'s broadsheet pages, and though there was overseas news on page 11, by page 12 the Queen was back again. The tone was set by a front-page story by 'the Editress of Our Women's Section' headed, rather unbelievably, 'Every Woman's Dream of Beauty Steps Ashore'. But it was believable in Australia, 1954.

Oliver Hogue, political correspondent of the Sydney *Sunday Sun*, was the press officer for the royal tour. He had become something of an expert in the planning of such events, having been involved previously with another tour which had had to be abandoned. The Queen's father, George VI, had been forced to cancel a visit because of ill health and the Queen, then Princess Elizabeth, was originally to come in his place. Oliver had been working on the preparations for that visit when the King's death caused it, too, to be cancelled. He had many unpublished anecdotes about his experiences, and one which appealed to me was about a gold-edged invitation which circulated in Sydney, to a party to be held at the home of a man I knew, Jo Fallon. It was a party—the invitation stated—at which Her Royal Highness, Princess Elizabeth, and the Duke of Edinburgh would be present. According to the director of the royal tour and the minister in charge, Eric Harrison, there was no such event. But on checking with Buckingham Palace they learned otherwise.

Jo Fallon was a press photographer who had unusual entrée to Sydney society, lived in a waterfront home in Vaucluse, and was a collector of notables. During World War II he had befriended the Duke of Edinburgh when, as Prince Phillip of Greece, he visited Australia as an officer in the

Royal Navy. When the royal visit was first announced Jo had written to Phillip and invited him and the missus to come to a party when they had some free time in Sydney. Phillip had written back and nominated a night when they had some time free and would both be delighted to call. But after Buckingham Palace heard about the invitations the King ordered that Jo's place be struck from the schedule. Earlier Phillip had tried to divert the tour to Alice Springs because he had just read Nevil Shute's novel, *A Town Like Alice*, but the King had told the organisers to take no notice of the young man.

Around the time of the royal tour Stewart Cockburn resigned as Menzies' press secretary. He had a tubercular condition which necessitated getting away from the pressures of the job. He went back to his home city, Adelaide, where—after lung surgery—he spent the rest of his working life as a respected and influential journalist, and wrote some significant books on politics and political issues. Stewart's unlikely successor on Menzies' staff was Hugh Dash.

Visiting Canberra some years later I went to see Reg Swartz, by then a minister, who had been Malcolm McColm's original room-mate in U65, 'the submarine'. Reg had now moved into a ministerial office downstairs where he had become mystified by a sound which started up in that part of the building shortly after six o'clock each night. It was a repetitive, rasping sound like some equipment in operation. He eventually discovered that it was Hugh Dash snoring in the thin-walled room next door as he slept away the dinner hour after the crowd left the Non-Members' bar.

Hugh was an old *Daily Telegraph* sporting journalist who had worked in Parliament House during the war, probably because of a wartime shortage of political journalists and sporting events. There was a story told in the gallery that a few ministers, wanting to get away from the strains of war, had gone out of town one day for a picnic lunch, which Hugh Dash heard about, in a garbled fashion. It was garbled enough for him to build it into a sensational story about a secret cabinet meeting on the banks of the Cotter River, a story which the prime minister, John Curtin, immediately denied, and which was so wrong that even Dash was ashamed. When he ran into the prime minister in Parliament House a couple of weeks later he had to say something. The words that came out were: 'Oh, hullo, Mr Curtin! I've been avoiding you for the past fortnight.' This is one story which I have not checked with the records to match recollection with fact. I have no idea when Hugh's exclusive account of the secret cabinet meeting was published, and haven't the heart to search through the *Daily Telegraph*'s files for the duration of the war to check the details. Knowing Hugh, I have no doubt that this piece of press gallery lore had a basis in truth.

I took Hugh's appointment as a demonstration of Menzies' contempt for the press. Stewart has subsequently told me, however, that he recommended him to Menzies. There was only a small band of ministerial press secretaries at the time to pick from. Hugh had been press secretary to Billy Kent Hughes, Minister for the Interior, but Kent Hughes was such an erratic individual and, I judged, such an ineffective federal minister (despite a reputation previously in Victorian state politics) that Hugh's working experience with him could have been disregarded. But as press secretary to a conservative prime minister, Hugh was too much of a comic turn to be taken seriously. I suspect that Menzies concluded that he didn't need a trier like Stewart any more, just someone who would perform the outward functions. There is no doubt that he found Hugh's low-life anecdotes relaxing. Most of us did.

I was leaving Canberra for Tasmania late in February when Menzies announced the next election date—29 May. As it turned out, no prime minister has ever timed an election better. The reason was soon apparent.

My reason for going to Tasmania was to hear Billie play Beethoven's *Emperor Concerto* in Hobart with the Tasmanian Symphony Orchestra. Of all my experiences of her concerts this is perhaps the one that I recall with the simplest pleasure. Hobart was free of the pressures of the bigger cities, and I was a more relaxed member of her audience than ever before or since. The music was appropriate; the *Emperor* is not as unswervingly masculine as the name suggests, and calls on many of the musical qualities that her playing possessed. After the concert we took a few days off for a slow drive from Hobart to Launceston through the centre of the graceful island.

Frank Green, a Tasmanian, insisted that we should stop at a certain pub on the way to celebrate the licensee's enlightened views. The man had once asked Frank whether he was a friend of Menzies. 'I hate the bastard,' Frank told him. 'Right!' said the pubkeeper. 'The drinks are on me.' I never knew the reason for the intense ill-will between Frank and Menzies, but I knew Frank as a warm friend and a warm hater. With Arthur Shakespeare, proprietor and editor of the *Canberra Times*, hating had crystallised into vendetta. When Frank caught the biggest trout of the season, one year while I was in Canberra, the *Canberra Times* carried a paragraph about it with an editor's footnote suggesting that it should more correctly be identified as the biggest trout caught out of season. Frank, who as I have said was a special magistrate of the Australian Capital Territory, threatened him with litigation, but I cannot trace the outcome. Beyond these minor affairs, though, there was tragedy in the Green household. Frank and his wife had one child, a son who became a doctor and an alcoholic, and died in circumstances suggesting suicide. Frank suffered so much that he could never speak of him.

After the Fairfax organisation bought Associated Newspapers it had a surplus of political correspondents. This problem was solved in a way which suited everyone. Alan Reid took over the *Sun-Herald* column and I began to write a Tuesday column for the *Sydney Morning Herald*, as John Pringle wanted. A *Herald* without its own political column was not his idea of an influential newspaper. So he and I began a much closer collaboration, and with Harry Kippax as news editor and John as editor I enjoyed, for a time, the best working relationships that I could hope for.

I have already mentioned one of the hazards of journalism, the cliché. Some journalists are insensitive to clichés and seem to write with no more effort than it takes to join a series of them together. Others are conscious of the way in which worn-out phrases reduce the power of writing. The problem is that they are so easy to use. Working to a deadline, especially, it is hard to fight off the ready-made phrases, however limp they may be. And I confess that too many of them found their way into my political articles. I shamefully failed to resist a last nail in the government's coffin, some red herrings, a straw in the wind, Evatt crying wolf, Liberal politicians letting sleeping dogs lie and someone even putting a cart before a horse. But one of my adventures with a cliché had more enduring significance than the others—I would like to say that it hung like an albatross around my neck.

It came in one of the first columns I wrote after John Pringle put them on his leader page. Parliament was meeting for a short pre-election session, but according to the latest polls the government was losing support again. It seemed to have peaked at the time of the Gwydir by-election and slipped then, despite the royal tour. But what was Menzies to do? 'As a prime minister who has had more than four years to carry out his policy,' I wrote, 'Mr Menzies cannot suddenly promise a social revolution—especially as the government has not performed one major act of policy for more than a year, except for cutting taxes.' And then the cliché. This one I didn't merely use—I patted it and took it for a little walk. 'The Liberal Party,' I wrote, 'is hoping that the Prime Minister, Mr Menzies, will pull a couple of rabbits out of the top hat which he wore with such assurance during the Royal tour. It looks as if he will have to do so if his government is to survive the election in May.' And this was the sequel:

Eight days later, after parliament's dinner recess, Menzies walked into the House of Representatives and announced the defection of Vladimir Petrov, agent of the Russian secret police, operating in the guise of a third secretary in the Russian Embassy in Canberra. Ever afterwards Evatt claimed that Petrov's defection was the rabbit, that Menzies had known about it and by implication that I, too, must have known that there was something sinister about when I wrote those words. The Petrov affair was to set Evatt on the path to destruction.

CHAPTER 13

A Good Home for the Dog

1954

We could not at first know that the slow fall of Bert Evatt had begun, and could not foresee its erratic course, his seeming recoveries along the way, or the landslides that would be touched off by his descent. There was something pathetic—and, to Labor supporters, most sinister—about his situation even on that first night when Menzies announced Petrov's defection: when we went looking for Evatt we found that, incongruously, he was away at an old boys' function at Fort Street, his old Sydney school. Menzies made his announcement that night so that a Royal Commission of inquiry into Petrov's revelations could be set up before the parliament rose, but his opponents naturally accused him of taking advantage of Evatt's absence. A Bill to establish the commission was introduced into parliament the next day. The day after that, the parliament was prorogued and MPs dispersed for the election campaign.

The defection of Vladimir Petrov led to the great upheavals of my time in Canberra. As for its immediate impact, I have never seen the press gallery more frantic for grains of information. None of us knew anything about Petrov, who had apparently decamped with documents and information that would blow the whole story of Russian spying in Australia, whatever that might amount to. Colin Mann went down that night to Petrov's house at no. 7 Lockyer Street, Griffith, only 300 yards from the Embassy. The embassy was in our home territory, halfway between Mugga Way and Telopea Park. I had been there previously for a reception and a night of films. In fact I had crudely disrupted an inspiring film about Joseph Stalin's workers, Joseph Stalin's factories, Joseph Stalin's collectives, et cetera. The scenario had moved on to the natural beauties of Russia ... now we were looking at a waterfall. 'And this is Joseph Stalin's water,' I said, just loudly enough for the journalists and their partners to hear; torches flashed in the little auditorium as puzzled Russians tried to fathom the reason for the sudden laughter.

When Colin reached Petrov's house near the embassy it was in darkness and deserted except for a tabby cat on the doorstep. Petrov had kept a dog, Colin learned from neighbours, but it had disappeared.

It was not till next day that I was able to fill in any significant parts of the picture beyond what Menzies had told the House. After leaving Parliament House on the night of Menzies' announcement I had gone for a drink at the Hotel Canberra with a small group including Neil O'Sullivan, a Liberal minister from Queensland. He told us something about the extent of the material that Petrov had brought with him. The next morning I found that one of the people I knew in the Department of External Affairs had a lot of background on the defection. Petrov had obviously been a spy, for he was forty-five, and real diplomats were not third secretaries at that age. I learned that he had had more freedom than any of the other Russian diplomats in Canberra, and didn't even act like one of them. He drank in bars, went trout-fishing with non-Russians, had long conversations with individuals whom other Russians would have met only in the safety of groups. Some months previously, I heard, he had told an Australian friend that he didn't know where he stood under the new regime since Stalin's death, didn't know what awaited him when he returned to Russia. He was afraid to go back. These were some of the points I had gathered for the first of the stories I wrote that day.

The political significance of Petrov's defection was my next story. Politicians thought it would help the government in the coming elections and some of them, on both sides—but only some—were already convinced that it would win the election for Menzies. They had no idea what new information Petrov might reveal, but even his claimed confirmation of Russian espionage in Australia gave support to Menzies' familiar warnings about the threats of international communism. Whatever these threats might amount to, Menzies was the activist against them. Evatt's earlier fights against Menzies' anti-communist legislation and referendum could be seen, however unjustly, as putting him in the opposite camp.

There was one other story to be written on the Petrov case at this stage, a human mystery yet to be unravelled. Mrs Petrov had not defected with her husband. She was not at home. She was reported to be at the embassy.

Was she a prisoner? Had she wanted to defect with her husband, but been detected and stopped? What would the Russians do with her? It was Colin Mann who scooped the rest of the press gallery on Mrs Petrov.

Colin did what any police roundsman would do and no sophisticated political journalist would dream of doing. Experienced Canberra hands merely assumed that the embassy would be uncooperative and Mrs Petrov inaccessible. Colin walked up to the front door and asked to see her. The ambassador himself, Mr Generalov, came to meet him, declaring that the reports circulating about Mrs Petrov were nonsense. Colin asked if she had elected to stay with the embassy. 'Yes, that is so,' he replied. Colin asked if he could meet her. The ambassador consulted the press attaché, then went to a phone. A few minutes later Mrs Petrov came into the room.

The story of this interview with Evdokia Alexeyevna Petrov was cabled around the world. It was by far the best exclusive story of the Petrov affair, and justified Colin's wasted days and weeks in Canberra. A red-eyed Mrs Petrov did not believe that her husband had defected. 'He wouldn't leave me, because we married each other,' she touchingly proclaimed. She believed him kidnapped. Otherwise he would have been allowed to meet an official of the Embassy. Her distress was beyond pretence. The following day the rest of the press gallery was on to the Russian Embassy to interview Mrs Petrov and salvage some journalistic honour after being so completely scooped by the *Herald*. Try as they did, they were unsuccessful. Mrs Petrov was not available.

Mrs Petrov's rescue in Darwin from a night flight to Europe is too well known to retell now. Dominating the front page of the *Herald* the following Tuesday was one of the great newspaper photographs, the picture of a distraught woman being dragged on to an aircraft at Sydney airport by two Russian security guards. Australia groaned. But there were no one-stop flights to Europe in 1954, and it was the refuelling stop in Darwin that made it possible for her to be taken aside and persuaded to speak to her husband by telephone. When she discovered that Petrov, far from being held, was acting of his own free will and was under Australian protection, she too defected. Then she disappeared behind a curtain of security. Politics were put aside as we searched for clues to Mrs Petrov's movements and news of her husband, the spy. Two days later a rumour flew through the press gallery that they were bringing her to Canberra in an RAAF aircraft. There was an emergency evacuation of the gallery, all into cars headed for the airport.

The RAAF and Civil Aviation occupied opposite sides of the same airfield in Canberra. We couldn't get into the RAAF base but we could watch from the civil airport side, and Elgin, a keen racegoer and punter, had called home for his racing binoculars. I went to the airport with him in his car, and felt increasingly helpless as time passed and we didn't know whether we were wasting the afternoon. Finally I had to tell Elgin that I needed to get back to town for something I *must* do before the close of business that day. Surprisingly Elgin, too, said he couldn't wait any longer, no matter what happened to Mrs Petrov—and a few minutes later both of us were queuing at a clerk's counter in one of the offices of the Department of the Interior, the rulers of Canberra. We had each received a final warning that our electricity would be cut off immediately unless we paid our overdue accounts by four o'clock that afternoon. But as soon as we left the Department of the Interior we found that Mrs Petrov wasn't coming our way at all. The story of the flight to Canberra was a blind.

The Petrov affair provoked countless questions: how had the spy operation run? what information had the Russians gained? what effects had it had on Australian or Western interests? Questions about the effect on the political contest in Australia were equally insistent. When I had written unworthily, just before, of Liberals' hopes that Menzies would pull a couple of rabbits out of the hat, the latest poll was showing that the government's position had recently slipped. But Menzies, I wrote, was at his best when he was down, whereas Evatt tended to panic. I was right about Evatt, though on this occasion you could hardly blame him. The Doc's immediate reaction when told of Menzies' announcement to parliament was that Labor would support the fullest inquiry. But by the end of the week he was railing against Menzies for his handling of the affair, claiming unjustified interference with the procedures of proper investigation. Menzies curtly dismissed Evatt's attack as incomprehensible, sneering at his 'curious and hysterical outburst'.

Just how much Evatt's election policy was woven in an atmosphere of panic created by Petrov, and how much of it might have emerged anyway out of his fever of ambition, there was no way of knowing. For he produced it virtually without consultation. The policy speech shocked even his own supporters. Despite some wild promises for individuals and industry— headed by a commitment to abolish the means test on pensions within three years—he rejected any increase in taxation. He explained the financing of his commitments in an extraordinary manner. He would simply direct the Commonwealth Bank to 'provide the credit necessary for an expanding economy'. The bank would 'use its credit resources to provide adequate supplies of cheap money for urgent development of the continent'.

Soon Evatt was claiming that 'hundreds of millions of pounds a year' could be saved to finance Labor's policy merely by 'honest accounting', and now he was not only denying the need for any tax increases to finance his promises but was even promising specific reductions. It was Mandrake the Magician politics, as if the Doc needed only to gesture hypnotically to make millions of pounds appear or vanish at will. Bill Bourke publicly rejected his leader's big promise. Labor, if elected, would have to re-examine its policy on abolition of the means test, he warned. 'Frankly,' he said, 'I am not happy about this idea of everybody getting pensions irrespective of their income.' Some of the left-wingers were appalled for different reasons: here was Evatt playing for the support of the capitalists with a costly depreciation allowance for industry. But where was socialism, the socialisation of 'production, distribution and exchange' that was still item one on the party platform? Sooner or later the Labor Party must explode. But at this time Bourke was the only one to protest publicly.

I began my election travels, as usual, with Menzies. He opened his campaign in a subdued manner. The policy speech, delivered two days before Evatt's, assured voters of more tax reductions in the next budget, as expected, promised a modification to the means test on pensions to meet 'the majority of hard cases' and little else, and Menzies knew better than to give any satisfaction to those who were waiting for him to exploit the Petrov affair.

Menzies began to attract huge audiences. On the night of Evatt's policy speech Menzies' appearance in Brisbane attracted a crowd of three-and-a-half thousand, overflowing the City Hall. The next night he was in Rockhampton.

It is often the irrelevant memories that stay. I see Rockhampton itself, a piece of purest Queensland, and its bridge, a fanciful example of Victorian-age engineering which, according to local folklore, had originally been intended for a river in India but was remaindered to Rockhampton instead. And I remember that the next morning Evatt's campaign speech in Brisbane was published on the front page of the *Rockhampton Bulletin* whereas you had to turn to one of the back pages for their coverage of Menzies' meeting in their own city. For its venue branded it as local news; the front page of the *Rockhampton Bulletin* recognised nothing less than national and international events, spurning the parochial affairs of its own city. What's more, the newspaper's editorials that morning ignored the election entirely—indeed they could hardly have been further removed from it. The most exotic of them was devoted to the Indian poet, Rabindranath Tagore, for it was a Saturday, and bookish editorials on Saturdays were a tradition for this newspaper. The first visit to Rockhampton by a prime minister in God knows how many years was not going to shake that.

Evatt's policy transformed the campaign immediately. The Treasury's costings on his promises reached Menzies a short time before the meeting in Rockhampton, and immediately I detected a new mood in him. The audience that crowded into the Rockhampton School of Arts that night witnessed a carnivorous attack on Evatt. Politicians always put on the mask of a victor until or unless someone tears it off, but you can tell when the real mood of victory is on them, and Menzies now seemed certain that he was going to win. Evatt's foolhardy promises counted more than any political fallout from Petrov in giving Menzies this surge of confidence, and from that night onwards Menzies' campaign was relentlessly negative, an assault on Evatt's credibility. Evatt would 'rather be prime minister of a bankrupt country than Leader of the Opposition in a solvent one,' he said. 'He is trying to bribe you with your own money,' he told one audience. He sneered at his opponent as being 'as innocent of financial knowledge as a frog is of feathers'. It was Menzies at his most lethal.

The cost of Evatt's promises are meaningless today, so much has inflation changed the significance of the numbers, but when Menzies claimed that the measurable items alone would cost £357,800,000 he was talking about a sum equivalent to more than a third of the entire Commonwealth budget. Menzies claimed that income tax would have to be doubled to pay for these undertakings, and though he was probably stretching it there was no doubt that the cost would be enormous. Yet those of us on the election trail were not convinced that Evatt could be written off. Whatever anyone wanted, it seemed, he would promise it. How many idealistic pensioners and prospective pensioners could reject his offerings, we wondered; and how many other groups could refuse what he held out to them, whatever common sense might say about its irresponsibility?

When I left Menzies to join Evatt I found the Doc campaigning in his unique manner. He, his staff and the press party with him hadn't had breakfast on the ground since their tour started. 'His idea of going from Hobart to Sydney,' I observed, 'is to drop across for a meeting in Adelaide on the way.' In the slow aircraft of the time, too. The economics of his election policy had got even more out of hand than before, as he had no inhibitions about adding new commitments as he went. And his manner was new. He was speaking faster, more incisively and more emotionally than usual, shouting into the microphone to override interjectors. He was as unpredictable as ever, as a meeting in Orange one night showed.

We had all driven over late in the afternoon from Bathurst. The journalists had gone ahead, so we didn't know that his car had broken down on the way. All we knew was that he was behind schedule. Finally he turned up at dinner time. Usually on these tours we ate together in the dining room, and on his arrival in a town Evatt, like Menzies, would first be welcomed by his local party branch. But by now he was so peevish that he brushed off his supporters, rejected their dinner in his honour, ignored the press party, disappeared into his room and stayed there. At eight o'clock a large crowd was waiting in a hall nearby for the meeting to begin, many of them obviously pensioners assembled to hear the words of their saviour. They all had their overcoats on but these were not enough, for the nights in Orange in late May are cold, and there was no heating in the hall. While we and the audience suffered, the Doc—I discovered later—was still in his hotel room with Mary Alice having chicken sandwiches and champagne which he had ordered from room service, taking his time and—in a mood of obstinacy, it seemed—deliberately making everyone wait.

Down the street a local Labor Party official was making his introductory speech without the leader he was supposed to be introducing, boring the audience as he extemporised to cover the delay. It was nearly a quarter to nine when Evatt arrived, and fate had taken a hand again with the failure of the loudspeaker system, so that when he did speak he had to shout to be heard. He got his message across, no doubt, but it was a miserable night, and would have been more miserable for the pensioners if they had known about the unhurried champagne snack with which he was consoling himself as they shivered.

Another irrelevant memory from this tour which, like Rockhampton's bridge, won't go away: who should come up to me in Orange but Jack Farland? I had no idea what had become of Jack, who was briefly one of my predecessors in the Canberra job. He was a man, I thought later, with an ambition that could have been boundless. I'd known him briefly in the Canberra office when he first went there as Ray Maley's offsider. Rodger Rea was the junior in the Sydney *Daily Telegraph* office throughout Jack's rise and fall in Canberra, and watched it all. Ray Maley, with his weakness for drink and gambling, was already in trouble when Jack arrived to work with him. And while Ray neglected the job, Jack began to get scoops that had the press gallery marvelling. The *Herald* recalled Ray to Sydney and installed Jack in his place. He moved into 29 Mugga Way with his family, but soon he overreached himself. He did so with a story that the Americans were refusing to exchange atomic secrets with Britain because they were afraid that they would leak to the Russians through Australia's CSIR, the government scientific research organisation.

Chifley denied Jack's story absolutely until Artie Fadden rose from the opposition benches in the House of Representatives, waving a document which, he claimed, confirmed it. It was a minute written following a meeting Chifley had had with British cabinet ministers. At this sensational point Chifley called in the Commonwealth Police, who searched *Herald* files in Sydney and Canberra. Farland was charged with having been party to an offence against the secrecy provisions of the Crimes Act. Evidence was given that he had been getting his documents from a young woman typist in the public service. For security reasons, no doubt, he was taken to court not over the British cabinet matter but over a story on the much less interesting subject of tobacco imports.

The *Herald* was threatening to support Farland all the way to the Privy Council in defence of the freedom of the press. But Rodger Rea was in the Canberra magistrate's court, covering the Farland case, when a mysterious document was shown to the *Herald*'s counsel, and then to Angus McLachlan. McLachlan went white, Rodger says, and the *Herald* instantly abandoned Farland's defence. The contents of the document were never publicly revealed. Farland was found guilty and fined £35 with costs; he left Canberra and left the *Herald*. Guy Harriott took his place.

Now I knew what had become of Jack Farland since those days: he was editor of the local paper in Orange. Here he was with his worn face, wanting to know everything about the press gallery in Canberra, and the office, and the job. 'And are you living in the Mugga Way house?' he asked finally. This I felt was his greatest pain. I suspect that he wanted to torture himself by meeting the man now living in that style to which journalists were not accustomed, occupying the house that once appealed, it was said, to Betty Fairfax, lording it in that stately garden, receiving guests in the circular drive, strolling in the precinct of the diplomats ... 'Yes,' I confessed almost guiltily, 'I'm living in the Mugga Way house.' I don't think he wanted to know any more, and that was the last I saw or heard of him.

The Royal Commission on Espionage met briefly during the election campaign. Victor Windeyer, senior counsel assisting the Commission, foreshadowed fragments of the evidence to come but played down the likelihood of political shocks. Some politicians on both sides of the House were mentioned in Petrov's documents, he said, but they were not prominent, and at most they were 'in-the-dark' informers. His most interesting disclosure was that one of the dossiers sent to Moscow was on journalists in the Canberra gallery. I wondered what Moscow had on file about me.

Meanwhile Menzies was having bigger election meetings than ever: five thousand in Forrest Place, Perth, one lunchtime. But those of us who were travelling with him didn't assume that these numbers foretold a result. Journalists who had been on the 1949 campaign tour said that Chifley was attracting big crowds of devoted supporters on the eve of his great defeat. And now, in 1954, Evatt's campaign was disrupting established allegiances, alienating many swinging voters yet winning new supporters at the same time. Seldom had a leader appealed so openly to voters' self-interest, but seldom had one left himself so open to scepticism and disbelief. Would self-interest win, or scepticism?

The election centre in the *Herald* office on election night in those pre-computer days was like an old army operations room. Sheets of paper with handwritten voting details from one electorate after another were being constantly put up on the walls around the room and pulled down again as soon as new figures came in. But I was not responsible for assessing the result. That task had been allocated to Reg Mahoney, a sound and experienced journalist who had spent weeks in preparation, analysing information on voting trends in previous elections. The art of making the quickest possible assessment of an election result lay in understanding the changing patterns that would emerge as counting proceeded. Country electorates were the trickiest, as the first figures in were from the towns, more favourable to Labor than the later ones from outlying polling booths which reflected the more conservative country vote. I had discussed these problems with Reg, but on election night I had the easy job. When he had pronounced the result, I would write a comment.

As soon as the figures meant anything that night they showed such a swing to Labor that later counting seemed unlikely to save the government. As more figures arrived, first impressions were strengthened. Everyone in the newsroom was convinced that Labor had won—everyone, I imagined, except me. I began to notice something different. The strong swing to Labor was still there, but not in enough of the marginal electorates which it had to win to gain office. My previous conclusion that Evatt's campaign had fractured normal voting patterns was justified. Labor was failing to win vital votes just where it needed them.

I had hesitated to interrupt Reg as he ceaselessly surveyed the figures and scribbled, but now I went over to him. 'I reckon the government's getting back,' he said. 'So do I,' I told him, 'Labor's not winning the seats it needs.' I was relieved to find that Reg's judgment had not been shaken by the rest of the newsroom crowd. Angus McLachlan was hovering nearby so that if the *Sun-Herald* made a spectacular mistake as it did when Irvine Douglas misread the result on election night, 1949, he would know why. Reg told him what he thought; Angus couldn't accept it. I said I agreed with Reg. It was too early to make a final judgment, but it would soon be time for the next edition, and by then Reg would have to commit the *Sun-Herald* to a verdict. In my mind the figures were continuing to confirm our reading, but the newsroom was aghast. 'I just hope you're right,' said Angus, grim and disbelieving. 'I don't know how you can arrive at that,' said Kate Commins, the *Herald*'s only woman executive on the general news staff, who had organised and run the war room that night.

As Reg bravely hammered out his 'Government back' introduction on his typewriter there was nothing else I could do until the late edition, so I had a few bets on the result, and won, for Menzies was back with a reduced majority. Some of the members whom I knew personally lost their seats. One was the mad, likeable, militaristic Liberal Bruce Graham, who'd lost his leg in the war, and another was Roy Wheeler, whose subsequent decline I have already recounted.

Although I had failed to forecast the result even just before the elections, the final figures justified my uncertainty. They showed that Labor had won slightly more votes than the government parties, more even than the combined votes of the government parties, the communists and the independents. It just didn't win enough votes in the right places. But Evatt's mighty gamble had almost succeeded.

My final thoughts about this time of the early Petrov hearings and the elections go back, as on other occasions, to something inconsequential. It came out in evidence in the Royal Commission later that one of Vladimir Petrov's conditions when negotiating his defection with Security was that they should find a good home for his dog. But it was Colin Mann who found the dog and fed it when it reappeared at the old address. Then it disappeared again. Was that because Security had lived up to its promise? I often wondered, but we'll never know.

CHAPTER 14

The Witch Hunt

1954

Canberra. It had its own attractions; I think we set ourselves against them because it wasn't Sydney, or London. But when you were under that pure, hard-edged summer sky, so different from the cloudy untidiness of Sydney's, sometimes you could forget the other places. Canberra seemed to be not only the political capital of Australia but the picnic capital as well. For picnics by the Murrumbidgee River, mainly, and swimming in its pebbly waterholes, and precious little sign of humanity there. Then there were the drives up to the top of Red Hill at dusk to watch the golden grassy slopes dissolve; this was another way of reaching into a storehouse of sensation that shared nothing with the other Canberra that dwelt in such worldly places as the bars and corridors and offices of Parliament House.

There were people, too, who began to give life in Canberra some variety for us. Some came from the diplomatic community. There was a young South African third secretary, Ray Killen and his wife Anne, whom the Reids and we greatly liked, and the acting head of their mission, Gerry Nel, who bravely put on a public showing of *Cry the Beloved Country*, a fine film that challenged the values of his government. Another young couple were John and Mavis Morrison. John was the British third secretary; on holidays the Morrisons drove far into the outback and made journeys that few Australians ever ventured on in those days. John disproved any notion that British aristocracy might necessarily be effete. He went on to inherit his father's title, Lord Dunrossil.

There was Henri Méhu, the French chargé d'affaires, who forgave Canberra because, after all, it had taken two thousand years for Paris to become what it was. Like us, he took refuge in Sydney as often as possible but unlike me, being an irresponsible bachelor, he drove a sports car and did the trip in not much more than three hours, a time which required insane speeding through the meanders of the undulating, crumbling old two-lane road called the highway. And the Greek chargé d'affaires, Dimitri Lambros, who entertained us with the Australian diplomat Mick Shann and his wife just after both of them had attended—as observers—the Bandoeng Conference, a historic meeting of unaligned countries. Remarkable though it seemed at that time, the conference was conducted in English, the only common language for its mainly Asian and African participants. But as Dimitri recounted the story of it and its significance Mick, edging behind him and out of his sight, mimed a silent commentary which suggested that Dimitri had no more comprehended the events of the conference than if it had been conducted in Sanskrit. We nodded and maintained impassive faces.

Harold and Elizabeth White were still the best of neighbours. Elizabeth was no longer producing breast milk for afternoon tea parties but had many other appealing eccentricities, such as scattering geranium blossoms in her toilet bowls, to the bewilderment of visitors. She introduced us to a charming elderly woman whom she had befriended. Billie felt sorry for Elizabeth's friend and, knowing that she lived alone, had her to Christmas dinner. Elizabeth mentioned afterwards that our guest had recently been released from an asylum for the criminally insane, having murdered someone, but perhaps she was past that sort of activity.

Harold White was a small man who lived behind a large moustache. Canberra gossip depicted him as a satyr. He sometimes stood on the end of the bed crying cock-a-doodle-doo before flinging himself onto his wedded partner, it was claimed, and one of his children was reputed to have been conceived in the bath. It was probably a love of tactile experiences that caused him to keep a cow to supplement the grass cutter, and the milking set the routine of his day. The garden was one of the few elements of informality in the Whites' world, for Elizabeth and her daughters never visited us, however casual the purpose and time of day, without dressing up and slipping into their high heels.

I gave the youngest of the White children, Kathy, a temporary job as our office junior in her time between school and university. My action in doing so was a fateful one. Kathy was a softly rounded sixteen-year-old who immediately attracted the junior reporter in the office, a red-headed young man named Harry Holgate. A liaison between them caused distress at no. 27 Mugga Way, for the Whites wanted no obstacles to Kathy's brilliant career, certainly not from a journalist, for they despised almost all journalists except, for some reason, me. Harold even asked me what I would do in his place. I couldn't imagine, and suggested sending her overseas for a year as, I understood, Victorian fathers did to cool daughters' ardour. Either he wisely didn't try to take my advice or it didn't work.

Harry and Kathy were married, Kathy was not diverted from her academic career, and Harry—presumably not to be too far outclassed in the academic stakes—did a university degree part-time. But the marriage didn't last, and to finish once and for all the story of Kathy and Harry, she later became Kathy West, and was one of the intellectual leaders and publicists of the misguided attempt to promote Joh Bjelke-Petersen as prime minister of Australia. For a while it was difficult to pick up *The Australian* without reading an article on Australia's political future by Dr Katherine West, but once the Bjelke-Petersen campaign collapsed and its folly became evident to nearly all, her name seemed to disappear from those columns. As for Harry, he became briefly a premier of Tasmania.

Of all politicians except Malcolm McColm, the one I became most friendly with away from the political scene was John Gorton. Billie and I liked him and Betty Gorton as a couple and we liked their close friends, Norman and Ruth Mussen, who were living in Canberra. John was a most engaging man, without pretences. He was a rank-and-file senator, as remote from the ministry as most of the rest of the 1949 crop of Liberal parliamentarians. He never became one of my political informants, never told me stories about government party meetings, but we shared a view of politics. Like me, he was impatient with Menzies' measured approach to government; we both looked in vain for a sense of opportunity. But I'd have liked John as well if he had been much more radical or more conservative. We liked Betty Gorton equally—a direct, genuine, intelligent, understanding woman who lacked any interest in the trivialities that politics offers to those on the fringe.

The Mussens were in many ways similar people, living in Canberra because Mussen, Mackay and Potter, architects, were supervising the construction of the John Curtin School of Medical Research, one of the first stages of Canberra's new Australian National University. This project must have been a frustrating experience in Canberra as Canberra was then, at a time of endless inefficiencies in the building industry. A young English architect in Norman's office named John Scollay, who sang at parties and accompanied himself on the guitar, long before the guitar took on, had a song beginning:

When I was a lad and a bit of a fool
I got mixed up in the medical school,
But even more mixed up than I
Were Mussen, Potter and Mackay.

Norman had gone ahead to Canberra when they got the medical school job, and lived at the Hotel Canberra until Ruth could join him. The often lonely life at the Canberra (which I knew so well) drove him to a bottle of whisky a day, and as he would have been embarrassed to buy that much at the Canberra he went over every second day to the Civic Hotel, on the outskirts of the city, alternating his purchases between the two places.

Our other life, in Sydney, continued. We stayed at Mum's flat and spent the rest of the time with our journalist and musician friends. Billie did a number of broadcasts for the ABC from the Sydney studios. One Sunday later that year, with Marta Zalan and Charles, I called at a flat in Manly where Neville Amadio, the flautist, lived. He hushed us, as a guest was trying to sleep in the Amadios' spare room. The sleeper was Michael Bialoguski, a doctor who was momentarily famous as the part-time Security operator who had cultivated Petrov and brought him to the point of negotiation with the Security chiefs. He was having an afternoon nap, with his revolver on the table beside him. I didn't seem able to escape the Petrov affair, which by then was in full swing.

This was also the year when Billie's sister Maxie came home to Australia, unable to stand her Norwegian mother-in-law or the straightlaced provincialism of Bergen, Norway. When she married, Lars claimed to be enthusiastic about migrating to Australia, but since then the time never seemed right for him. Maxie eventually left with her three-year-old daughter Britt, judging this to be the only way of persuading Lars to follow. There was movement also in my own family. Mum's youngest sister Rea, who had still been living with Nanna, was getting married, so Nanna moved in with Mum, while Max and Britt moved in to Nanna's flat in Waverley, a real-estate prize because of rent control. And we, too, were looking at real estate. In 1954 I reached thirty, and that, I thought, was the age to be moving on, if you were in a place and a job that you didn't plan to stay in for a long time.

It was also time for me to take steps towards home ownership if I didn't want to finish up like Dad, never having a place of his own. But so far I'd still been spending everything I earned. So to get started we bought a piece of land in Mosman for £1000, mainly financed by loans of a few hundred each from Mum and Charlie Zalan. Then we started trying to live on my expenses, mainly the gardening allowance for 29 Mugga Way. We—especially Billie—did all the gardening in the *Herald* estate from then on. I also picked up extra money as the Australian correspondent of *The Economist* and by occasionally standing in for the AAP-Reuter representative in Canberra. AAP paid at a standard rate for each story or instalment of a story you sent them, and I sent everything I could. So, if I was lucky, I might at least arrive back in Sydney without any debts. But I didn't.

Alex Sverjensky wanted my help. The Sverjenskys were White Russians who had gone from Russia to Shanghai. Alex's mother and brother stayed on there but now, many years later, his mother had died and his brother wanted to join him in Australia. Alex nominated him as a migrant and went to see the Department of Immigration a number of times about his application. They assured him that there was no problem but he became convinced that there was.

I was lucky to have a contact who could check the Sverjensky file, and discovered something quite unexpected: the application had been blocked by Security. When I investigated further the result was even more of a surprise: the Security objection didn't concern Alex's brother but Alex himself. I wondered how to approach him. Could he have a secret past, or present? Do you ask directly: 'Are you a spy?' If the real answer is yes you will get no, and if it is really no you wouldn't know whether to believe it anyway. But I could see no alternative to the direct approach, so the next time I was in Sydney I took it. What would they be holding against you? I asked him. I haven't the slightest idea, said Alex. If there's nothing about you that they could object to, I said, have you any friends with a political background that could put you under suspicion too? Or have you ever been a member of any organisation that they could object to? Alex assured me that he had always kept away from politics, and his friends weren't political. I decided to believe him.

The situation was hard to resolve. I didn't know any Security people. There was no point in going to the Immigration Department, as I could offer no evidence to justify ignoring a Security report. I thought about these problems on the drive back to Canberra and decided that the only solution was to go to the top. Harold Holt, then Minister for Immigration, was a politician I had never known well—mainly because he came from Melbourne, so I didn't have the same opportunities to meet him often on his home ground as I had with the ministers from Sydney. But he was a liberal-minded man, and I felt sure he would act if he could be convinced that Alex's case was genuine. I saw him soon afterwards, told him the story, and said I felt that Alex had told me the truth. Holt listened sympathetically and told me he would ask the department for an explanation. Shortly afterwards his private secretary told me that they had made inquiries, and Alex's application would go ahead. As soon as I could, I thanked Holt and asked him the reason for the change of mind. He told me that when Security were asked the reasons for their recommendation they 'didn't come up with much to back it up', so he decided to ignore them. A few months later Alex's brother opened a delicatessen shop in Coogee.

I was impressed by Holt's approach. It showed him as a reasonable and open-minded man, and this was his reputation. Another example of his liberal-mindedness was his quiet relaxation of the White Australia Policy as inflexibly applied by his recent Labor predecessor, Arthur Calwell. The numbers of Asians admitted under Holt as minister were small, but their significance was not.

Bill McMahon had the office next to Holt. Bill became Minister for Navy and Air about the time I went to Canberra in 1951, and Minister for Social Services after the 1954 elections. He was a successful minister. He was well equipped, with his degrees in economics and law, but he pursued self-interest with scarcely a gesture of concealment. False modesty, or any modesty at all, was foreign to him He was going deaf, and though he had an operation later to improve his hearing, at the time I describe he spoke unnaturally loudly as some deaf people do. One afternoon when I went to see him after a cabinet meeting he suddenly said to me: 'Harold Holt made an absolute fool of himself in cabinet this morning'. This outburst had nothing to do with the topic I was there to talk about, and I stayed silent while he declaimed. The cabinet had been discussing economic issues on which Holt, according to Bill, had talked nonsense. None of the rest of the cabinet was much better for that matter, he told me, for most of them knew nothing about economics. Bill was telling me what he thought of Holt and his other colleagues in his excessively loud voice and I felt sure that the thin internal walls between the offices in the old temporary parliament building were incapable of stopping such a volume of sound. Surely Holt in his office next door would be able to hear him, I was thinking, and if he could he would be fascinated by this outburst..

Bill became even more extravagant. He was the best equipped of the entire cabinet on economic issues, he told me—the only one with an economic background, better qualified for the position of Treasurer than

Artie, the incumbent, who was only an accountant; for that matter Bill was also the best equipped of all the ministers for the prime ministership after Menzies. This was another shot at Holt, the likely successor.

I wouldn't have been surprised to discover that McMahon had thoughts along these lines, but it was hard to believe that he was telling them to me without provocation and with no sense of indiscretion. To me the idea of Bill McMahon as prime minister was ludicrous. He had ability; his weakness was character. There was his unconcealed disloyalty towards colleagues, which he was now demonstrating, and his undisguised lack of scruple. Angus McLachlan had told me of a discussion with McMahon in which McMahon said simply: 'If there is anything the *Herald* ever wants from cabinet, just let me know and I'll support it.' 'How can you respect a man like that?' asked McLachlan, who was something of a puritan. How, indeed! I came away from my own encounter with McMahon wondering whether anyone would believe me if I told them about it. People would think I was exaggerating.

Lou Leck became news editor of the *Herald* that year. It appeared that the organisation was being kind to Harry Kippax because of his difficult divorce. They sent him to the United States—where he took up a writing role again with distinction, as always—and later to London. The acceptability of my job depended on my relationship with the news editor more than anything else, and I was uncertain at first about Lou. Unlike Harry, he wasn't a personal friend or one who shared my interests. Whether he would give me the free hand that I now expected, only experience would tell.

Lou began our working relationship with only a few minor requirements. It was coming up to budget time in Canberra, and his main message was to forget budget speculation. This was an activity which gave Ken Schapel something to write about for weeks every year. And as it was only speculation it didn't matter, really, whether it was right or wrong. Things expected to happen didn't happen, that was all. No-one could prove that they had not been considered, or that there hadn't been a change of mind. But I was happy enough not to have to cover myself this year every time Schapel wrote one of his pre-budget beat-ups.

As budget day approached, Schapel produced his normal speculation and fantasies. His big story was that the government would introduce a 40 per cent initial depreciation allowance to encourage industry to invest in new plant. Chifley had brought in such an allowance but the Menzies Government had abolished it when the economy turned bad at the beginning of the '50s. Now that the economy was recovering there was much speculation that it would be restored, and the *Telegraph* was running a campaign in support of it. Frank Packer, the *Telegraph*'s proprietor, must have had major investment plans. And, like other self-interested campaigns of his, this one had nothing subtle about it. Schapel's stories may have seemed to provide support for his employer's campaign. But as his series of budget forecasts continued I rang Lou Leck each time, assured him that they were pure speculation, and ignored them.

This was the background to my conversation with Artie Fadden at a reception in the members' dining room of Parliament House on the day the new parliament opened. Billie was standing with me when I said hello to him, and our conversation at first was purely social. But suddenly he said to me: 'You don't want to take any notice of those stories the Crow is writing about an initial depreciation allowance. There won't be any. It isn't in the budget.' Artie must have been goaded by Packer's pressure to the point where he had lost all patience. I was glad to hear his denial, but it was only the beginning. 'As a matter of fact, the main points in the budget are ... ,' he began, and then he listed ten of them, an outline of the whole budget.

An exclusive story on a budget was the biggest scoop of all in Canberra, for it was the hardest to get. In London in 1947 Hugh Dalton, the Chancellor of the Exchequer, resigned because he had indiscreetly mentioned just one feature of his budget to an evening newspaper journalist as he was on his way into parliament to deliver the budget speech. When the next edition of the paper came out Dalton may have already announced the point he had told the journalist in the corridors, but the act of disclosure had still been premature, and he regarded resignation as his only choice. The rules might not be so unyielding in Australia but it was only occasionally, in my experience, that a journalist might get a genuine story on a single important point in a budget. Now, here I was with the lot. And I had got it direct from the Treasurer at a function at which any politician or pressman in Canberra could have seen him talking to me in a corner.

Although Artie didn't impose any restrictions, out of consideration for him I felt that I couldn't write the story that night, and decided to take the risk that he might give it to someone else. But the next afternoon I rang Lou. I've got the front-page lead story for you tomorrow, I told him. You know we've agreed that I won't write anything on the budget unless it's right: well, I'm writing a budget story today. It's the whole story. I have it from an unquestionable source, so you can have complete confidence in it. Every word will be right.

Lou knew Canberra. He knew exactly what a leaked budget meant. He knew that he didn't have to worry about the accuracy of the story, either. As for me, I went home that night knowing that I'd got one of the best Canberra scoops for years. But when I collected the paper the next morning I couldn't accept what I saw. The story was there, but it wasn't the front-page lead. It wasn't even the second story on page one. You had to go down to the third story, under the picture, to find what the *Herald* had done with it. My disappointment and anger were mixed with bewilderment. How could Lou Leck do this?

The answer, when I got it, was unimaginable. My budget story had been too good. It was such an important story that Lou had shown it to Angus McLachlan, who had shown it to Rupert Henderson, who didn't believe it because he didn't believe that the depreciation allowance could have been rejected. Someone like Bill McMahon must have encouraged him to expect it. I must have got this story from Menzies, he decided. There must still be an argument going on about it. Menzies must be trying to knock it on the head, and I had obviously been taken in by Menzies' line. Despite Henderson's attitude Lou wouldn't give up the story, but played it down.

The reaction was quite different in Canberra. The rest of the press gallery knew that this story couldn't be mere speculation—it wasn't written that way—but I got no direct reaction from the government side until the next day, Saturday, when Artie rang me from the Hotel Canberra in the morning. Could I come over and see him? I drove there, announced myself, and waited in the most obscure corner of the large lounge of the old hotel. The woman on the front desk said that Sir Arthur had a delegation with him but wouldn't be long.

I expected to meet Artie in his room, for privacy, after his visitors left, but a few minutes later he excused himself from his meeting, came into the lounge and sat down with me. If he'd been trying to disguise himself as anyone but the Treasurer of the Commonwealth of Australia he could not have done a better job, for he was still wearing his pyjamas and a woollen dressing-gown. But although he didn't look like a federal treasurer he was certainly unmistakable as Artie Fadden.

He hunched forward. 'Have you told anyone where you got that budget story?' he asked. 'Certainly not, Artie,' I told him. 'I never talk about my sources. Even my own office doesn't know where this one came from.' 'Good!' he replied, and explained what had happened since my budget story appeared. Menzies had one of his witch-hunts on, he said, because there were some points in my story that hadn't even gone to cabinet at that stage.

This meant that they were known to only six people—Menzies and himself, Roland Wilson, head of the Treasury, and three others whom he named, whose identity I have forgotten. But so long as I hadn't revealed my source to anyone, everything would be all right. Then he got up and went back to his delegation. They must have been Queensland farmers, I calculated, otherwise even Artie would not have met them in his pyjamas.

What fascinated me, apart from Artie's dress code, was his revelation that not even the cabinet knew some of the points the *Herald* had published about the budget. That was probably why Henderson didn't believe them. Like Packer, but more discreetly, he too had probably been lobbying for the depreciation allowance, and would have been drawn to the section of my story which said that it had been rejected. If so, he may have tried to check immediately with one of the *Herald*'s cabinet contacts. Almost any member of cabinet would have denied at least parts of my story, not realising that Artie had told me more than he had told them. 'I can assure you, Rupert,' Henderson's source would have said, 'cabinet has made no such decision.'

My indignation was slightly assuaged on budget day when I wrote the official budget story. Everything I had written earlier was, of course, confirmed.

CHAPTER 15

Document H

1954 and 1955

Menzies went fishing in New Zealand after the 1954 elections, but Evatt wouldn't have had time for a picnic by the river. He had just sacked my former colleague Fergan O'Sullivan, who had been his press secretary for the past year. I knew nothing of the sacking then, but soon everyone knew. When the Royal Commission on Espionage resumed its hearings after the elections Fergan was identified as the author of Document H, a report on members of the press gallery that had been provided to one of the Russians, which the Russian Embassy had passed on to Moscow. It had nothing to do with the Doc; Fergan had written it while he and I were working together in the *Sydney Morning Herald* office in Canberra in 1951. But two other members of Evatt's staff were named as informants by another Canberra journalist, Rupert Lockwood, who wrote for communist and trade union papers.

Lockwood had given the Russians a much wider-ranging and more scurrilous document than Fergan's. It became known in the Commission as Document J. Later one of Evatt's former stenographers also admitted having given information to the Russians while working in his office. When Evatt accused Menzies of buying Petrov's documents to embarrass him politically, Menzies asserted that if he had told parliament what he knew about Evatt's staff before the elections, Evatt 'wouldn't be here now'.

These were only some of the Doc's problems; there were just as many within the Labor Party. Not only were Bill Bourke and others attacking him from the Right, but the Left was threatening him, too. It gained control of the federal executive of the party at a meeting which expressed 'complete dissatisfaction' with Evatt and the parliamentary executive for going their own way on election policy. The Federal Executive was formally demanding full consultation in future. For the next few months Evatt's battles with these critics inside the ALP and with the Royal Commission were the two themes in counterpoint which dominated Australian politics and my working life. I covered the political scene and 'Our Industrial Correspondent'—my troublesome colleague Fred Coleman Browne—was reporting on the combat inside the union-dominated ALP organisation.

The news about Fergan O'Sullivan was hard to take. The contents of Document H were unrevealed at the time, but apparently it was a series of unflattering personal assessments of many members of the press gallery, plus gossip and some scandal about their private lives. Fergan didn't deny authorship, saying that he had written it at the request of Pakhamov, Canberra representative of Tass, the Russian news agency. As he described it, its purpose was to help Pakhamov in his contacts with journalists to try to get more favourable material on the Soviet Union published in the Australian press.

I don't think that the press gallery regarded Fergan as anything quite so theatrical as a fully credentialled spy or traitor, nor did I, but he was revealed as a man moved by hostility and contempt for almost everything and everyone around him. The evidence from the Royal Commission brought to mind the occasions when I had invited him home to eat with us, but found that he had other commitments—so often that it became obvious that he didn't want to come. At the time I took his refusals personally. But Elgin Reid pointed out now that Fergan had always avoided fraternising with other members of the press gallery, except for one or two. Thinking back, I had to agree. Fergan had emerged as a radical driven by an ideology that was poisonous to ordinary relationships.

I didn't see him again till thirty years later. Then I found him confronting me at a friendly round-table lunch in Sydney, smiling and cordial, as if Document H had never existed. Eventually its contents were published—except for the scandalous bits. 'Hal Myers. About 26–28,' he had written. 'Likes to think himself totally detached. Conservative under test. Wife is pianist of near-concert standard (Leonie Stredwick). On London staff for 2–3 years.' To what degree the reference to Billie was intended as a sneer I do not know, as she was still in London when he wrote the document. The part that I found most indigestible was the phrase: 'under test'. What was the test, I wondered. Who had devised it, this devious technique, whatever it was, for classifying friendly and unwary associates?

The rest of the document was scornful of most members of the gallery except for a few whom he regarded as politically progressive, and one, John Bennetts in the Melbourne *Herald* office, about whom he may have been quite mistaken. John was rumoured at the time to be a Security informant, and much later did become an intelligence officer. Some of Fergan's judgments were clearly astray: 'Courier-Mail. Elgin Reid. Only representative here, about 26, completely naive.' Some reflected standard press gallery opinion: 'Melbourne Herald. Harold Cox. About 45. Complete conservative. In Canberra for about 15 years, very snobbish, talks only to heads of service and those wishing to push themselves on him.' Irvine Douglas was also a 'complete conservative'.

Fitchett did not appeal to him, being dismissed with the observation: 'Considers himself great wit so adopts no political stand.' Fergan rejected the Labor credentials of Alan Reid, the only known member of the Labor Party in the gallery, with the comment: 'Likes to think himself pro-Labour', adding tartly: 'Wealthiest man in gallery. Owns station outside Canberra.' He reported that Schapel was 'believed to be' a Security agent. It was a collection of the conclusions and indiscretions of a young man ('About 25 . . . Radical', he called himself in Document H) who hadn't spent long in the press gallery and didn't know quite as much about its members as he or his Russian friends might have supposed. I've always wondered what he thought of it afterwards.

Evatt survived as leader of the opposition after the elections only because the most threatening challengers bided their time and missed their opportunity. A West Australian member of the caucus executive, Tom Burke (father, incidentally, of the West Australian premier, Brian Burke, who went to gaol in his political retirement for financial impropriety during his premiership) was so disgusted at his colleagues' inaction that he mounted a quixotic challenge of his own, without warning or lobbying, and therefore without a chance of success, so that Evatt's greatest troubles still lay in the future. But in ballots for the caucus executive the left-wingers, led by Eddie Ward, emerged as the strongest faction and therefore possibly the greatest threat to Evatt. Ward's verdict, I wrote, was stark: 'Evatt must go—but not for six months.' And Eddie Ward, a big man, an ex-boxer, unforgiving and unshakeable, with the hardest, grimmest face I have ever seen, pursued his causes relentlessly.

I was lucky to have got close to Bill Bourke just when I needed a dependable informant on the showdown which was obviously coming. I began to spend more time in Melbourne, sometimes dining at the Bourkes' home, sometimes meeting Bill over long lunches at the Latin Cafe, an Italian restaurant favoured by the Catholic intelligentsia. The Bourkes' house was a revelation to me, so remote was it from the Labor style of the '50s when most of the Labor MPs had come from the ranks of union officials, self-made and self-educated. It was less than a mansion, more than a house—the sort of building that estate agents respectfully call a residence. It was two-storeyed, standing back from its street frontage in well-heeled Toorak. Within, it was on the gloomy side and conservative. Bill Bourke *was* conservative, and might have been at home among the Liberals except for some political ideas and traditions which flourished in the Catholic Labor environment. But at the time one political issue overshadowed all others for people like him. It was communism.

Every Tuesday during parliamentary sittings I loitered in the halls and corridors, had Bill paged, sent notes to him by messenger into the House, and kept trying until I could contact him to check what had happened in caucus that morning. If there had been any outbursts I would arrange a meeting place where I could hear the full story. I might pick him up in my car in a side street near the House. Sometimes we met on the deserted roof of Parliament House after dinner, stumbling in the dark over whatever the last workmen had left there. Anywhere that offered secrecy.

Only a week after Tom Burke's unsuccessful challenge, Bill Bourke was telling me about the two Labor members who had been throwing punches in the party room that morning. Their fight started after a row about a government Bill to remove doubts about the powers of the Petrov Royal Commission. Ward, predictably, had moved that they should oppose the Commission, but his motion was heavily defeated. Then Les Haylen was belligerently telling him to stop beating his chest as if he was running the party. That was when Ward the ex-boxer hit Haylen the ex-journalist—and Haylen, fighting out of his class, hit back. Their blows were a foretaste of what was in store for Labor.

Evatt—as usual, without consultation—suddenly appeared before the Royal Commission a few days later as counsel for two members of his staff who had been named in evidence. Rupert Lockwood had identified the Doc's private secretary, Alan Dalziel, and assistant secretary, Albert Grundeman, as sources of information in Document J, a 'closely typed' thirty-seven-page report which counsel assisting the Commission had described as a 'farrago of facts, falsity and filth'. Rupert was a likeable if misguided man whom I'd seen and chatted to from time to time around the press gallery. He produced his document in response to a Russian request for a survey on the economic, political and military penetration of Australia by the Americans.

I knew Dalziel and Grundeman only slightly. Dalziel was an unworldly intellectual who didn't mix with the press, and probably wasn't much at home with politicians, either. A strange choice as private secretary to a man who lived in the vortex of politics. A choice that reflected, I felt, the unworldly side of Evatt. Grundeman seemed no more and no less than a bag-carrier who travelled with the Doc and faithfully attended to his practical needs. The Doc's defence of these two men (and, by association, of himself) was to be built on a conspiracy theory which he pursued with supreme ingenuity, and which had only one fault: the conspiracy had been born in Evatt's overworked imagination and nowhere else. It was spy fiction, not fact, and did Evatt great harm. It even proved unnecessary. It had been made clear in the Commission already that there was nothing discreditable to Evatt in the documents that Petrov had handed over.

Lockwood proved to be an unreliable witness and, in Document J, an unreliable reporter, and the Commission soon accepted that Dalziel wasn't the source of information which Lockwood had attributed to him. As for Grundeman, the Commission's only interest in him was that Lockwood's efforts to cultivate him gave some evidence of the methods that were being used to try to gain information useful to the Russians. So the Petrov affair would have been less damaging to Evatt if he had let it take its course. But he immediately saw a conspiracy when four people from his past and present staff figured in Petrov's revelations. And once he cried conspiracy he must try to discredit Petrov, the Commission itself and, he decided, Fergan O'Sullivan. His efforts to do so were at the heart of the turmoil in the Labor Party with which the press gallery was absorbed.

Evatt quoted my 'rabbits out of the hat' comment in the Commission. The conspiracy he alleged was between the Petrovs, Fergan O'Sullivan and the government, with the Security service as go-between. He had quickly decided that Fergan was expendable and, therefore, could be cast in the part of the greatest conspirator. He alleged that Fergan, not Lockwood, had written Document J: Fergan's and the government's motives were to discredit Evatt, and Petrov's purpose was to acquire documents which he could trade for money and political asylum in Australia. These were bizarre suggestions. Fergan's role in such a conspiracy would have required enormous effort (which was foreign to him) and enormous ingenuity on his part, and for Evatt to prove that the conspiracy existed he had to demolish a mass of internal evidence in the document and all the circumstantial and expert evidence besides. As Evatt developed his case Lockwood began to modify his own evidence to match it, while Evatt branded Document J a fabrication and forgery, and the Commissioners were telling him to stop shouting. When he quoted my unfortunate pre-election comment about the rabbits, the chairman of the Commission, Justice Owen, observed wryly: 'It is no use reading newspaper cuttings to us.' A few days later the Commissioners threw the Doc out of the inquiry because of his inability to separate his personal and political interests from his role as Dalziel's and Grundeman's self-appointed advocate.

The day after that, Eddie Ward was at it again. He was trying to punch another Labor member at the end of a caucus meeting which had just heard a long, emotional speech from Evatt justifying his role in the Petrov inquiry. It went on for so long that there was no time for anyone who disagreed with it to speak. The next day I went to a press conference which the Doc called to deny the newspaper reports on the fracas, including mine. 'It was a wonderful meeting,' he insisted.

Two weeks later there was a meeting which even he couldn't call wonderful. In it, Bill Bourke attacked him in what was called the most savage speech ever made in the Labor caucus. The split, or I should say the Split, was coming. Bill was heard in shock and silence as he accused Evatt of 'doing the communists' dirty work' at the Royal Commission. He claimed that Evatt was in reality acting as Rupert Lockwood's senior counsel and that his appointed counsel, a Melbourne barrister named Hill, frequently visited Evatt in his chambers. Evatt was trying to confuse the public and discredit the Commission, Bill claimed, to get in first 'in case any of his former appointees became involved in the inquiry later'. Evatt denied these assertions and the left-wingers supported him. It took only two weeks more for him to make the historic attack on his opponents which fragmented the Labor Party.

When I first came to know Bill Bourke his decision to expose what was happening in the party gave me a scoop. But never again. After that, the details of every caucus meeting leaked to the whole of the press. I knew, though, that Schapel wasn't getting any. The *Daily Telegraph*'s stories were being written by his offsider, George Kerr. And I could easily guess where they were coming from: Stan Keon, Member for Yarra, leader of the right-wing Catholic group in parliament. George Kerr was a lapsed Catholic member of an orthodox Catholic family from Melbourne.

Some of Stan Keon's views were so extreme that I tended to avoid him professionally, though I had nothing against him personally. My longest conversation with him had been at the Latin Cafe in Melbourne one day, after the short stayers had finished their lunch and left. By then he was on his own, and came over with a bottle of red to sit down with Bill and me; we went on for the rest of the afternoon, and I had no complaint about the company. So the first time I couldn't find Bill after a caucus meeting I paged and found Keon, who gave me a full description of events without hesitation. By now, the confidentiality of the party room had ceased to exist. This was war in the Labor Party, with no Geneva Convention to set the rules.

Evatt bypassed the Canberra press gallery when he made his move. He issued a statement in Sydney attacking a small, increasingly disloyal minority in the party, mainly from Victoria, saying it seemed certain that their activities were directed from outside the labour movement. He said he would bring these activities before the next meeting of the ALP federal executive so that 'appropriate action' could be taken by the ALP Federal Conference in January. His cryptic statement was the first public hint of an organisation known as the Movement, a shadowy group run by the Catholic church's most powerful layman, Bob Santamaria, whose name was unknown even to most of the Canberra press gallery. Evatt gave no details, no explanations; he knew that others would rush to fill them in for him. And so the Split was assured. I was about to live through and report one of the great acts in the Australian political drama.

Harold Cox was president of the press gallery when I went to Canberra in 1951. The president, elected by—in press gallery terminology—the heads of service, called and chaired meetings on matters of common interest and represented the gallery in taking them up if necessary with the government, the Speaker, the President of the Senate or any other authority. The position was officially recognised within and outside the parliament. Harold, we knew, was invited to represent the gallery at cabinet lunches for visiting dignitaries, and received invitations from diplomats to some of their smaller, more select functions. For all Harold's disconcerting qualities he was appropriate to the role: he was a senior member of the gallery, and knew how to conduct himself as its representative. His position as president was accepted, and he had been re-elected unchallenged for several years. Harold clearly relished the status that the presidency of the gallery gave him—and when the Queen visited Canberra he, as president, was awarded an OBE.

Some time in 1953 Elgin Reid and Stan Hutchinson wanted to talk to me about the presidency. Harold Cox, they'd heard, wasn't going to stand again. They were concerned that there might not be an acceptable alternative ready to take on the job, and wanted me to do so.

I thought it would be presumptuous to put myself forward, and wanted to nominate one of them instead. Harold was probably the oldest head of service in the gallery and I was the youngest; he had long experience in political journalism and I had comparatively little. But they persuaded me that my position as the *Sydney Morning Herald*'s representative gave me all the status I needed. Shortly after, I was elected president, knowing that Harold would hate having me as his successor. I believe he hated it even more than I expected, for I heard later that he hadn't wanted to give up the presidency at all. He had merely been piqued about something and wanted to be persuaded to change his mind.

One of my first experiences as president was very educational. It was a cabinet lunch for Solomon Bandaranaike—then opposition leader, later prime minister, of Ceylon. Bandaranaike gave a neat little speech in which he congratulated Australia on the advances it had made. Ceylon still had a long way to go to achieve its social objectives, he said. Its eventual aspiration was to provide adequately for all its citizens from the cradle to the grave. But Australia had gone even further, said Mr Bandaranaike: here we looked after our people from the erection to the resurrection.

It was in my first term as president that Menzies accepted my invitation to be guest of honour at the annual press gallery dinner. We had a short head table with three places, one for Menzies, one for me, and one for another member of the gallery. I foolishly made what I saw as the courteous gesture of inviting Harold, as immediate past president, to occupy the other seat at the head table, with the guest of honour between us. Harold couldn't monopolise Menzies but took revenge for the slight that he imagined I and the gallery had done him by refusing to recognise or respond to anything I said. This episode didn't tell me anything I hadn't known about Harold; it was merely confirmation. Menzies, on the other hand, was a perfect guest. There was no hint of animosity towards me, and we could have been mistaken that night for old friends. He did his best in every way, not only giving one of his usual witty and elegant after-dinner speeches, but also bringing some topical verse he had written for the occasion.

The potential for advantage as president of the gallery was strikingly demonstrated when the American Embassy offered me a six-month, expenses-paid visit to the United States. It was a Smith Mundt fellowship, which was granted to young journalists from a number of countries, giving them a chance to see the United States and work in an American newspaper office. I was intensely interested, not knowing the US at all. But I turned down the opportunity because they wouldn't have paid for Billie to go, we hadn't the money to pay for her, and I wasn't prepared to leave her for so long. I recommended that they offer the trip to Elgin. They did, and he accepted, for the furthest Elgin had ever been outside Australia was in Bougainville, where he served as a gunner in the army during the war. He went to the US in 1955 in time to miss the split in the Labor Party— reporting, instead, on local affairs in Rapid City in the badlands of South Dakota. This was near the site of Custer's last stand. Back at home we thought we were watching Evatt's.

My decision to turn down the American offer was strengthened by a hope that I might have a good chance of getting an even better one. I had my eye on a Nieman Fellowship, which took a young journalist to Harvard for a year, and covered a spouse's expenses as well. A Nieman Fellowship was offered annually to one Australian, and was rotated among the states. Jack Flower from the *Sydney Morning Herald* had just had one. It was certain that the choice wouldn't come back to New South Wales for several years, but I imagined that when it did, I would have a reasonable chance. But my theory about the Nieman Fellowship was never tested: I left journalism before even the possibility arose. All I ever got out of it was Jack Flower's dog, Dash, which we looked after while Jack enjoyed himself at Harvard.

Dash was a huge stupid German pointer—or maybe he wasn't, as he had no pedigree—who wagged his tail so much that it had a permanent bleeding sore on the tip. He gave a typical performance once when the Bonneys came to see us in Mugga Way not long after Garnet had taken delivery of his last Pontiac, the one he shipped out when they left America. Dash first jumped up and scratched the car, then used his tail to embellish Garnet's new palest grey Yankee summerweight suit with his bloody graffiti. A week before Jack Flower got back to Sydney and would have taken him back, Dash was shot by the owner of the sheep property across the road from us. The same landholder also killed our own dog, Paddy, whose only misdemeanour was to keep bad canine company.

In 1955, though I had no specific plan for leaving Canberra, Billie and I were still working towards our return to Sydney. She was getting more engagements—ABC concerts and broadcasts and music club recitals in Sydney, as well as country tours with other Sydney musicians—and was going up to Sydney for rehearsals. In this year, also, Maxie's husband Lars

Larsson arrived in Australia and made a good debut with the Sydney Symphony Orchestra, playing the Khachaturian piano concerto and, in a later concert, the first Beethoven piano concerto. He looked set to establish himself in Sydney but, having arrived almost without warning, still had to build a career here. Fortunately Maxie's job would support the two of them and their daughter Britt until Lars got more work; meanwhile he locked himself in a church hall each day and practised.

Our visits to Sydney were both musical and social, and we spent as much time as possible there with Max and Lars, our friends and relatives Ron and Kath Giovanelli, Marta and Charles Zalan, Ross and Pat Westcott, and other musicians and journalists. On Sunday mornings we often visited a Russian family, the Harrises, in Kensington for a banquet called breakfast. The daughter, Lelia, would have been a professional pianist if she hadn't done medicine. The Harrises were White Russians who had arrived in Australia via Shanghai and turned to the manufacture of handmade chocolates of great excellence to set themselves up in Sydney. They were a cultured and spirited family. Their Sunday breakfast of wonderful Russian cakes and delicacies was prepared by Mrs Harris and granny, who had never learned English, and sat at the table in silence, beaming, throughout the feast. Mrs Harris' own command of the language was good but imperfect, and produced at least one masterpiece of its kind. A rolling stone, she told us, does not gather any moths.

In Canberra the procession of visitors staying with us continued, and there was a new face among them. It was Gabrielle Keefe, the fifteen-year-old daughter of Mum's sister Myra and her husband Stan Keefe. Myra was very Irish in appearance, dark-haired, dark-eyed, with an alert, engaging personality. Stan was a big, slow, smiling man who worked as a clerk in the railways. He was too easy-going for Myra's liking. 'You never do anything to provide for the future,' she complained. 'Of course I do,' he protested. 'I buy a lottery ticket every week.' It is a detail which seems quite improbable in the light of Gabrielle's subsequent life.

Gabrielle stayed with us just after she had been thrown out after a year in the convent, which she entered when Myra died from cancer. The mother superior had correctly discerned that she was unsuited to religious orders, and Gabrielle's rehabilitation from the experience began immediately at our house as she took to bed with Van der Velde's *Ideal Marriage*, the sex manual of the '40s, from our bookshelves. After that she flitted across our path from time to time in London and Sydney until her life became caught up in almost unimaginable events in South Africa. She had much of her mother's attractive but complex personality. I knew her better than my other cousins and would probably have nominated her as my favourite then, but the South African story disclosed another Gabrielle. She became prominent in the most extreme right-wing politics, wrote as a journalist for the Conservative Party publication, *Die Patriot*, and had a second marriage to a prominent Conservative Party MP, Clive Derby-Lewis. He was one of two men sentenced to death for the assassination of Chris Hani, a man who had been regarded as a possible successor to Nelson Mandela. Gabrielle herself, now known as Gaye Derby-Lewis, was one of the accused and was acquitted of charges of murder, conspiracy to murder and illegal possession of a firearm. The Sydney *Sunday Telegraph* ran a full-page article about her under the heading 'Sydney convent girl to vampire'. 'A former Sydney convent girl, dubbed the "vampire", is rapidly emerging as the most hated woman in South Africa,' it said. It reported that the African National Congress believed her to be the 'brains' behind the killing.

Bert Evatt's attack on the 'small, increasingly disloyal minority' was the most extreme move open to him. It would split the party, it destroyed any remaining chance of achieving his ultimate ambition, the prime ministership, but it was the only way to save his party leadership. Having lost the support of the right wing, which had given him the leadership in the first place, he now set out to destroy it. The ingenuity of his strategy lay in the fact that the left wing now had to either dump him immediately or support him indefinitely, for he had suddenly appointed himself as the voice of their cause. And as the press gallery followed the events in caucus over subsequent weeks we were astonished to see his likeliest challengers outwitted, Eddie Ward missing his chance altogether and Arthur Calwell missing the moment. Arthur challenged Evatt eventually but too late.

A little later I was writing about a notable party meeting which ended with Evatt standing on a table. He had just faced another challenge, the opposing forces were ranged on two sides of the party room as votes were being counted, one Evatt supporter was demanding that names be taken, Ward was pencilling and shouting 'We'll take their names'. The Doc was declaring: 'We don't want names' but had jumped up on to the table where he could get a better view of the enemy nevertheless. Even his still solid supporter, the ex-journalist Allan Fraser, was thumping the table and protesting: 'This is pure intimidation.' This party meeting has passed into Labor history, and various politicians have recounted it. Their apparent powers of recall are clearly indebted to the stories that I and others wrote that day, full of quotes and stage directions received hot and fresh as our informants emerged from the party room with all the detail still circulating in their over-stimulated minds.

Despite the cryptic nature of Evatt's attack on the Labor disloyalists, the *Herald* to my surprise published a well-informed editorial on the subject and a feature article on the leader page by 'A Political Correspondent', headed: 'Catholic Action, the "Movement" and the Labor Party'. I confess that I had never heard of the Movement, and although my ignorance was hard to excuse, most of the press gallery shared it. The anonymous political correspondent was John Pringle who, it emerged, was already better informed on the background to Evatt's attack than most Australians. John's wife was a Catholic, and his personal interest and intellectual curiosity had brought him, since becoming editor of the *Herald*, into contact with the Catholic hierarchy—not only in Sydney. Thus he knew exactly what Evatt's campaign was about: the forces behind what were known as the Industrial Groups, and their shadowy intrusion into the affairs of the Labor Party. These were groups of anti-communist unionists which had been organised within communist-dominated trade unions to fight and destroy the communist leadership. Behind the formation and operation of the groups was a shadowy force known—to those in the know—as the Movement. Behind the Movement was Catholic Action, the Catholic lay organisation. And behind all this was Santamaria, a then mysterious figure who was the Catholic Church's most influential layman. These connections formed a secret chain, and Evatt's revelations about an outside influence in the Labor Party were in some ways exaggerated but not unjustified.

It was this situation that led to the only effort ever made by the *Herald*'s management to influence my political reporting. Angus McLachlan rang me to say that in future, when we mentioned politicians who were supporters of Santamaria, Mr Henderson wanted us to identify them as such. My defences went up instantly like the quills of a disturbed porcupine (I know, because I used to scream at the porcupines in the zoo when I was a kid, just to produce the effect). As I saw it, Henderson's directive would make us part of Evatt's campaign. I argued that automatically identifying people in this way could be quite misleading. I wouldn't know whom to identify, because some of Evatt's greatest opponents weren't supporters of Santamaria at all. For instance, I said, I knew that Bill Bourke, though a Catholic, was completely opposed to any attempt by Santamaria to interfere in parliamentary politics, so you couldn't lump him in with the Santamaria group.

I knew that Keon and Mullens would back Santamaria unquestioningly, but they might even be the only ones. There wouldn't be much point in a list of just two names, I said, but if we had a list it had to be correct: it would be just as bad to exclude any of the right people as it would be to include any of the wrong ones. And on this note of non-cooperation we ended the conversation. This wasn't a matter on which McLachlan was likely to give me an instruction, and he probably realised that I wouldn't be receptive to it if he did. So no more was heard of the idea. But my attitude could not have improved my standing with McLachlan and Henderson.

The reason I hadn't hesitated to contest Henderson's proposal lay in a story that Bill Bourke had previously told me about a move by Santamaria to call a meeting in Melbourne of Victorian Catholic Labor MPs, and Bill's refusal to have anything to do with it. Bill made it known that as far as he was concerned it was effrontery on Santamaria's part to call a meeting of elected parliamentarians. Their responsibility was to their electors, not to any other person or organisation. Santamaria, he told me, was very annoyed at this rebuff.

I was also aware that some of Evatt's opponents in caucus were not even Catholics, let alone members of a Santamaria group. I had in mind particularly the Victorian, Bob Joshua, an Anglican who would later become titular leader of the rebels. A subsequent event confirmed the situation between Santamaria and Bourke. It occurred at one of my lunches at the Latin Cafe. Bourke and Santamaria had known each other and been friendly for years, going back to university days, I believe, but as Bill and I edged towards our lunch table we almost collided with Santamaria, who cut him completely. Even Bill was surprised at this display of animosity.

In the following months I met a new visitor in Malcolm McColm's room. Helping us to open and consume Malcolm's warm, late-night bottled beer supply was the Queensland Labor premier, Vince Gair, taking part in the fight against the Doc. Vince was a short, bloated figure with qualities you wouldn't have suspected from his appearance. The most convincing evidence of qualities not apparent was that his wife had been a nun, and had left a convent to marry him. The fact that Queensland Labor had chosen him as leader was less surprising: he was the sort of rough, shrewd operator you would expect them to pick. I found it an irresistible symbol of Labor's upheavals that the men whom Vince turned to for companionship in Canberra now were two Queensland Liberals, Malcolm and his new, very right-wing room-mate, Bruce Wight. They were three outsiders together enjoying an old mateship—with nothing missing, I felt, but the camp fire. Vince may have been a state premier and a formerly powerful force nationally, but he joined other delegates who boycotted the ALP Federal Conference around this time, returning to Brisbane to advocate Evatt's departure in the interests of Labor unity. He was on the losing side.

Before 1954 was out, while the Gallup poll showed the Labor Party to be at its most unpopular for twenty years, Menzies celebrated a record term as prime minister. On 29 November, 1954 he had been seven years, fifteen weeks and one day in office, a day longer than Billy Hughes. But most of his prime ministership was still ahead, and the Labor Party was setting it up for him.

On the personal front, Billie finished the year recording another broadcast for the ABC on the eve of Christmas in its sound and rehearsal studio on top of the Woolworths store at Kings Cross. In January we went off to have a holiday with the Bonneys in the new house they had bought at Avalon, one of Sydney's northern beaches, having finally broken their ties with Melbourne and Canberra. Life in the press gallery, the hours, the drinking, the travel, the tension of a year of political crises, were not good for a marriage, and Billie and I needed time to relate better to each other. This we did, but the case for making our intended break with Canberra and political life was more apparent than ever.

Early in 1955 the government faced economic problems again and was introducing new import restrictions, but Menzies had nothing to worry about as the Labor Party cracked apart. The ALP Federal Executive moved in and set up a new state executive in Victoria, expelling Bourke, Keon, Mullens and three other federal MPs as well as many members of the state parliament. Days later the expelled groups formed the Anti-Communist Labor Party. It subsequently became the Democratic Labor Party, and it was the DLP that kept Labor out of office for years. Meanwhile the Cain Labor Government in Victoria fell, state elections were called, Labor lost, and on the day of the Victorian elections Billie and I went to Heather Menzies' wedding. Distasteful as it must have been to the father of the bride, there wasn't room for anyone from the press gallery except the president.

CHAPTER 16

The Split

1955

A series of events was about to occur which would wholly change my direction, but at first there was no hint of their significance. They began with a discussion I had with Angus McLachlan about a new journalists' award which was imminent. Newspapers always reviewed salaries in the light of new awards, and some members of their staff found themselves less well off than they expected. Some found their grading reduced; some lost a margin which they had previously been paid above the award salary for their grade. I wanted to be sure that nothing like this happened to me.

I was, at this stage, being paid at the top rate under the journalists' award. This was not a big salary for the job, but with the other advantages I enjoyed and the prospects that it could open up I was not dissatisfied. What did worry me slightly was that my formal grading did not measure up to the salary I was getting, and I wanted this anomaly corrected. Soon afterwards a note from Lou Leck informed me that I had been upgraded to the top of the scale. This move had no effect on my salary but provided the assurance I wanted. I rang and thanked McLachlan, but the issue was far from closed.

I went to Sydney for one of the biggest political events of the year. It was the state conference of the ALP, at which the left-wing forces were planning to overturn the right-wing group in control, just as they had in Victoria. As in Victoria, the Federal Executive stepped in, this time to ensure that the conference would be run in a way which didn't prejudice these plans. The Federal Executive even intended to vet the delegates and issue its own delegates' badges to ensure that Evatt's opponents couldn't introduce any last-minute ring-ins. But the state headquarters outwitted them by issuing its own badges just before the conference. By the time the federal secretary, Jack Schmella, arrived from Brisbane carrying his own collection of badges in a brown-paper bag, the right-wing state officials had got in first with theirs.

I mention the badges because it was the tightness of the security control on the conference that caused my first difficulties. No-one had thought of issuing press badges, for the conference was being reported by the old-time industrial reporters including my *bête noir*, Fred Coleman Brown, who had known all the officials and most of the delegates for years. I was attending as a political commentator, not a reporter of the union scene, and didn't know the state ALP officials at all. The delegates were assembled and the doors of the Sydney Town Hall were shut when I arrived, and when I knocked, Bill Colbourne, the state secretary, opened up but refused to let me in. We had a row, I asked him to get Fred to identify me, but he refused and went back in, slamming the door behind him. Naturally I didn't intend to be left out of this piece of political history. I waited until Colbourne had had time to get lost in the hall, and knocked again. This time someone else appeared. When I told him who I was, he let me in without argument.

It was a two-day meeting over a weekend, an angry meeting, and on the first morning among shouts, cheers and booing the pro-Evatt group won a series of votes. Fred wrote a front-page lead story for the country edition of the *Sun-Herald*, which went to press very early, saying that Evatt's supporters had gained control of the conference. Then he went off to lunch, and to my amazement (he did everything to my amazement) did not reappear. By the afternoon his story was obviously wrong. The voting began to swing one way and the other, depending on the motion, and by the end of the day the conference was completely split. I couldn't leave the *Sun-Herald* without a news coverage of these events, so I stepped in and wrote an entirely new front-page news story to replace Fred's. At least the *Sun-Herald* got it right in its late editions.

Fred emerged again the next morning—with an agonising hangover, I hope—and this time stayed for the day. By the end of it the Industrial Groups appeared to be still in control of the party in New South Wales despite the efforts of the federal executive and the left-wing faction. Fred said nothing about the previous day. He probably assumed that I had been telling his masters about Saturday's events, but I hadn't—I had merely written my news story and delivered it without comment. I may even have saved him from the sack, but got no thanks.

Sitting down to write my weekly column after that, I recounted some of the extraordinary attempts by the left-wingers to tie up the conference votes. Among the seven-man delegation representing the builders' labourers, for instance, were a commercial traveller, a fruit-barrow operator and two men who were not even members of the union. But even extravagant manoeuvres such as these had failed. I didn't see how Evatt could continue as leader for very long after this, though I rated him the most resourceful and unpredictable man in Australian politics, and admitted that any forecasts about him were almost always wrong. I was wrong myself this time. He did survive. I also wrote immediately after the conference that government members were forecasting a joint Senate and House of Representatives election in December. That forecast proved to be right, and the election campaign at the end of that year was my final assignment for the *Sydney Morning Herald*.

The stories I wrote in 1955 weren't all about the Labor Party. Some were about restive Liberals, some were about the not-so-serious sidelights of politics; but the strangest of them was certainly the Malayan story. Not so much the story as the way I got it.

Menzies had just spent a leisurely ten weeks overseas, taking in a Commonwealth Prime Ministers' Conference in London, where he said that on his return he would be consulting the cabinet on Malaya. There had been talk of Commonwealth action to strengthen joint defences in Asia, especially to aid the Malayan government against communist rebels. It was now a Thursday afternoon at the end of March 1955, a cabinet meeting had just broken up, ministers were racing to the airport to get home to their states, and I was trying to find one who hadn't left. I went down to Richard Casey's office and found that he was still there, but Schapel was there ahead of me, waiting in Casey's outer office. 'He's said he would see Ken,' said the secretary, 'but then he's going off to catch his plane. Would you like to see him together?' 'No thanks,' I told him, 'I'll wait.' With Casey, Minister for External Affairs—now Foreign Affairs—I had a good relationship; I was pretty confident that I could get more out of him than Schapel could. But the secretary warned that his boss was short of time, so I would have to see him with Schapel or not at all. I grudgingly accepted the offer, and a few moments later was shown in.

I was probably unfair to Casey in those days. He had a military moustache and an accent that I couldn't take seriously—a huntin' and fishin' accent which I found ridiculous. He'd come back to Australia in 1946 after some glamorous jobs overseas—member of the British War Cabinet, Governor of Bengal—with the reputation of being Menzies' likeliest rival. He was ambitious, painstaking and experienced, certainly, but I didn't find him very bright, and couldn't understand how anyone could see him as a prime minister. On his travels as Minister for External Affairs he kept a diary, and took to sending it to John Pringle. 'It seems extraordinarily indiscreet to me,' said Pringle. 'I can't imagine any other Foreign Minister in the world sending his personal diary to a journalist.' A different kind of indiscretion: late one night I'd seen Casey come into the House of Representatives in his dinner suit, so drunk that he was having difficulty getting his words out. I couldn't understand why a man of the world didn't stay well away at moments like that. But I must say that I always found Casey likeable, courteous and, whenever possible, helpful.

So here I was in Casey's room, hearing that he had nothing to tell us and wondering if I could briefly hang back when Schapel left. Time was going by, but Casey began showing us some photographs which we both knew would be of no interest to our papers. Schapel said thanks, but the *Telegraph* didn't have space for any of them. He was standing near the door. I was standing by Casey's desk. But Casey continued to shuffle through his pictures, laying them down on the desk one by one in front of me. Schapel couldn't even see them from where he stood. I became aware that Casey was putting the pictures down beside the only other thing on his desk, his out-tray. There was one document in it: the text of a cable. Perhaps he wanted me to read it; I did. It was about a decision to send an Australian army battalion to Malaya and to commit other Australian forces to a Commonwealth South-East Asian Strategic Reserve. Even the concept of this reserve was news.

While I was speed-reading the document on Casey's desk as well as I could, Elgin Reid was in the office of Jos Francis, the Minister for the Army. While Casey was making it possible for me to get the drift of this cabinet decision without Schapel seeing it, Jos Francis had strangely excused himself and left his office, apparently intending that Elgin should scan the sole document on *his* desk. It was the same cable. Elgin and I agreed that, for some reason which we never divined, both ministers were glad to get this news out immediately through journalists they trusted. Menzies planned to announce the despatch of the battalion and the establishment of the strategic reserve the next morning. The announcement was being delayed till then so that other governments, especially the British, could be advised. Elgin and I were able to publish it in advance of Menzies' announcement, including the fact that the battalion would have front-line duties, fighting with British forces engaged in the local war against the Malayan communist rebels.

The story itself was more important than we realised immediately. The cabinet decision was the precursor of other Australian intervention in South-East Asia, and it quickly became significant in Australian politics because Evatt loudly opposed it, in keeping with his new political stance. But what I recall about this story has less to do with its significance than with Elgin's and my mysterious experiences in getting it.

Other, less consequential items remain from that year. One was the column I wrote on Frank Green's retirement. It was not often that you could devote a whole newspaper article to a farewell to a friend, but Frank left in mid-year when parliament was in recess. There was a brief pause in political activity, so I wrote of his career and his parting thoughts after nearly thirty-four years in the parliament. He regretted the decline of the parliament—no longer master in its own house, he said, since it had been taken over by the government machine. And he regretted the decline of the old spirit in Canberra, with comradeship, which he valued, replaced by success-ship, which he did not, and the public service classification become a worshipped social register. Everyone knows that men of this age regret, and to them change and decline are often synonymous. And many people don't take much notice of them. But I thought that Frank Green's last plea or groan on behalf of vanishing values deserved a final notice.

Finally, again, there was the speech by the politician who didn't make speeches—the human equivalent of the unspotted leopard or the unstriped zebra. Billy Jack, Liberal Member for North Sydney, had made a maiden speech some time after his election in 1949 and claimed not to remember whether he had made one or two more speeches since then, until he stood up in late 1955 during the debate on the Estimates. He was a sprightly little man who cultivated his electors but not journalists, as he had nothing to say to them. He explained that he didn't make speeches in parliament because other people said what he wanted to say, and said it better. And when he did break his silence in parliament for the third or fourth time in six years, he got it wrong. I noted in my column that he read a prepared speech which referred to legislation which wasn't before the House. It appeared that he was speaking in the wrong debate.

The new party in which Bill Bourke found himself had a very limited life for its members in the House of Representatives. They would lose their seats at the next elections, and Bill would have to go back to business or the law. Meantime he, with the other Anti-Communist Labor politicians, set out to reveal as much dirt on his former party opponents as possible— not to destroy the party but, as he would have believed, to cleanse it. One of the scandals he alleged was in New South Wales, where he claimed to have secret information on widespread corruption. I told him after one of these speeches that he should have kept quiet until he had more evidence. I didn't doubt that there was something in what he was saying, but if he couldn't do better than seemingly rely on rumour and gossip he would only undermine his credibility. 'I know you're right,' he admitted. 'I shouldn't have done it. I hadn't intended to get on to that one yet—I was going to find out more about it before I said anything. I just got carried away.'

It is easy, years later, to see these people as fanatical destroyers, blind to reason. It is easy to say that history has debunked their obsession with communism—after all, no communist force has ever threatened Australia's shores, let alone taken over the world, and now that particular threat is dead. What I know of this group, however, especially through my friendship with Bill Bourke, shows them in a different light. What everyone now knows about the communist world has justified much of their determination to resist it, even if one might reject some of their methods. And the communist control of some of our most important trade unions, which others fought to break, did little to make Australia a better place, and much to set it back. If the extremism of the communists provoked a degree of extremism among their opponents, should we be surprised?

Bill Bourke and his friends wanted to be social reformers. Communism and circumstance diverted them.

I was much more comfortable writing my political column for the *Herald* than I had been when it ran in the *Sun-Herald*. My contacts among politicians and public servants had increased with my time in Canberra, and so had my knowledge of government and politics. But I also gained from writing for a newspaper with a perceptive editor who followed politics closely. Pringle and I were in constant contact, and always lunched or dined together when I was in Sydney. He surprised me over dinner one night with the question: 'Would you like to be the next editor of the *Herald*?' Yes, I would.

I didn't imagine that he was offering me his job, or even suggesting that I would get it, but he was obviously testing me. I wasn't surprised that he was foreshadowing his own departure. He had said when he first arrived that, interesting as he found Australia and the job, he couldn't imagine staying for life—London was where he would always feel most at home. 'I'd always miss my club,' he said. I was flattered though not carried away by his inquiry, and began to hear that he had posed the same question to a number of others. A colleague, discussing him, saw it sceptically as one of Pringle's ways of winning friends and influencing people. It was, nevertheless, a question that again focused my mind on the future.

What *would* I do when I left Canberra? How many other jobs were there in journalism that would attract me? I was thinking about these questions when a printers' strike stopped production of the Sydney *Daily Mirror*. The dispute spread to the Fairfax organisation through an attempt to have the *Mirror* printed on the *Sun*'s presses. Next, all the Sydney dailies were on strike. The proprietors agreed to produce a combined newspaper, and members of the Australian Journalists' Association met to vote on a strike in support of the printers. I was in Sydney having a few days' break, and asked Rodger Rea to vote for me in Canberra. 'Please say that I think it would be bloody stupid for the AJA to be dragged in,' I told him, knowing that the striking printers did not even have the support of their own union. But I said that if the decision was for a strike I would accept it. And a journalists' strike it was, with a promise of all the animosity that followed an earlier one which was still poisoning relationships in the *Herald* office when I got back after the war.

The proprietors then sought journalists willing to work on their 'strike edition'. It would have been foreign to me to do so, for when you got down through whatever layers of sophistication I may have acquired, a fine deposit of the Australian workers' culture survived beneath. I found it ridiculous for professional journalists to be caught up in such a dispute but I couldn't go against them. What I should have done, being off-duty for a few more days, was to stay quiet and hope that the strike might end before the *Herald* tracked me down and was able to ask my intentions. Instead, I took the initiative and rang Jack Flower, who was now chief of staff. 'I'm just calling to let you know that I'm on strike,' I told him.

By an unlucky coincidence the new journalists' award had been announced just before the strike began. But back in Canberra I was preoccupied with something different, as my old drinking injury had come against me. I had done permanent damage to a disc when I tried to jump through Elgin's daisy hedge in Telopea Park, and now it flared up again so badly that it was agony for me to move. A local doctor, a progressive thinker, wanted to put me in hospital for a few hours and give me a manipulation under general anaesthetic. Anything seemed better than the pain, so I tried his treatment.

Billie was sitting beside my hospital bed as I tried to shake off the anaesthetic. After the obligatory inquiries about my condition, which at least seemed no worse than before, she handed me an opened envelope. 'Have you got a strong right arm?' she was asking as I took out a sheet of paper and began to read. I remember the incident like seeing the poster, President Kennedy Assassinated; this one was: Shots Fired at Hal Myers. For I was reading a memo from Lou Leck on the review of staff gradings following the new award. My salary hadn't been touched, but I had been cut back by a grade, and therefore missed out on a rise. The *Herald* had done exactly what I had tried to avoid in my recent discussion with Angus McLachlan. Most of the after-effects of the anaesthetic vanished. 'My right arm is quite strong enough,' I said. 'I'm not going to do anything about this until I'm ready, but I'm not going to work for people who think they can treat me like this.'

The *Herald* management thought they would punish me for disloyalty in the strike. I learned afterwards that 'they' had been extremely surprised by my action. I, on my part, had expected them to be realistic. If I had worked during a strike they would have had a damaged political correspondent, for a strikebreaking political journalist would be ostracised by half the politicians—the Labor half. And I didn't believe they could really have much respect for me if I sided against my colleagues. Some *Herald* journalists did. I was contemptuous of some of these and sorry for others, for I'd seen how a few like them had been treated before. The *Herald* was still a private, family company whose proprietors had never really faced the fact that its journalists were not family servants. I had seen it discipline and humble senior journalists for errors and other lapses, handing out suspensions or downgradings. I pitied those who through insecurity, I assumed, had accepted such treatment, and I had no intention of doing so myself.

I decided to leave journalism. I would have seen it as a step down to work for any of the other Sydney newspapers. I could have accepted the *Daily Telegraph* but not the afternoon papers, and the *Telegraph* had few openings for my kind of journalism. The national paper, *The Australian*, did not yet exist. Television had not started in Australia, so the possibility of switching to television journalism did not arise. But I had a problem familiar to many people who want to change careers: there was almost nothing else that I was qualified to do. The only other occupation in which, it seemed, I could exploit my experience was in the largely unknown field of public relations.

Some of the public-relations people I knew were second-rate journalists who were doing less work for more money in companies that employed them for writing and publicity work. A few more respected former journalists ran small public-relations consulting firms with major companies as clients, or were employed directly by industry associations. I didn't know much about their work, but if public relations for an organisation meant establishing productive relationships with the groups on which it depended, the relevance of a journalist's experience was apparent. Journalists knew more than most people about the way things ran in the world, the centres of power and influence and the political environment. And if mediocre, burned-out journalists could survive in public relations, I figured, anyone with brains and energy should be able to do well. As for pride in your work, I decided hopefully that most jobs were what you made of them. Public relations would never have been my first choice, but if I could find a reasonable opening in this field I would see where it led me.

I talked to public-relations consultants in Sydney. Then I had an unexpected approach from Eric White, a man whom I knew only slightly. Eric published a private subscription newsletter, *Inside Canberra*, in partnership with a former Sydney *Daily Telegraph* journalist, Don Whitington. When parliament was sitting they took turns week and week about to come to Canberra and get inside it. I saw Don more often because he spent more time at the Non-Members' bar in Parliament House.

Don and Eric were a complementary pair. Don matched most people's idea of a journalist, interested in books and politics and excessively devoted to grog, talk and late nights. His face had a worn look which hadn't been earned easily. He had enough acquaintances of similar tastes among politicians and journalists to provide an acceptable quota of stories for *Inside Canberra*, though I discovered that he had a strange notion of his readers' interests. The publication had mainly business subscribers, and Don fancifully believed that they bought it because their chairmen and managing directors wanted to pass off these stories as their own, over port and cigars in the club, as evidence of their familiarity with the corridors of power. What they really wanted, on the contrary, was information that would help them in their businesses, and this was mainly provided by Eric and by a moonlighting press secretary, Bill Prehn, on the staff of the Minister for National Development, Senator Bill Spooner. Prehn was *Inside Canberra*'s unofficial Canberra correspondent.

Don motioned me over to one of the little tables along the wall of the

Non-Members' bar—a bare and somewhat battered article of furniture randomly decorated with intersecting rings from generations of beer glasses. 'I hear you want to go into public relations,' he began. Or, to report him more accurately, 'I h-h-h' ... pause ... 'I hear you want to g-g-g' ... silence ... 'go into p-public relations'. Then I gathered (rather slowly) that he and Eric had a couple of other publications apart from *Inside Canberra* and a couple of public-relations clients as well, and wanted to expand. But by the time we had finished a couple of drinks I'd learned that Don wasn't really interested, and didn't think that I would be interested, in public relations, and it was hard to fathom why he had even raised the subject with me.

Eric sought me out on a visit to Canberra soon after. He was clearly the businessman in the partnership, and knew what he was there for. Don had 'no right' to talk to me as he had, said Eric, who proceeded to sketch out his own plans and investigate mine.

Eric White had made his name in Canberra as public-relations director of the Liberal Party while Menzies was leader of the opposition, and was credited with having helped Menzies overcome some of his reputation for arrogance by means of 'meet the people' tours. Unlike Don Whitington, Eric wasn't a journalist, didn't look like and didn't behave like one. He had the good fortune to look distinguished; he was tall, well put together and physically strong. He was just over forty, and his straight, glued-down hair was silvering on top but dark at the back. The only disconcerting element in his appearance was his eyes, which you perceived through spectacle lenses prescribed for unusually bad astigmatism. These seemed to draw special attention to the eyes, which appeared remote, probing, and even inquisitorial. They tended to set him apart from the person he was looking at, and reinforced his 'man of distinction' appearance. There was no doubt that Eric White was impressive.

When Eric left Menzies to take a chance with *Inside Canberra* he already had commercial public relations in mind after political public relations. His and Don's business expanded with the publication of another newsletter, *Money Matters*, written by a contributor, and the ownership of two newspapers, the *Mount Isa Mail* and the *Northern Territory News*. Eric also used the contacts established through his work with Menzies to begin developing a small public-relations consulting business. By the time we talked he had already decided that this was where his best prospects lay, but he couldn't make progress without support. He had brought in another *Telegraph* journalist, Bill Rodie, promising him a share of the business, but the experiment failed.

Rodie didn't turn up at the office one morning, and Eric didn't know what had happened until a client rang to ask: 'What's this chap Rodie up to? He's been on to me trying to get my business.' Others began to tell the same story.

By now, Eric was ready to start again. I was impressed enough with what he told me to decide to try this new business, and over the following weeks we worked out a basis for an association. There was no bargaining, and that pleased me. I was to get the salary I wanted, a car, and a share of the business. Eric undertook to sell me shares at book value, which wasn't much, to be paid for out of profits. I found this offer very fair, we shook hands, and I resigned from the *Herald*.

I would work out my obligatory period of notice, for it seemed certain that Menzies would call an election before the end of 1955, and it would be unrealistic for the *Herald* to try to break in a new Canberra correspondent in time for the campaign. But for all practical purposes I ended there and then the career that had occupied half my lifetime.

How Billie handled her musical activities during the disruptive period that followed, I do not know. She even had another solo recital, the most demanding of all forms of performance, coming up late that year at the Sydney Con. As always in the periods leading up to major concerts, I played my role as her critical test audience, hearing her through movements and works many times, and occasionally through the whole program. The program itself was an ambitious one, imaginative and somewhat unconventional in its layout. I was glad to have been able to contribute some ideas to it.

Only a month before the election campaign began, the Doc committed one of the most irrational acts of his career, one which must have ensured his defeat if any doubt about the elections had remained. Defending his actions in the Petrov case, he revealed to parliament that he had written to Russia's Foreign Minister Molotov, seeking to learn the truth of evidence given before the Petrov Royal Commission. A reply from 'a representative of Molotov', he said, stated that the documents Petrov had given to the Australian authorities were false. In a two-hour speech Evatt declared that he attached great importance to this letter showing that the Soviet government denied the authenticity of the documents.

Government members in the House laughed. Fred Osborne called Evatt's behaviour 'the sad spectacle of the decay of a great mind', and I think Fred was being genuine and not merely political. Some have claimed subsequently that Evatt was mad before he left politics; I've often said it myself, but only in a loose sense of the word. From my own dealings with him I saw nothing to suggest that he was in reality anything but sane then, though obsessed. And although he had never liked what I wrote about the Labor Party in the period leading up to the split and afterwards, he was always civil, and our personal relationship did not change. But it is still hard to relate the wild illogic of the Molotov letter to the normal mental processes of an intelligent man.

The *Herald* paid me an apparent compliment by repeating the sort of experiment it had tried with me. It brought back a young man, John Malone, from New York to succeed me. John was an Irish-Australian type, apparently attuned to politics. He arrived back in Australia in time to report some of the election campaign, writing a most engaging piece on Artie Fadden's campaign in Queensland. I cannot resist quoting a story from his reports of Artie's meetings, because it is so typical of Artie as I knew him:

> When a man refused to stop interrupting at a meeting in Dalby in Southern Queensland he [Fadden] retorted with a story.
> 'When I was a young fellow a circus came to my little town,' he said. 'There was a donkey tethered to a rope. We used to throw sticks at the donkey. My mother said: "Artie, one of these days that donkey will haunt you."
> And I had to come to Dalby to learn the truth of her words.'

Artie could go on like that for days. I had always believed that the most entertaining book that could be written on Australian politics would be Artie's story put together from Artie's stories, exactly as he told them. Eventually Elgin and a Country Party character, Ulrich Ellis, did help him to write his autobiography but, anecdotal and revealing as it was, it did not have quite the tone of Artie's live performances. I suspect that Artie had too much respect for the written word.

The election result was so inevitable that there is not much to say about it. Some of the time the *Herald* did not even run its campaign stories on page one—it was more interested in strikes in Sydney. Election night produced the inevitable landslide, Bill Bourke was out, the Doc himself was nearly out—his seat of Barton was seriously in doubt till the end of counting—and when it was all over I was out, too. By Christmas Billie and I had gone from Mugga Way.

Since my Canberra days my feelings about Menzies have softened somewhat. He was certainly in most ways an essential conservative. No-one could doubt his intellectual power, but he did not use it to initiate much, except in a few matters which appealed to him personally. He was a man of set attitudes who, as I saw it, had done his real thinking years before. And by the end of each day the mellowing effect of his relaxant, Scotch whisky, had taken over, though he never showed the signs of excess.

Menzies was not in a mood for change. Yet this picture of the man gives insufficient credit to his sanity and judgment. He had too much sense to rush to hasty decisions, and he refused to be swept up in the latest wave of opinion. What I regarded as inertia on his part was sometimes wisdom. Menzies never left a trail of foolish decisions behind him.

He is accused of having been devious and of misleading the people on some great issues, and he does appear to have occasionally made questionable manoeuvres to achieve his objectives. But the objectives were honourable if sometimes debatable, and Menzies stands as a man of principle. Critics who claim otherwise are not talking about the Menzies I knew.

My views on Evatt have not changed. He was a man whose devotion to some notable libertarian causes was hopelessly compromised by his ambition. He was an intellectual who tried to play the populist, and would seize on even nonsensical causes if they suited him; in the end he was chasing fantasies. Subsequently for a time he was sanctified by one section of political opinion but I remember none in the press gallery, seeing him at close quarters, who was ever caught up in Evatt worship. I myself had little respect for his character, yet I confess to a perverse liking for the man, and that has not changed in retrospect, either.

Evatt perhaps tried harder and did more than anyone else has ever done in an unsuccessful effort to become Prime Minister of Australia. Who else has a record anything like his?—President of the General Assembly of the United Nations, Deputy Prime Minister under Chifley, Leader of the Opposition for nearly nine years, leader of his party in four federal elections—and so close to success in one of them that he won a majority of the vote, yet still failed to win government. He even promised more than any other political leader has ever promised in an election campaign. Evatt to me is the Icarus of Australian politics, who soared too high, and fell to earth, and was destroyed.

I thought that I was taking two interesting remnants of my journalistic life away from Canberra. I had to give up my spare-time role as Canberra correspondent of *The Economist*, but an Australian named Brian Crozier, who edited their confidential newsletter, *Foreign Report*, asked me to continue writing for it. And Tom Fitzgerald, who'd started his challenging publication, *Nation*, asked me to write for that, too. It was a good brief. 'You can write anything you like, about anything—we'll publish it,' said Tom. Regrettably I soon became so preoccupied with my new activities in Sydney that I let both of these attractive invitations lapse. But I had learned much in Canberra, and brought some close, lasting friendships away from it—especially with the Reids and the Reas, and Malcolm McColm, and a group of others with whom we did not lose touch.

When the time came, though, I was glad to put Canberra behind me, glad to be able to set out on life in Sydney again, and hopeful about my experiment in a new career. 'Good luck!' said Elgin as we left. 'I'm sure you're going to make a lot more money in public relations. But I wonder if you'll be as happy.' Driving to Sydney, I put such doubts aside.

Our departure from Canberra was more than the end of a chapter. I never returned to journalism. Or to life with the politicians. But, looking back on the events I have told, the story remains incomplete. I have left some acrobats in mid-air, some actors in mid-gesture. Before I close the book on them I feel bound to let some of them finish.

PART V

After

CHAPTER 17

Whatever Happened To ... ?

1956–

'You'll love working with Eric,' said Frank Green when he heard of my move just before he left Canberra for Tasmania and retirement. To me his opinion counted for more than most, and he had been friendly with Eric White for years. But I was to learn that there was much about Eric that Frank did not know. I should have paid more heed to Elgin Reid's sceptical, discomforting questions.

For the first few years, though, my association with Eric succeeded beyond any expectations. At first we worked together in a shabby first-floor office that overlooked a dilapidated streetfront awning in one of the old buildings near Circular Quay. Eric and Don Whitington were mainly occupied with their publications, and at first I didn't have enough to do. Yet before the end of the '50s we had opened offices in every state and Canberra, and in London and New Zealand. Don and the publications had gone. And we had grown to be bigger than any other public-relations firms outside the United States and bigger than all but the top three in America, even though public relations had been flourishing there since before World War II. Then in the early '60s we set up in Singapore, Hong Kong, Kuala Lumpur and Bangkok, and in 1964 our company was listed on the Sydney Stock Exchange. It was the first listed public-relations company in the world.

There was a turning point in Billie's life, and therefore in mine, which occurred in London in 1962. I spent 1961 and 1962 trying to put Eric White Associates' troublesome London office on its feet. Billie saw our time there as an opportunity for musical experience. She auditioned with the BBC, did a solo broadcast on BBC radio and was offered another. She began to prepare for it as soon as we got back from a holiday in Italy. Having chosen a program that included a technically difficult work which was new to her, she jumped immediately into heavy practice to make up for the time lost during our holiday. This was a mistake. She over-practised and injured her hand, and then, on medical advice, did entirely the wrong thing. A London doctor diagnosed arthritis and gave her a powerful painkiller so that she could keep practising ('otherwise it will stiffen up').

Weeks later, when her trouble was much worse, she saw an arthritis specialist. 'You have absolutely no sign of arthritis,' he told her. 'You should never have taken those pills. You must stop them immediately and stop practising. You could have ruined your hand.' She cancelled the BBC. The pain and swelling gradually subsided after the specialist put her on a course of injections, heat treatment and rest. But even later, after we returned to Australia, each attempt to start practising again brought a recurrence of the trouble.

Only then did I understand that Billie's career as a pianist was finished. Finished by a doctor in London.

The end of everything she had worked for as a musician led to a painful period of meaninglessness, attempted reappraisal and the search for something to substitute for what she had lost. But nothing really worked. Even the greatest of setbacks, however, can also have compensations. If Billie had picked up her career in Australia in 1963 it is unlikely that we would have taken the step which we did take a year later when we put our names down to adopt two children. We would have missed the countless experiences and pleasures we have had with Roger, born in 1966, and Lucy, two years younger. Roger is a fine violist who now lives in the United States and has a growing career as a teacher and performer. He works at one of the large US universities and plays and teaches at summer schools and festivals in America and Europe. Lucy is an all-rounder who played the cello but chose science. She has excelled academically, and did an unusual Master of Science degree in medical demography at London University. Back in Australia now, she works in the field of public health. She is married, and is now Lucy Snow.

Billie and I are as devoted as any parents, and more so than many.

After we left Canberra I continued to see some of my political friends and contacts. I often spent time with Bill Bourke in Melbourne. I found myself, later, working with organisations with which Fred Osborne and Allen Fairhall were involved. And when Eric White Associates opened an office in Brisbane I had Malcolm McColm appointed to our local board there. But Malcolm had no political future. I remember seeing him in a chastened mood at lunch one day after he'd been to a function the night before. Before the end of the evening he had had an argument with Menzies during which he became very insulting. But it didn't matter in the long run, because he didn't have a long run in politics after that. He lost his seat in parliament in the 1961 elections.

Nothing ever went totally right for Malcolm, and the rest of his life disintegrated with his political career. He lived with his wife Berta and their children in one of those big Queensland timber houses that are as comfortable as old slippers. Casually disposed around the walls, domesticated almost like household pets, was a collection of European paintings, among them two Corots, that his father had once acquired in a barter. But even before Malcolm lost out in politics this scene of domestic well-being was changed for ever by his passionate, out-of-control love affair with a friend of Elgin and Thea Reid. Malcolm still loved Berta in his way, and still lived with her. And soon he had more reason to do so, for they discovered that Berta had cancer. After she died Malcolm married his lover, Nell, got a good job in New Guinea and went there with Nell and his son Malcolm. And suddenly, before their new life even started, he died.

Change the names and the time and place, and it is a story that to me has the elements of Greek drama, except that it had just happened, and it was about a good friend, one that I didn't want to lose.

I didn't see John Gorton again for several years, but had made friendly contact with him again before Harold Holt was drowned and the prime ministership was vacant. John McEwen fortunately (I thought) put Bill McMahon out of the contest to succeed Holt by declaring that the Country Party would not work in a coalition government with him as prime minister. Allen Fairhall, I believed, had the ability to do the job. But the Liberals were looking for a popular hit, and that was how they fixed on John Gorton. I was glad for him, but can't deny that as a public relations consultant I also valued, potentially, having access to a prime minister. I thought there might be times when access might be crucial for a client with a view to put forward on a matter which merited the prime minister's attention but otherwise mightn't get it.

He asked my advice on finding a press secretary. I suggested someone I'd known and respected for years, but after several days' consideration my nominee declined with thanks. If he had accepted, my later problem with

John Gorton would not have occurred. When Billie and I visited Canberra we were invited to lunch at the Lodge. Our relationship with the Gortons was as warm as ever.

I asked John to be guest speaker at a major conference in Sydney which I had suggested to one of our big clients, the Australian Finance Conference. On the night of the conference dinner I waited downstairs at the Wentworth Hotel for him so as to introduce the chairman of the conference. As soon as this formality was over he grabbed my arm and set off rapidly in the direction of the function, dragging me ahead of the others. 'Well, Hal, how're we going?' he asked, to my surprise. I hadn't expected the need for reassurance. But everyone knew that he was a controversial prime minister. I said something comforting.

Just over a week later it would have been hard to find anything comforting to say. That was when a member of his government, Ted St John, recounted in the House of Representatives how the prime minister had bundled a young woman from the press gallery into his car after a party at Parliament House, gone to the American Embassy, called for the ambassador—who had already gone to bed—and demanded a drink. St John (pronounced singe-'n) branded him as unfit for his office, and John Gorton's real political decline probably dated from that night. His appointment of a young friend, Ainslie Gotto, as his secretary, and the power she overtly exercised, were seen as possibly scandalous and certainly outrageous, but it was the incident at the US Embassy that gave him the label of the larrikin prime minister. He was really anything but a larrikin but he could obviously be terribly indiscreet.

For a time after I left the *Sydney Morning Herald* it went back to its old habit of changing political correspondents. My successor, John Malone, was in the job for about a year. His successor, George Kerr, was soon sacked over an error on a highly controversial issue, parliamentary salaries. George successfully sued for wrongful dismissal and joined Eric White Associates as our first government-relations consultant. For a time then the *Herald* job was divided between Max Newton, who also represented the *Australian Financial Review*, and Rodger Rea. When Newton went to Sydney to edit the *Review*, Ian Fitchett from *The Age* replaced him and Rodger soon resigned. Fitchett was the last of the old Canberra crew as I knew it to hold the job.

Ken Schapel, the Crow, remained the competitor for some years. His days in Canberra ended when his employer, Frank Packer, decided to sent him to take charge of the London office of Consolidated Press. But in

London something went to Schapel's head. Rumours of strange behaviour reached Sydney, and Packer eventually sent his editor-in-chief, David McNicoll, to see what was happening.

McNicoll appeared unannounced in the London office at half past eight one morning and the staff came in at fashionable London hours between nine and ten-thirty—except for the Crow. When the unsuspecting Schapel arrived to start work at midday, McNicoll sacked him. Back in Canberra, Schapel set himself up as an independent. He died a few years later.

I was flying back to Sydney from Canberra on the same plane as Artie Fadden when I saw him sitting alone. I changed seats and joined him. Artie had left politics by then and taken up some directorships. He was on his way back to Brisbane after a trip to Canberra for a company he was associated with. In earlier times I'd sometimes seen Artie show the effect of the drink quite quickly, and this might have been one of those days. He was distressed and sorry for himself because his old ministerial colleague Bill Spooner had been too busy, or unwilling, to see him. There were tears in Artie's eyes as he told me of this rejection by a man he had worked with so closely for so many years.

The next and last time I saw Artie I expected him to be even more fragile. He was to be guest speaker at a lunch being held in Sydney by the Institute of Chartered Accountants, a client of my new consulting firm after I left Eric Whites. I'd rung to ask if I could pick him up and take him to the lunch. Artie was pleased, and told me that I'd find him in the boardroom at Hooker House in Angel Place—he was then on Hooker's Queensland board. But he was not expecting to be in good shape—he was getting over eye surgery and was going up to Macquarie Street that morning to get some stitches out. I expected to find a shrunken Artie Fadden sheltering behind dark glasses in the safe haven of a directors' retreat. Instead, I found the once deputy prime minister waiting downstairs in the street, a pathetic-seeming figure, alone in the lunchtime crowd, with his cabin bag on the footpath beside him, ready to go straight on afterwards to the airport. And then, revived by a couple of Scotches and an audience, and speaking without a note, he kept about three hundred accountants and businessmen laughing from the start to the finish of his speech. How could I have imagined that maybe Artie could no longer do it?

What, I reflected, should you make of Artie Fadden, the treasurer who once so indiscreetly gave me the whole budget, the deputy prime minister who said things about Menzies behind his back that he would never say to his face? Could you respect such a man? I believed so. He was a man of much strength and of human weaknesses. But the weaknesses went with the humanity, and he had more of that than most politicians I have known. He also had political courage.

Colin Bednall, managing editor of the *Courier-Mail*, had seen Elgin Reid as its next editor. But Bednall left newspapers for television, Elgin stayed in Canberra for some years after we left, and by the time he returned to Brisbane his opportunity had gone. He settled into—for him—the undemanding position of leader writer on a newspaper that lacked the fortitude to tackle the main issue of the time. Only the mildest criticism of Queensland's unsavoury premier, Sir Joh Bjelke-Peterson, could ever be allowed.

Elgin was eventually given some recognition as associate editor of the *Courier* but never had a real opportunity to show what he could do. He became also the part-author of two books. One was Fadden's autobiography, *They Called Me Artie*, which — as I have mentioned—he helped write. The other was an Australian version of a book called *Scientific Racegoing*, written by a professor of English and a professor of political science from an American university. Scientific Betting would have been the accurate title. Elgin had to find real examples from the Australian turf to substitute for the American form and performances which the authors had quoted. Of course he adopted the principles of *Scientific Racegoing* for himself, and won enough at first to pay his children's school fees. But each year the returns got smaller. I've known several people who made money from an apparently sound betting method. It requires so much self-discipline that almost all of them eventually stopped winning.

Elgin is the only person who could ever make me enjoy a day at the races. He analysed racing and politics similarly, and made the two activities seem like interchangeable forms of gambling.

Unhappily I have to add that he died of cancer in 1984.

Eric White had not failed to take advantage of my relationship with John Gorton. They had known each other before though they had never been friendly. But after John became prime minister Eric offered him any help we could give him. And just before the 1969 elections the prime minister rang him to say that he didn't have a good enough speech-writer for the election campaign, and wondered if we could provide someone for the duration.

My co-director Peter Golding's job at that time was to advise the chairmen and chief executives of some of our major clients, and we agreed that he could put these activities aside for a few weeks to help the prime minister. He had the ideal qualifications. Not only did he have great experience in public relations, but he had previously been one of Melbourne's best journalists.

We considered what would happen when Peter began to travel with John Gorton on the campaign tour. There would be questions to the PM, questions to Peter and, no doubt, questions to us back in Sydney. We decided how we would deal with them. If we handled Peter's temporary appointment diplomatically, his appearance on the campaign team should soon be taken for granted. The press gallery must have known that there was no first-class speech-writer on Gorton's staff.

Peter went to Canberra and began working from Liberal Party headquarters. There was a change in what we'd first imagined to be the plan: he didn't travel with Gorton but stayed on in Canberra, having daily consultations on the issues on which new speech material was needed. Probably by then both Eric and Peter already realised that he would not travel with Gorton at any stage and that, therefore, his activities would remain completely behind the scenes. But this wasn't communicated to me.

Nothing more had happened when word of Peter's activity somehow reached the press just as a public-opinion poll showed a big drop in John Gorton's popularity. It was the front-page lead story in the Sydney afternoon paper, the *Sun*.

GORTON HIRES HELP
Another Poll Shock

said the headlines.

The Prime Minister's popularity has fallen sharply according to a new Gallup Poll released to-day.

The latest Gallup shock coincides with news that the Prime Minister has co-opted a top public relations consultant as a special adviser for the last days of the election campaign.

The consultant's job: to find flaws in Labor's campaign and plan a late counter-attack for Mr Gorton.

The consultant is Mr Peter Golding, a director of the public relations firm, Eric White Associates.

Neil O'Reilly, touring with the Prime Minister, reports from Adelaide:

'Mr Golding's appointment will be widely interpreted by Government supporters as a panic move.'

And so on. Almost everything in the story was half-wrong.

The *Sun* had rung me, and also quoted 'the joint managing director of Eric White, Mr A. H. Meyers' as confirming that 'a consultant had been made available to the Prime Minister during the campaign period'. This was what we had originally agreed to say but, I discovered, contradicted what everyone else now wanted to say. The new party line was that Peter was working temporarily for the Liberal Party, not the prime minister. As for the prime minister himself, he hated this story, which broke in the final stages of a tense campaign which he could easily lose. He was especially distressed that I had said the wrong thing and given weight to this embarrassing report.

The embarrassment wasn't over. Eric and I still failed to tie down the situation precisely enough between ourselves, and when a newspaper rang me to clarify it the next day I rather flippantly, though unintentionally, gave the story some more currency. 'He's doing it deliberately!' John Gorton wailed into the telephone.

The government narrowly won the election. The story about Peter had no bearing on the result. The serious newspapers ignored it, and the others dropped it after a couple of days. But I knew that a nervous John Gorton was very unhappy about anything connected with this story of his 'panic move', including my part in it. And looking back on what had happened I knew that I should have kept my mouth shut. Eric and I should also have prepared ourselves for possible slip-ups in the campaign as carefully as we would have prepared a client.

I saw John Gorton afterwards to try to repair the damage. I explained how I had been the victim of a misunderstanding, and he accepted what I told him. But the friendliness seemed somewhat forced this time, and I went away convinced that our old relationship had been a casualty of politics. Regretfully, I never went to see him again. I had grown away from Canberra and the political scene.

Garnet Bonney worked for some years after his retirement. His term as Director of Information in New York had been a post-retirement job. When he moved to Sydney and lived near Avalon Beach he was offered another, as Australian representative of the British Travel Association, on a part-time basis which suited him. But after the association appointed someone full-time and his arrangement ended he was not sorry. He had passed the seventy mark and was a devil for work no longer. He took advantage of living close to the beach. Whenever possible Minnie and he were there for a swim before the Sydney nor'-easter got up in the late morning. At weekends Billie and I sometimes went down with them. In February 1959, the story came to an end. Garnet got up one morning, stood by the bed, complained of a pain in his left arm and fell down dead.

I think that my mother was able to close the book on Garnet's life with acceptance. Their relationship had survived to the end and, to be practical, Garnet had made his usual success of things even in dying. Seventy-five, no pain, no slow destruction, no loss of the mind. He had just got up one day and died.

My father-in-law, Stred, who was just as big a figure in my consciousness as Garnet, lasted several more years. Not by looking after himself, though— he just happened to be a few years younger than Garnet. Indeed Stred was a living checklist of everything the Heart Foundation warns you about: too much beer, too much whisky, too many cigarettes, too much weight, no exercise. But he made a special effort to keep going while we were in London in 1961 and 1962. He was so determined to see his daughter again that he gave up drinking for all that time.

Stred was staying with us in Sydney to get treatment from a heart specialist when Billie went in one morning and found him dead with a book from our shelves on the floor beside him. It was one of Gavin Souter's, with the eerily appropriate title, *The Last Unknown*.

Mum lived on into her eighties, long enough to experience a late grandmotherhood, to her delight. The longest lived of the group intimately associated with my life from the older generation was Minnie. We stayed close to her but I still don't know whether she knew of my relationship with Garnet. If not, she must certainly have suspected it. It is only since her death that I have felt able to tell the story. I have no overwhelming urge to do so, but without it my account of this part of my life would simply not be true. Some people may suppose that in telling it I have intruded on my mother's memory, but I am sure that, on the contrary, she would have been glad. In a more tolerant age she would not have been so secretive in her lifetime, certainly not if she could have revealed the truth without hurt to others.

The successes of Eric White Associates had another side to them. Problems emerged as our growth outran our capacity to manage the business, especially to recruit enough good people and keep them. Troubles with clients followed inevitably, but by then the greatest trouble was in our boardroom. The more we grew the more we were divided by rivalries. One director who left us after many disputes became our most damaging competitor. In his territory, Melbourne, we had no-one capable of matching him. And he knew every weakness that could be exploited in the organisation that he had left behind. Our Melbourne office collapsed into a decline which greatly damaged the whole organisation.

Unexpected aspects of Eric White's personality were emerging. He was a typical entrepreneur, addicted to starting ventures, not always well chosen, and leaving it to others to make them work. He invested his confidence in a series of people but became disillusioned with every one of them in turn. Then he began to cut himself off from all but a few of our own staff and most of our clients as well. Most of our newer clients had never met the man whose name was on the door.

With Peter Golding, my most senior colleague, I struggled to overcome our problems as Eric became more remote. A mood of depression spread through the organisation, and all pleasure in working with Eric had gone. This wasn't merely my own experience: no-one else enjoyed working in the company then and Eric didn't enjoy it, either. He became preoccupied with the idea of selling out to one of the American public-relations firms. In this, eventually, he was to succeed.

When Eric White Associates Limited became a listed company we had two outside directors. One was an accountant and professional director whose main role, as I saw it, was to act as the professional mourner at our board meetings. He was Eric's mouthpiece, putting pressure on Peter and me whenever a problem emerged. Eventually after one of his performances I walked out of the boardroom and immediately wrote a letter of resignation, saying that this was not the way I wanted to live and work. So I handed over my responsibilities as joint managing director to Peter Golding. With Eric as the other joint MD, it was an uncomfortable position for anyone to inherit.

I sold my shares off-market at a premium to Eric, cashed in the funds that I had been putting into a directors' superannuation scheme and left the company with more money than I ever expected to make from it. Then, aided by associations that I'd formed in public relations and journalism, I helped to build up, and eventually sell, very profitably, two other companies. One was a firm of public-relations consultants of which I was chairman. I was happy to be in it, glad of the independence it gave me.

But that was another life, another story.

Index